A Fanny Fern Reader

A Fanny Fern Reader

Selections by a Pioneering Nineteenth-Century Woman Journalist

Edited and with an Introduction by
EMILY E. VANDETTE

Cover Credit: Sara Payson Parton, known as Fanny Fern, c. 1866. Library of Congress, Photograph. https://www.loc.gov/item/95502453/

Published by State University of New York Press, Albany

For information, contact State University of New York Press, Albany, NY www.sunypress.edu

Library of Congress Cataloging-in-Publication Data

Name: Fern, Fanny, author. | Vandette, Emily E., editor.
Title: A Fanny Fern reader : selections by a pioneering nineteenth-century woman journalist / Fanny Fern, edited and with an introduction by Emily E. VanDette.
Description: Albany : State University of New York Press, [2024] | Includes bibliographical references and index.
Identifiers: ISBN 9781438498522 (hardcover : alk. paper) | ISBN 9781438498539 (ebook) | ISBN 9781438498515 (pbk. : alk. paper)
Further information is available at the Library of Congress.

Contents

ON SCHOOL REFORM

Introduction

In the middle of the nineteenth century, the highest paid and most famous newspaper writer in the United States was a woman known to the world as Fanny Fern, the nom de plume of Sara Payson Willis. Entertaining (and often provoking) readers with her engaging, conversational style that blended satire and sentiment, Fanny Fern wrote with an unbridled candor that was unexpected for a woman of her time. While she also authored two best-selling and controversial novels (*Ruth Hall* in 1853 and *Rose Clark* in 1855), it was Fern's newspaper columns that made her a household name in the 1850s and 1860s and were her most significant outlet for social commentary.[1] Fern's voice, despite being widely recognizable in her time, was virtually eliminated in the male-centered literature canon that took shape in the twentieth century. However, readers today will find in this celebrity columnist's writing a compelling glimpse into the past, as well as prescient cultural discourse that is still relevant today. Indeed, in nearly two decades of teaching college courses in American literature and women's literature, I have found that the writing of Fanny Fern consistently fascinates my students. They are intrigued by the variously snarky, subversive, quirky, sentimental, witty ideas of this author who defied the rules of her society for women to remain docile and demure.

The selected works in this volume represent Fern's perspective on a range of topics: from pushy department store salesmen to the hazards of secondhand smoke; from the joys and hassles of life in New York City to the inhumane conditions of schools, prisons, and asylums; from dealing with people's annoying habits and personalities to coping with trauma and grief. Above all else, Fanny Fern was known for her advocacy for women's rights and financial independence, and her writing on those issues was shaped by her own fight for professional equity in the male-dominated newspaper world.

The story of Fanny Fern's meteoric rise to stardom is one of perseverance and triumph in the face of substantial obstacles. Before becoming "Fanny Fern," Sara Payson Willis's life was conventional for a white, elite-class woman of the 19th century. But a sudden change of fortune following the untimely death of her husband left her a destitute widow with two young children to support, during a time when there were few options for women to earn a living. With a talent for writing and familiarity with the newspaper business, Fern turned to writing for newspapers in an effort to provide for her family. She would have to advocate fiercely for fair compensation as a professional writer; in doing so, she confronted the substantial obstacles to a woman's voice and financial independence in a patriarchal society. The lessons Fern learned in the early struggles of her career stayed with her throughout her entire life, and she used her platform to advocate for women's independence and to call out patriarchal hypocrisy when she saw it.

The fifth of nine children, Sara Payson Willis was born in Portland, Maine, on July 9, 1811, to Nathaniel Willis and Hannah Parker Willis. The year after Sara was born, her family moved to Boston, where her father continued his work as a newspaper editor and served as a church deacon. Sara enjoyed a close relationship with her mother, judging from the loving recollections she would later share in such pieces as "Mother's Room" (included in chapter 6). In her biography of Fern, Joyce W. Warren points out that she especially appreciated her mother's affectionate cheerfulness, even in the face of her father's cold and stern personality: "Fern respected her mother for having the patience she felt that she herself never could have had under such [harsh] treatment. She recognized the cost to her mother of this effort and recognized also that it was only because of this effort that her mother was able to make their childhood home the warm and cheerful place that it was."[2]

Sara's father and her eldest brother, Nathaniel Parker Willis, were both editors of periodicals. Her father founded the Congregationalist newspaper the *Boston Recorder*, as well as the children's magazine the *Youth's Companion*, and Sara helped proofread and wrote copy for her father's periodicals. Her brother was a successful author and editor, eventually establishing the extremely popular magazine the *Home Journal* (which is still running today, with the title *Town & Country*). This early exposure to the world of authorship and publishing shaped Sara's own budding interest in reading and writing, but when it mattered most, her brother and father failed to support her writing career. In 1828 Sara began attending Catherine Beecher's Hartford Female Seminary in Hartford, Connecticut, where she began to develop her voice, as well as a reputation for her sense of humor and a mischievous sparkle in her personality.

Sara married Bostonian banker Charles Harrington Eldredge in 1837, and the couple had three children between 1838 and 1844: Mary, Grace, and Ellen. After several years of a relatively conventional life as a nineteenth-century wife and mother, the trajectory of Sara's life was derailed by a series of tragic deaths: her youngest sister, Ellen, died in 1844 from complications in childbirth, and her beloved mother died six weeks later; her firstborn, Mary, succumbed to meningitis in 1845; and her husband died from typhoid fever in 1846. Compounding the trauma of these personal tragedies, Charles Eldredge died in serious debt and left his widow and children in poverty. Sara took in sewing work, but it was not enough to support herself and her children, and she received little financial support from her family and in-laws. Eager to rid himself of financial responsibility for his daughter and her children, Sara's father pressured her into a poorly matched marriage to Samuel Farrington in 1849. Sara's second marriage brought more hardship and heartache, as Farrington proved to be an emotionally abusive and jealous husband. Two years into their marriage, Sara took her two daughters and left Farrington—a bold and risky choice for a woman in the nineteenth century, when marriage laws favored men and divorce scandalized women. Farrington spread malicious rumors meant to tarnish Sara's reputation, and he eventually filed for divorce on the grounds of desertion. Sara was left financially destitute yet again, and her family refused to offer her and her children support, essentially punishing her for the scandal caused by her divorce.

Faced with the need to earn a living for herself and her daughters, Sara turned to writing essays and columns for Boston-based newspapers under the pseudonymous persona that would make her famous. As a woman working in the male-dominated newspaper business, Fanny Fern's compensation in the early days of her career was paltry. Warren notes that Fern's first contribution to the *Olive Branch* earned her fifty cents, and when she was later writing for both the *Olive Branch* and *True Flag*, both papers paid her two dollars per column.[3] On top of the usual obstacles facing women writers of the era, Fern's difficulties breaking into the business were exacerbated by the hostility of her own brother, the prominent editor and author Nathaniel Parker Willis. Rather than lending support to his sister's budding career as a newspaper contributor, Willis harshly rejected his sister's writing. He went so far as to forbid James Parton, who was editing Willis's magazine the *Home Journal* at that time, from publishing anything written by Fanny Fern or even positive reviews of her publications. Parton resigned from the *Home Journal* in protest. Undeterred by her brother's rejection and the discrimination she faced as a woman writer, Fern continued to publish in various newspapers and gained a devoted fan base. She later exposed her brother's betrayal, as well as the exploitative practices of the newspapers that grossly underpaid her for her writing, in her 1854 autobiographical novel *Ruth Hall*.

In 1852 Fern was hired as a regular columnist by the New York-based paper *Musical World and Times*. The following year, in a turning point in her professional career, she published her first collection of columns, *Fern Leaves from Fanny's Port-Folio*, with the Auburn, NY, publisher Derby and Miller. In a savvy move, she negotiated to receive royalties at ten cents per book rather than a flat fee of one thousand dollars; her decision paid off when the book became a bestseller, with seventy thousand copies sold in the US and twenty-nine thousand in England in 1853.[4] With her financial success and increasing fame from *Fern Leaves*, Fern relocated permanently to New York City, which she found to be a better fit than Boston both professionally and personally. Derby and Miller published two more successful books by Fern, a second collection of columns, *Fern Leaves from Fanny's Port-Folio, Second Series*, and a collection for children, *Little Ferns for Fanny's Little Friends*. Reviewers praised Fern's collections for her original style and bold perspective. A review of *Fern Leaves from Fanny's Port-Folio, Second Series* that appeared in *Godey's Lady's Book* points out the value of Fern's collected columns in preserving and curating the author's newspaper writings: ". . . unlike meteors, which fade away after a brief flash, Fanny's flashes are designed for preservation, and are carefully collected together and made to form a brilliant galaxy for permanent usefulness and lasting admiration. Her originality, industry, and proficiency in all departments of life and human knowledge are wonderful, indeed, and therefore wonderfully widespread is her popularity."[5]

Following the success of Fern's collections of columns, Fern's next book sold even more impressively, while provoking an onslaught of negative criticism. A roman à clef, *Ruth Hall: A Domestic Tale of the Present Time* revealed the significant obstacles of a nineteenth-century woman writer who sought to lift herself out of poverty and support her family. Closely based on Fern's life experiences, the novel tells the tragedies and triumphs of the title character as she overcomes the circumstances of grief, poverty, and patriarchal oppression to achieve financial independence, professional success, and fame, as well as builds a supportive personal network. In her account of Ruth's trials and triumphs, Fern based her fictional characters on the people in her life who mistreated her and withheld support when she needed it most. She exposed her family and in-laws for failing to provide compassionate care and assistance in the aftermath of her husband's death. She also satirized her famous but vain brother Nathaniel Parker Willis, named Hyacinth Ellet in the book, who, like Willis, refused to support his destitute sister's budding writing career despite his powerful position in the literary world. The novel also included fictional counterparts to the editors who exploited Fern's popularity and discriminated against her. One of the editors who felt attacked by the novel, *True Flag*'s William U. Moulton, retaliated by outing Fern's well-protected identity and publishing an unauthorized "biography" of the author.[6]

While *Ruth Hall* was a spectacular commercial success, reviewers criticized the novel and its author, primarily for transgressing deeply entrenched gender codes in nineteenth-century society. Simply put, Fern's decision to expose her family for their heartlessness and her former editors for their exploitation was considered unwomanly. Perhaps critics reacted so vehemently against *Ruth Hall* not solely because of the private family business aired in the novel, but also because of the inconvenient reality that the injustices and hypocrisy it revealed were all too common. *Ruth Hall*, and Fanny Fern, represented the threat of a woman writer lifting the veil on the power structures that hinder women from achieving success and independence in a patriarchal society. Never one to be deterred by critics and scandal, Fanny Fern continued to speak out on these issues for the remainder of her writing career. A notable exception to the trend of disparaging reviews was one that was written by the prominent women's rights activist Elizabeth Cady Stanton for the feminist magazine *The Una*. Stanton praised Fern's candid depiction of the obstacles that prevented a woman from being self-supporting and financially independent.[7] In response to the largely hostile criticism of *Ruth Hall* as unwomanly, Fern offered a more docile female protagonist in her second novel, *Rose Clark* (1856), but she included a secondary protagonist whose marriage closely paralleled Fern's own experience with her emotionally abusive second husband. "In *Rose Clark*, she cannily constructs the title character as a conventional female protagonist (that is, one based on the conventions of fiction) and then plays off against her a protagonist derived from Fern's own life."[8] While the autobiographical parallels are less elaborate in *Rose Clark* than in *Ruth Hall*, both novels incorporate events from the author's own life that call into question cultural gender codes in the nineteenth century.

Despite the controversies surrounding her best-selling first novel, Fern's fame and fan base continued to grow. In 1855, Fern accepted an offer from *New York Ledger* owner Robert Bonner that would make her the highest paid newspaper contributor in the US: one hundred dollars for each installment of her serialized story, "Fanny Ford." She began a weekly column for the *Ledger* in January 1856, and her column appeared in its pages every week until her death in 1872. The arrangement between Fern and Bonner proved to be mutually beneficial. Fern was already famous by the time she began writing exclusively for the *Ledger*, and her popularity led to a surge of subscriptions for the fledgling newspaper. In turn, Bonner showed his support for Fern, not only by paying the unprecedented sum for her weekly column, but also in the free range he granted her voice. Even when they disagreed, Bonner did not restrict or censor his star columnist. In "A Break-fast Reverie on Ledger Day," which is included in chapter 9, Fern playfully comments upon the reciprocal benefits of her arrangement with Bonner and the *Ledger*. She acknowledges the freedom she enjoyed with an employer who "gives me a wide pasture to prance in, because he is sure that I will not jump the fence, though the conservatives sometimes needlessly hold their breath for fear I will." In turn, Fern comments that she was inclined to give "three cheers for Robert Bonner, whose heart is as big as his subscription list, and that's saying considerable, and who deserves, a hundred times told, every mill that his industry and energy have earned; and now, when he reads this, he may blush if he likes—I shan't." Following the success of his experiment in drawing Fern's dedicated fan base to his paper, Bonner recruited other prominent authors to write for him, and the *Ledger* became one of the most popular and influential papers of the era.

Fern's writing style was recognizable for its combinations of satirical irreverence and sentiment; seriousness and levity; and subversive ideas and conventional values. Her readers knew to expect layers of meaning in her columns, as she often wove her more radical messaging into more playful and lighthearted commentary. It is from an early column of Fern's, "Hungry Husbands" (chapter 2), that we get the adage "the way to a man's heart is through his stomach," a conventional enough sentiment that seems to be in-line with women's traditional domestic roles. But the statement sets up a bold discussion about a husband's potential for brutality when his carnal demands are not satisfied, as well as sardonic advice for wives to help them avoid the repercussions of their husband's hunger: "Yes, feed him well, and he will stay contentedly in his cage, like a gorged anaconda." Ironically, Fern's powerful satirical commentary in that article was reduced to a light-hearted axiom about men's appetites, reflecting a broader erasure of this fascinating author's voice.

Fern was known as an advocate of women's rights and economic independence, and, unlike many feminist voices of the day, even her more radical messages were tolerated by her readers. Fern's candor, relatability, and humor enabled her to reach a broad spectrum of readers, even when her critique of gender roles and double standards would have otherwise lacked mainstream appeal.[9] In a *Ledger* column that appeared in 1856, "Moral Molasses; or, Too Sweet by Half" (chapter 2), she points out the absurdity of guidelines for wives in domestic advice manuals: "'Always meet your husband with a smile.' That is one of them. Suppose we put the boot on the other foot, and require the men to come grinning home? no matter how many of their notes may have been protested; no matter how like Beelzebub, their business partner may have tormented them; no matter how badly elections go;—when they do it, may I be there to see!" When she wrote on the same topic a year later in her article "A Word on the Other Side" (chapter 3), she dropped the humor and leveled a more direct critique of the misogynistic domestic advice manuals policing women's lives: "I have no patience for those who would reduce women to a mere machine, to be twitched this way and twitched that, and jarred, and unharmonized at the dogged will of a stupid brute . . . I have no patience with those who preach one code of morality for the wife, and another for the husband."

At the same time that Fern was embarking on her new partnership with the *Ledger*, she also began a new chapter in her personal life with her marriage to James Parton, the editor who resigned in protest when her brother forbade him from publishing or promoting Fern's writing. A successful author himself, well respected as a biographer, Parton was supportive of Fern's career and the pair were equal partners in their marriage. While she maintained a strict sense of privacy when it came to her family, she often wove references to her playful and mutually respectful dynamic with "Mr. Fern" into her columns, modeling for her readers an ideal egalitarian marriage. Sadly, Fern experienced the tragic loss of a child for a second time, when her daughter Grace died shortly after childbirth. She and Parton raised Grace's daughter "Effie" from infancy, and her later columns frequently referred to the challenges and joys of grandmotherhood.

Fern continued to write her weekly column for the *New York Ledger* until just before her death from cancer in 1872. Over the course of her career, she also published two novels (*Ruth Hall* and *Rose Clark*); three books for children; and a total of six collections of her newspaper columns. The collections of columns are especially important for providing a sense of permanency to an otherwise ephemeral form of commentary, and for many years they served as the main source for readers to access Fern's newspaper writing.[10] Several articles and compilations of articles that appeared in Fern's collections are included in *A Fanny Fern Reader*, along with uncollected articles from the *New York Ledger*. While the thematic categories of this volume are not exhaustive, they indicate the range of topical areas Fern addressed in her career as a newspaper columnist. Fern's writing varies as much in the seriousness of its content as it does in its style and tone: she addressed universal realities of the human condition that ranged in intensity from the complex processes of grief and trauma to the petty annoyances of busybodies and whistlers. She often called on her readers to sympathize with the downtrodden, and she advocated for a more compassionate approach to prisons, schools, mental health care, and newspaper reporting. She also laid the groundwork for later methods of investigative journalism in pieces like her exposés of the asylum and prison located on Blackwell's Island (featured in chapter 6). But the most frequently recurring theme in Fern's writing is gender in society: the roles of men and women in domestic, civic, and professional spaces. Given her experience confronting gender-based discrimination in the newspaper world, she was a passionate advocate for women's economic independence. In addition to addressing the subject frequently in her column, in 1868 she cofounded a New York-based professional women's club, Sorosis, the first club of its kind in the US.

While her newspaper writing regularly delighted, inspired, and provoked her nineteenth-century readers, perhaps equally remarkable is its capacity to do the same for readers today. Teaching Fanny Fern's writing to college students has allowed me to appreciate the complex ways in which this famous author from the nineteenth century still speaks to modern-day readers. In nearly two decades of teaching, my students consistently value Fern's voice for its engaging style, and for the conversations and debates it stimulates. Indeed, we even learn from paying attention to the limitations and biases that are revealed regarding Fern's progressive concerns as a white, elite-class woman writing to an audience of mostly white, middle-class readers in the nineteenth century. Whether grappling with the entrenched cultural attitudes *resisted* in Fern's writing, or those that are *revealed* in it, my students marvel that a celebrity author from the past is unknown today outside of the world of women's literature classrooms. This volume is dedicated to the many students over the years who have appreciated Fern's boldness and humor, and her prescient discussions about gender and power.

Note on the Text

The works included here are selected for their representation of the author's voice and opinions, as well as their potential relevance to modern-day readers, with the hope of inspiring further interest in Fern beyond academic settings. In most cases, the essays are based on the versions published in the *New York Ledger*, accessed mainly through America's Historical Newspapers (by Readex) and the Digital Library @ Villanova University. Unless otherwise noted, the dates indicate when the column appeared in the *New York Ledger*. Several essays are based on the versions published in Fanny Fern's collections of columns (including some thematic compilations of articles that were included in those books), as noted throughout the text. While archaic spellings and grammar have mostly been retained, silent emendations have been made in cases of obvious typographical errors. Minor changes to punctuation have been made for the sake of consistency.

I

"These are some of the annoyances of authors; but, verily, they have their rewards too"

On Authorship and Authors

If there was one subject that Fanny Fern's devoted readers could never get enough of, it was the author's life as a celebrity columnist. Fern frequently offered her readers insights into her professional life, the ups and downs of a writing career, as well as advice for budding writers. But she shared those glimpses into the world of authorship while preserving the privacy of her personal life, a particular challenge in a celebrity-loving society. Excerpts from her correspondence from readers, which she frequently included in her columns, illustrate the typical requests she received, from inquiries about her personal appearance to requests for her help with unsolicited manuscripts. Fern gave her readers a peek behind the curtain of the writing profession, while reminding them of the humanity of the celebrity authors they admire. She also confronted the discriminatory treatment of women writers, whose personal lives often took precedence over their literary publications in the eyes of the reading public and critics. Her essay "American Female Literature" is a particularly powerful argument about the arbitrary criticism too often leveled at women's literature.

Borrowed Light
From Fern Leaves from Fanny's Port-folio, *1853*

"Don't rely too much on the torches of others;—light one of your own."

Don't you do it!—borrowed light is all the fashion. For instance, you wake up some morning, fully persuaded that your destiny lies undeveloped in an ink stand. Well, select some popular writer; read over his or her articles carefully; note their peculiarities and fine points, and then copy your model just as closely as possible. Borrow whole sentences, if you like, taking care to transpose the words a little. Baptize all your heroes and heroines at the same font;—be facetious, sentimental, pathetic, terse, or diffuse, just like your leader. It may astonish you somewhat to ascertain how articles which read so easy, are, after all, so difficult of imitation; but, go on, only take the precaution, at every step, to sneer at your model, for the purpose of throwing dust in people's eyes.

Of course, nobody sees through it; nobody thinks of the ostrich who hides his head in the sand, imagining his body is not seen. Nobody laughs at your servility; nobody exclaims, "There's a counterfeit!" Nobody says, what an unintentional compliment you pay your leader.

In choosing your signature, bear in mind that nothing goes down now-a-days, but *alliteration*. For instance, Delia Daisy, Fanny Foxglove, Harriet Honeysuckle, Lily Laburnum, Paulena Poppy, Minnie Mignonette, Julia Jonquil, Seraphina Sunflower, etc., etc.

If anybody has the impertinence to charge you with being a literary pirate, don't you stand it. Bristle up like a porcupine, and declare that it is a vile insinuation; that you are a full-rigged craft yourself, cruising round on your own hook, and scorning to sail under false colors. There's nothing like a little impudence!

That's the way it's done, my dear. Nobody but regular workies ever "light a torch of their own." It's an immensity of trouble to get it burning; and it is sure to draw round it every little buzzing, whizzing, stinging insect there is afloat. No, no!—make somebody else light the torch, and do you flutter round in its rays; only be careful not to venture so near the blaze as to singe those flimsy wings of yours.

Mrs. Adolphus Smith Sporting the "Blue Stocking"
From Fern Leaves from Fanny's Port-folio, Second Series, *1854*

Well, I think I'll finish that story for the editor of the "Dutchman." Let me see; where did I leave off? The setting sun was just gilding with his last ray—"Ma, I want some bread and molasses"—(yes, dear,) gilding with his last ray the church spire—"Wife, where's my Sunday pants?" (*Under the bed, dear,*) the church spire of Inverness, when a—"There's nothing under the bed, dear, but your lace cap"—(Perhaps they are in the coal hod in the closet,) when a horseman was seen approaching—"Ma'am, the *pertators* is out; not one for dinner"—(Take some turnips,) approaching, covered with dust, and—"Wife! the baby has swallowed a button"—(*Reverse him,* dear—take him by the heels,) and waving in his hand a banner, on which was written—"Ma! I've torn my pantaloons"—liberty or death! The inhabitants rushed *en masse*—"Wife! will you leave off scribbling?" (Don't be disagreeable, Smith, I'm just getting inspired,) to the public square, where De Begnis, who had been secretly—"Butcher wants to see you, ma'am"—secretly informed of the traitors'—"Forgot *which* you said, ma'am, sausages or mutton chop"—movements, gave orders to fire; not less than twenty—"My gracious! Smith, you haven't been *reversing* that child all this time; he's as black as your coat; and that boy of yours has torn up the first sheet of my manuscript. There! it's no use for a married woman to cultivate her intellect—Smith, hand me those twins."

American Female Literature,
Letter from Fanny Fern
Published in the New York Tribune, *June 16, 1854;
reprinted in the feminist periodical* The Una:
A Paper Devoted to the Elevation of Women, *August 1854*

To the Editor of the N. Y. Tribune.

Sir: In *The Daily Times* of the 5th inst. appeared an article entitled "American Female Literature," in which the following passage occurs:[1]

"Whatever differences of opinion may exist as to the merit of our recent female writers, there can be no doubt as to their popularity and influence. Neither Irving nor Cooper has been read in anything like the same numerical ratio as Fanny Fern, Miss Wetherell,[2] and others of the same class. The fact is significant. No doubt their talents have had a due share in this unprecedented popularity. But it were folly to attribute the results to this cause mainly. There is no sort of proportion between the genius shown in these volumes and the immense sale they have had. The true reason is in a combination of circumstances, among which are to be enumerated the present prepossession of the public mind in favor of any good thing that ladies undertake to do, and consequently the ease with which they secure the public ear—Women of any intellectual force find the American world more than ready to do them justice. They are really anxious to admire them. If an American woman of pretension and position writes an inferior book she cannot be half so sorry for it as the tender-hearted public."

Will the editor of *The Times* inform us why, if "the American world" is so "really anxious to admire" female talent, and more than ready to do it justice, that editors take so much pains to persuade the public that the sale of a popular book by a female writer is owing to such a combination of circumstances as he names? Why (with such chivalric feelings as he claims that men entertain for our sex) not *allow* these ladies, without any disclaimer, the full benefit of their success, even though, in his opinion, it be mainly owing to adventitious causes? Why "damn with faint praise," after this fashion—"Very good for a *lady* book"; or huddle literary ladies together with this contemptuous expression—"Petticoat rush for print"; or why whine at all, like a vexed school-boy, *"because a girl has got up to the head?"*

Why, if "women of any intellectual force find the American world *more* than ready to do them justice," did the writer below alluded to, at whose literary baptism the editor of *The Times* himself stood god-father, receive the following unmistakable rebuff:

The Myrtle Wreath. By Minnie Myrtle. Dedicated to Henry J. Raymond, Editor of *The New York Daily Times*. New York: Charles Scribner. Boston: Redding & Co.

"A collection of newspaper articles, in prose and poetry; the former evincing at times some little originality—the latter of the most common place description. As a whole, the book is not above mediocrity."—*Boston Saturday Evening Gazette.*[3]

Why did those gallant "American" fingers so unceremoniously wring the neck of this lady's first literary bantling?

Why, on the first appearance of "Uncle Tom's Cabin" did some of the gallant editors of the "American world" pronounce it "too powerful to have been written by a woman" and, when driven from this "chivalric" opinion, why did they still sneakingly cling to the belief "that her *husband* must have assisted her in writing it?"—And if the American world (including of course, American Editors,) is so "anxious to admire" the female sex when developed literarily, why was a coarse anecdote stating that "Mrs. Stowe, when traveling, was mistaken by a gentleman for an Irish servant-woman," passed from one editorial hand to another with so much *gusto*?[4]

Again the editor of *The Times* says: "There is something in this to be remembered by our aspiring women. To make men, you must treat them as air-condensers treat the water in a fire-engine—put six or eight additional atmosphere in pressure on their brains, and by resistance call forth their strength. They must have obstacles to surmount—suffering to test their fortitude—dangers to arouse their courage. Facility, in the sense of easiness, is the worst enemy of manly genius. But for the impediment in Demosthenes's utterance—the misfortunes in Sir Walter Scott's circumstances—the poverty of Burns, and the deformity of Byron, their genius would never have impressed the world so potently. But womanly mind loves sympathy, admiration, praise. The fragrant atmosphere which these create, must float around the plant of her genius ere it can flower in Summer fullness."

Is this *true*? Have literary women no obstacles to encounter—no dangers to surmount—no impediments to overcome? Can a literary *woman*, how talented soever she may be, command on her *début* as great remuneration for her literary contributions as a *man* can obtain under the same circumstances?

Has she a *flowery* path, who, reared in luxury, shrinking, delicate, sensitive—suddenly finds herself thrown by misfortune upon her own exertions for her daily bread for herself and her little ones, and, casting a timid eye about her for the best means of support, finally resorts to her pen? Who ignorant of the avenues to public favor—ignorant of the chords to which the public heart vibrates—tremblingly takes her first manuscript, and finding her way, haphazard to some office, blushingly hands it to the Editor, who with his heels higher than his head, and a cigar in his mouth, leisurely finishes the story he is telling to other heels and cigars, before attending to her request. Has *she*, think you, Mr. Editor, no "difficulties to surmount?" And when she "calls again in the course of a week," and finds the same smoking party convened, and encounters the same broadside of curious glances, and the added disappointment of a rejected manuscript, only to renew that experience a second, a fourth, a sixth, or a *twelfth* time in other places, returning to her gloomy room at intervals to weep over her famishing children—is there nothing in *this*, Mr. Editor, to "test the fortitude and courage" of a woman ? Was the "stuttering of Demosthenes," or the "deformity of Byron" harder to bear than this?

Do successful literary ladies *always* pen their contributions with a golden nib, in a damask chair, on a tapestry carpet, inhaling the luxurious aroma of hot-house plants, clad in purple and fine linen, and faring sumptuously every day?

No, no, no, Mr. Editor. I tell you, with a dark picture of suffering indelibly daguerreotyped on my memory—*no!* Oh, Man, be magnanimous! Be just to Woman. The World is wide enough for her and you. As far as any remarks relate to me, it matters little; but in God's name, drive not, by this tone of patronising tolerance, one literary female aspirant (more easily discouraged) back to "The Song of the Shirt." Pluck not one leaf from a *woman's* laurel wreath; gathered too often 'mid the night-shade of sorrow, and whose *envied* leaves, perchance, in the brightest hour of her triumph, may press an aching brow.

FANNY FERN.

My Old Ink-Stand and I;
or, the First Article in the New House
July 19, 1856

Well, old Ink-stand, what do you think of this? Haven't we got well through the woods, hey? A few scratches and bruises we have had, to be sure, but what of that? Didn't you whisper where we should come out, the first morning I dipped my pen in your sable depths, in the sky-parlor of that hyena-like Mrs. Griffin? With what an eagle glance she discovered that my bonnet-ribbon was undeniably guilty of two distinct washings, and, emboldened by my shilling de laine, and the shabby shoes of little Nell, inquired "if I intended taking in slop-work into *her* apartments?" How distinctly I was made to understand that Nell was not to speak above a whisper, or in any way infringe upon the rights of her uncombed, unwashed, unbaptized, uncomfortable little Griffins. Poor little Nell, who clung to my gown with childhood's instinctive appreciation of the hard face and wiry voice of our jailor. With what venom I overheard her inform Mr. Griffin that "they must look sharp for the rent of their sky-parlor, as its tenant lived on bread and milk, and wore her under-clothes rough-dry, because she could not afford to pay for ironing them!" Do you remember *that*, old Ink-stand? And do you remember the morning she informed me, as you and I were busily engaged in our first article, that I must "come and scrub the stairs which led up to my room"; and when I ventured humbly to mention, that this was not spoken of in our agreement, do you remember the Siddons-like air with which she thundered in our astonished ears—"Do it, or tramp!" And do you remember how you vowed "if I did tramp," you would stand by me, and help me out of the scrape? and haven't you *done* it, old Ink-stand? And don't you wish old Griffin, and all the little Griffins, and their likes, both big and little, here and elsewhere, could see this bran-new house that you have helped me into, and the dainty little table upon which I have installed you, untempted by any new papier-mache modern marvel?

Turn my back on *you*, old Ink-stand! Not I. Throw you aside, for your shabby exterior, as we were thrown aside, when it was like drawing teeth to get a solitary shilling to buy you at a second-hand shop? Perish the thought!

Yes, old Ink-stand, Griffin and all that crew, should see us now. Couldn't we take the wind out of their sails? Couldn't we come into their front door, instead of their "back gate?" Didn't they "*always know* that there was something in us?" We can forgive them, though, can't we? By the title deed, and insurance policy, of this bran-new pretty house, which their sneers have helped us into, and whose doors shall always be open to those who have cheered us on, we'll do it.

Dropped many a tear into you, have I? Well—who cares? You know, very well, that every rough word aimed at my quivering ears, was an extra dollar in my purse; every rude touch of my little Nell, strength and sinew to my unstrung nerves and flagging muscles. I say, old Ink-stand, look at Nell now! Does any landlady lay rough hands on those plump shoulders? Dare she sing and run, and jump and play to her heart's content? Didn't you yourself buy her that hoop and stick, and those dolls, and that globe of gold-fish? Don't you feed and clothe her, every day of her sunshiny life? Haven't you agreed to do it, long years to come? And won't you teach her, as you have me, to defy false friends, and ill-fortune? And won't you be to my little Nell a talisman, when my eyes grow dim, and hers brighten? Say, old Ink-stand?

Answers to Fern Correspondents
November 15, 1856

Michael Dolan's request "for $500 to establish himself as a market gardener," is respectfully declined.

Miss H. F., of Bangor, who "wishes $20 to buy a silk dress to go to church in, she not owning one"—ditto.

To Katy——, who would like the writer to "make six taste-ful pincushions in the form of a Fern Leaf, for her table at the——fair"—ditto.

To BRIDGET JONES, who "has been a servant-girl in a tavern for many years, who is now married, and lives humble, but who would be willing to give the undersigned house-room while she put into words, her (Bridget's) remarkable history, to be published for her (Bridget's) personal benefit"—ditto.,

To JOSEPH——, who "is willing to pay the undersigned a reasonable sum for composing a moving love-letter for him to a cruel coquette"—ditto.

To FRANKLIN——, who "wishes the undersigned to meet him at the corner of——and——sts., that he may see how she looks"—ditto.

To MOSES WOLF, who "would like to know how much the undersigned receives for copyright—how much she has made by writing, and how it is invested"—ditto.

To THOMAS——, who "is an invalid, and who has been a long time out of cigars; and who wishes the loan of $2 to buy some"—ditto.

To JOHN CRAM, HENRY STUFF, ARTHUR COOK, AND WILLIAM WELLS, Committee, who "will place all the writings of the undersigned in their village library, if the author will forward them, post-paid, and handsomely bound"—ditto.

To SIX young ladies of the——Ericson Seminary, who "implore the writer to forward for their use, a quantity of compositions, and French exercises, at her earliest convenience"—ditto.

To PROF.——, who wishes the published opinion of the undersigned on this question, "What was the first thing Adam said to Eve when he saw her?"—ditto.

To THOMAS ROHAN, who is "Editor of a paper with an unprecedented subscription, who likes to encourage lady-writers, and who is willing to give the undersigned the advantages of this unprecedented circulation by publishing *gratis* one of her articles every week"—ditto.

To JAMES——, who "respectfully solicits the honor of dedicating a work on the raising of Hens, to the undersigned"—ditto.

To MARY M., who desires a frank expressions of opinion from the undersigned, with regards to her marrying an old bachelor.

Ans. Don't do it. A man who for so long a period has had nobody but himself to think of, who knows where the finest oysters and venison steaks are to be found, and who has for years indulged in these and every other little selfish inclination unchecked, will, you may be sure, (without punning,) make a most miserable *help-meat*. When you have tea, he will wish it were coffee; when you have coffee, he will wish it were tea; when you have both, he will desire chocolate; and when you have all, he will tell you that they are much better made at his favorite restaurant. His shirts never will be ironed to suit him, his cravats will be laid in the drawer the wrong way, and his pocket-handkerchiefs marked in the wrong corner. He will always be happy to wait upon you, provided *your* way is his way; but an extra walk round a block will put him out of humor for a week. He will be as unbending as a church-steeple—as exacting as a Grand Turk, and as impossible to please as a teething baby. Take my advice, Mary; give the old fossil the mitten, and choose a male specimen who is in the transition state, and capable of receiving impressions.

To Literary Aspirants
December 6, 1856

My heart aches at the letters I am daily receiving from persons who wish to support themselves by their pens; many of these letters, mis-spelt and ungrammatical, show their writers to be totally unfit for the vocation they have chosen; and yet, alas! their necessities are for that reason none the less pressing. Others, unexceptionable in these respects, see no preliminary steps to be taken between avowing this their determination, and at once securing the remuneration accorded to long-practiced writers, who, by patient toil and waiting, have secured a remunerative name. They see a short article in print, by some writer; it reads easy—they doubt not it was written easily; this may or may not be the case; if so—what enabled the writer to produce it in so short a space of time? Long habit of patient, trained thinking, which the beginner has yet to acquire.

You are taken sick; you send for a physician; he comes in, stays ten minutes, prescribes for you a healing medicine, and charges you three or four dollars. You call this "extortionate"—forgetting the medical books he must have waded through, the revolting dissections he must have witnessed and participated in, and the medical lectures he must have digested, to have enabled him to pronounce on your case so summarily and satisfactorily. To return to our subject. These practiced writers have gone through (as you must do), the purgatorial furnace which separates the literary dross from the pure ore. That all who do this should come out fine gold, is impossible; but I maintain, that if there is any thing in a literary aspirant, this process will develop it, spite of discouragement—spite of depression—nay, on that very account.

Now what I would say is this. Let none enter this field of labor, least of all shrinking, destitute women, unless they are prepared for this long, tedious ordeal, and have also the self-sustaining conviction that they have a God-given talent. The reading community is not what it once was. The world is teeming with books—good, bad, and indifferent. Publishers have a wide field from which to cull. There is a great feast to sit down to; and the cloyed and fastidious taste demands dishes daintily and skillfully prepared. How shall an unpracticed aspirant, whose lips perhaps have not been touched with the live coal from the altar, successfully contend with these? How shall the halt and maimed win in such a race?

Every editor's drawer is crammed—every newspaper office besieged—by hundreds doomed to disappointment; not two thirds of the present surfeit of writers, born of the success of a few, obtain even a hearing. Editors have any quantity of MSS. on hand, which they know will answer their purpose; and they have, they say, when I have applied to them for those who have written me to do so, neither time nor inclination to paragraph, punctuate, revise and correct the inevitable mistakes of beginners, even though there may possibly be some grains of wheat for the seeking.

To women, therefore, who are destitute, and rely upon their pen for a support, I would say, again, Do any thing that is honest that your hands find to do, but make not authorship, at least, your *sole* dependence in the present state of things.

Now, having performed this ungrateful task, and mapped out faithfully the shoals and quicksands, if there are among you those whose mental and physical muscle will stand the strain with this army of competitors—and, above all, who have the "barrel of meal and cruse of oil" to fall back upon—I wish you God speed! and none will be happier than she, who has herself borne the burden and heat of the day, to see you crowned victor.

Leaves of Grass[5]
May 10, 1856

Well baptized: fresh, hardy, and grown for the masses. Not more welcome is their natural type to the winter-bound, bed-ridden, and spring-emancipated invalid. "Leaves of Grass" thou art unspeakably delicious, after the forced, stiff, Parnassian exotics for which our admiration has been vainly challenged.

Walt Whitman, the effeminate world needed thee. The timidest soul whose wings ever drooped with discouragement, could not choose but rise on thy strong pinions.

> "Undrape—you are not guilty to me, nor stale nor
> discarded;
> I see through the broadcloth and gingham whether
> or no."

****

> "O despairer, here is my neck,
> You shall *not* go down! Hang your whole weight
> upon me."

Walt Whitman, the world needed a "Native American" of thorough, out and out breed—enamored of *women* not *ladies, men* not *gentlemen;* something beside a mere Catholic-hating Know-Nothing[6]; it needed a man who dared speak out his strong, honest thoughts, in the face of pusillanimous, toadeying, republican aristocracy; dictionary-men, hypocrites, cliques and creeds; it needed a large-hearted, untainted, self-reliant, fearless son of the Stars and Stripes, who disdains to sell his birthright for a mess of pottage; who does

"Not call one greater or one smaller,
That which fills its period and place being equal to any";

who will

"Accept nothing which all cannot have their counterpart of on
the same terms."

Fresh "Leaves of Grass!" not submitted by the self-reliant author to the fingering of any publisher's critic, to be arranged, rearranged and disarranged to his circumscribed liking, till they hung limp, tame, spiritless, and scentless. No. It were a spectacle worth seeing, this glorious Native American, who, when the daily labor of chisel and plane was over, himself, with toil-hardened fingers, handled the types to print the pages which wise and good men have since delighted to endorse and to honor. Small critics, whose contracted vision could see no beauty, strength, or grace, in these "Leaves," have long ago repented that they so hastily wrote themselves down shallow by such a premature confession. Where an Emerson, and a Howitt[7] have commended, my woman's voice of praise may not avail; but happiness was born a twin, and so I would fain share with others the unmingled delight which these "Leaves" have given me.

I say unmingled; I am not unaware that the charge of coarseness and sensuality has been affixed to them. My moral constitution may be hopelessly tainted or—too sound to be tainted, as the critic wills, but I confess that I extract no poison from these "Leaves"—to me they have brought only healing. Let him who can do so, shroud the eyes of the nursing babe lest it should see its mother's breast. Let him look carefully between the gilded covers of books, backed by high-sounding names, and endorsed by parson and priest, lying unrebuked upon his own family table; where the asp of sensuality lies coiled amid rhetorical flowers. Let him examine well the paper dropped weekly at his door, in which virtue and religion are rendered disgusting, save when they walk in satin slippers, or, clothed in purple and fine linen, kneel on a damask *"prie-dieu."*[8]

Sensual!—No—the moral assassin looks you not boldly in the eye by broad daylight; but Borgia-like[9] takes you treacherously by the hand, while from the glittering ring on his finger he distils through your veins the subtle and deadly poison.

Sensual? The artist who would inflame, paints you not nude Nature, but stealing Virtue's veil, with artful artlessness now conceals, now exposes, the ripe and swelling proportions.

Sensual? Let him who would affix this stigma upon "Leaves of Grass," write upon his heart, in letters of fire, these noble words of its author:

"In woman I see the bearer of the great fruit, which is immortality **** the good thereof is not tasted by *roues,* and never can be.

****

Who degrades or defiles the living human body is cursed,
Who degrades or defiles the body of the dead is not more cursed."

Were I an artist I would like no more suggestive subjects for my easel than Walt Whitman's pen has furnished.

"The little one sleeps in its cradle,
I lift the gauze and look a long time, and silently
brush away flies with my hand.
The farmer stops by the bars of a Sunday and looks
at the oats and rye.

****

Earth of the slumbering and liquid trees!
Earth of departed Sunset,
Earth of the mountain's misty topt!
Earth of the vitreous pour of the full moon just tinged with blue!
Earth of shine and dark mottling the tide of the river!
Earth of the limpid grey of clouds brighter and clearer for my sake!
Far swooping elbowed earth! Rich apple-blossomed earth!
Smile, for your lover comes!"

I quote at random, the following passages which appeal to me:

"A morning glory at my window, satisfies me more

****

Logic and sermons never convince.
The damp of the night drives deeper into my soul."

Speaking of animals, he says:

> "I stand and look at them sometimes half the day long.
> *They* do not make me sick, discussing their duty to God.

****

> —Whoever walks a furlong without sympathy, walks
> to his own funeral dressed in his shroud.

****

> I hate him that oppresses me,
> I will either destroy him, or he shall release me.

****

> I find letters from God dropped in the street, and
> every one is signed by God's name,
> And I leave them where they are, for I know that
> others will punctually come forever and ever.

****

> ———Under Niagara, *the cataract falling like a veil
> over my countenance."*

Of the grass he says:

> "It seems to me the beautiful uncut hair of graves."

I close the extracts from these "Leaves," which it were easy to multiply, for one is more puzzled what to leave unculled, than what to gather, with the following sentiments; for which, and for all the good things included between the covers of his book Mr. Whitman will please accept the cordial grasp of a woman's hand:

> "The wife—and she is not one jot less than the husband,
> The daughter—and she is just as good as the son,
> The mother—and she is every bit as much as the father."

Charlotte Brontë
June 6, 1857

Who has not read "Jane Eyre"? and who has not longed to know the personal history of its gifted author? At last we have it. Poor Charlotte Brontë! So have I seen a little bird trying bravely with outspread wings to soar, and as often beaten back by the gathering storm-cloud—not discouraged—biding its time for another trial—singing feebly its quivering notes as if to keep up its courage—growing bolder in each essay till the eye ached in watching its triumphant progress—up—up—into the clear blue of heaven.

Noble Charlotte Brontë! worthy to receive the baptism of fire which is sent to purify earth's gifted. I see her on the gloomy moors of Haworth, in the damp parsonage-house—skirted by the grave-yard, sickening with its unwholesome exhalations, crushing down, at the stern bidding of duty, her gloomy thoughts and aspirations; tending patiently the irritable sick, performing cheerfully the most menial household offices; the days "passing in a slow and dead march"; cheered by no mother's loving smile, or rewarding kiss; waiting patiently upon the hard, selfish, unsympathizing father, who saw, one by one, his gifted daughters sink into untimely graves, for want of the love, and sympathy, and companionship for which their yearning hearts were aching.

I see these sisters at night, released from toil, when their father had retired to rest, denied the cheerful candle-light, pacing up and down, in utter darkness, the dreary little sitting-room, talking of the vacant past and present, and trying vainly to pierce the impenetrable future for one glimmering ray of hope; and as years passed on, and vision after vision faded away—alas! with those who wove them—I see Charlotte, the last survivor of that little group, pacing *alone* that desolate sitting-room; while the winds that swept over the bleak moor, and through the church-yard, and howled about the windows, seemed to the excited imagination of the lonely, feeble watcher, like the voices of her sisters shrieking to be again enfolded in her warm, sisterly embrace. Alone—*all* alone!—no shoulder to weep upon—no loving sister's hand to creep about her waist—the voices of her soul crying eternally, unceasingly, vainly, give, give—and he who gave her life, sleeping, eating, drinking, as stoically as if ten thousand deaths were not compressed, to that feeble girl, into each agonized moment.

One smiles now, when the praise of "Jane Eyre" is on every tongue, at the weary way the author's thumbed MS. traveled from publisher to publisher, seeking a resting-place, and finding none; and when at length it did appear in book form—the caution of the sapient book-dissecting "London

Athenæum" containing only "very qualified admissions of the power of the author"—also of "The Literary Gazette," which "considered it unsafe to pronounce upon an unknown author"; also at "The Daily News," which "did not review novels"—but found time soon afterward to notice others. Mistaken gentlemen! you were yet, like some others of your class, to take off your publishing and editorial hats to the little woman who was destined to a world-wide fame, but, (and if ye have manly hearts they must have ached ere now to think of it,) not until the bitter cup of privation and sorrow had been so nearly drained to the dregs by those quivering lips, that the laurel wreath, so bravely, hardly won, was twined with the cypress vine.

Literary fame! Alas—what is it to a *loving* woman's heart, save that it lifts her out of the miry pit of poverty and toil? To have one's glowing thoughts handled, twisted, and distorted by coarse fingers; to shed scalding tears over the gravest charge which can be untruthfully brought against a woman's pen; to bear it, writhing in silence, and have that silence misconstrued, or speak in your own defense, and be called unwomanly; to be a target for slander, envy, and misrepresentation, by those of both sexes who can not look upon a shining garment without a wish to defile it—all this, a man's shoulders may be broad enough to bear, but she must be a strong *woman* who does not stagger under it.

I see Charlotte Brontë in the little parsonage parlor, at Haworth, draperied, hung with pictures, furnished, at last, with books from the proceeds of her own pen; and upon the vacant chairs upon which should have sat the toiling, gifted sisters, over whom the grave had closed, I see inscribed, Too late—Too late! and I look at its delicate and only inmate, and trace the blue veins on her transparent temples, and say, Too late!—even for *thee*—Too late! Happiness is not happiness if it be not shared—it turns to misery. But, thank God, at last came the delirious draught of love, even for so brief a space, to those thirsting lips—but which, incredible as it may seem, the father, in his selfishness, would have dashed aside; relenting at last, he gave up this tender, shrinking flower to more appreciative keeping; but the blasts had been too keen that had gone before—the storms too rough—the sky too inclement. We read of a wedding, the happiness of which the selfish father must cloud at the last moment, by refusing, for some inexplicable reason, or no reason at all, to give away the bride in person according to Episcopal usage—we read of a short bridal tour—of a return to a love-beautified, love-sanctified home—we read of a pleasant walk of the happy pair—of a slight cold taken on that occasion—of a speedy delirium—of a conscious moment, in which the new-made bride opened wide her astonished eyes upon her kneeling husband, pleading with God to spare her precious life; and we read the heart-rending exclamation of the latter as the truth flashed upon her clouded intellect—"Oh! I am not to die *now?*—when we have been so happy?" and with streaming eyes we turn away from the corpse of Charlotte Brontë.

Facts for Unjust Critics
June 13, 1857

A few scraps from the "Life of Charlotte Brontë," that I would like to see pasted up in editorial offices throughout the length and breadth of the land:[10]

"She, Miss Brontë, especially disliked the lowering of the standard by which to judge a work of fiction if it proceeded from a feminine pen; and praise, mingled with pseudo-gallant allusions to her sex, mortified her far more than actual blame."

"Come what will," she says, "I can not, when I write, think always of myself, and of what is elegant and charming in femininity; it is not on these terms, or with such ideas, that I ever took pen in hand, and if it is only on these terms my writing will be tolerated, I shall pass away from the public and trouble it no more."

"I wish all reviewers believed me to be a man; they would be more just to me. They will, I know, keep measuring me by some standard of what they deem becoming to my sex; where I am not what they consider graceful, they will condemn me."

"No matter—whether known or unknown—misjudged or the contrary—I am resolved not to write otherwise. *I shall bend as my powers tend.* The two human beings who understood me are gone; I have some who love me yet, and whom I love, without expecting or having a right to expect they shall perfectly understand me. I am satisfied, *but I must have my own way in the matter of writing.*"

Speaking of some attacks on Miss Brontë, her biographer says:

"Flippancy takes a graver name, when directed against an author by an anonymous writer; we then call it *cowardly insolence.*"

She also says:

"It is well that the thoughtless critics, who spoke of the sad and gloomy views of life presented by the Brontës in their tales, should know how such words were wrung out of them by the living recollection of the long agony they suffered. It is well, too, that they who have objected to the representation of *coarseness, and shrank from it with repugnance, as if such conception arose out of the writers, should learn, that not from the imagination, not from internal conception—but from the hard cruel facts, pressed down, by an external life upon their very senses, for long months and years together, did they write out what they saw, obeying the stern dictates of their consciences.* They might be mistaken. They might err in writing at all, when their afflictions were so great that they could not write otherwise than as they did of life. It is possible that it would have been better to have described good and pleasant people, doing only good and pleasant things (*in which case they could hardly have written at any time*): all I say is, that never, I believe, did women possessed of such wonderful gifts exercise them with a fuller feeling of responsibility for their use."

A friend of Miss Brontë says:

"The world heartily, greedily enjoyed the fruits of Miss Brontë's labors, *and then found out she was much to blame for possessing such faculties.*"

Mrs. Gaskell says:

"So utterly unconscious was Miss Brontë of what was by some esteemed '*coarse*' in her writings, that on one occasion, when the conversation turned upon women's writing fiction—she said, in her grave, earnest way, 'I hope God will take away from me whatever power of invention, or expression I may have, before he lets me become blind to the sense of what is fitting, or unfitting to be said.'"

Fanny Fern says:
I would that all who critically finger women's books, would read and ponder these extracts. I would that reviewers had a more fitting sense of their responsibility, in giving their verdicts to the public; permitting themselves to be swayed neither by personal friendship, nor private pique; speaking *honestly*, by all means, but remembering their own sisters, when they would

point a flippant, smart article *by disrespectful mention of a lady writer; or by an unmanly, brutal persistence in tearing from her face the mask of incognito-ship, which she has, if she pleases, an undoubted right to wear.* I would that they would speak respectfully of those whose pure, self-denying life, has been through trials and temptations under which *their* strong natures would have succumbed; and who tremblingly await the public issue of days and nights of single-handed—single-hearted weariness and toil. Not that a woman's book should be praised because it is a woman's, nor, on the contrary, condemned for that reason. But as you would shrink from seeing a ruffian's hand laid upon your sister's gentle shoulder, deal honestly—but, I pray you, *courteously*—with those whose necessities have forced them out from the blessed shelter of the home circle, into jostling contact with rougher natures.

To Writers
August 22, 1857

Be original. Don't filch whole sentences from other writers, without honest quotation marks. Don't treat us to Dickens and water—or Thackeray and water—or Brontë and water—or any other writer and water. Be yourself, or be nothing. (I *have* known the terms synonymous!) Always remember, that in this reading age and community, *an imitation is sure to be seen through;* and that in attempting servilely to copy the style of another, you not only fail of gaining his style, but you lose every chance of individuality for your own. If you have nothing to say, don't say it; if you have, for patience' sake, use your own words to do it in, though they may be rough as a nutmeg-grater. Second-hand literary goods are a drug in the market.

Fresh Leaves, by Fanny Fern[11]
October 10, 1857

This little volume has just been laid upon our table. The publishers have done all they could for it, with regard to outward adorning. No doubt it will be welcomed by those who admire this lady's style of writing: we confess ourselves not to be of that number. We have never seen Fanny Fern, nor do we desire to do so. We imagine her, from her writings, to be a muscular, black-browed, grenadier-looking female, who would be more at home in a boxing gallery than in a parlor,—a vociferous, demonstrative, strong-minded horror,—a woman only by virtue of her dress. Bah! the very thought sickens us. We have read, or, rather, tried to read, her halloo-there effusions. When we take up a woman's book we expect to find gentleness, timidity, and that lovely reliance on the patronage of our sex which constitutes a woman's greatest charm. We do not wish to be startled by bold expressions, or disgusted with exhibitions of masculine weaknesses. We do not desire to see a woman wielding the scimitar blade of sarcasm. If she be, unfortunately, endowed with a gift so dangerous, let her—as she values the approbation of our sex—fold it in a napkin. Fanny's strong-minded nose would probably turn up at this inducement. Thank heaven! there are still women who *are* women—who know the place Heaven assigned them, and keep it—who do not waste floods of ink and paper, brow-beating men and stirring up silly women;—who do not teach children that a game of romps is of as much importance as Blair's Philosophy;—who have not the presumption to advise clergymen as to their duties, or lecture doctors, and savans;—who live for something else than to astonish a gaping, idiotic crowd. Thank heaven! there are women writers who do not disturb our complacence or serenity; whose books lull one to sleep like a strain of gentle music; who excite no antagonism, or angry feeling. Woman never was intended for an irritant: she should be oil upon the troubled waters of manhood—soft and amalgamating, a necessary but unobtrusive ingredient;—never challenging attention—never throwing the gauntlet of defiance to a beard, but softly purring beside it lest it bristle and scratch.

The very fact that Fanny Fern has, in the language of her admirers, "elbowed her way through unheard of difficulties," shows that she is an antagonistic, pugilistic female. One must needs, forsooth, get out of her way, or be pushed one side, or trampled down. How much more womanly to have allowed herself to be doubled up by adversity, and quietly laid away on the shelf of fate, than to have rolled up her sleeves, and gone to fisticuffs with it. Such a woman may conquer, it is true, but her victory will cost her dear; it will neither be forgotten nor forgiven—let her put that in her apron pocket.

As to Fanny Fern's grammar, rhetoric, and punctuation, they are beneath criticism. It is all very well for her to say, those who wish commas, semi-colons and periods, must look for them in the printer's case, or that she who finds ideas must not be expected to find rhetoric or grammar, for our part, we should be gratified if we had even found any ideas!

We regret to be obliged to speak thus of a lady's book: it gives us pleasure, when we can do so conscientiously, to pat lady writers on the head; but we owe a duty to the public which will not permit us to recommend to their favorable notice an aspirant who has been unwomanly enough so boldly to contest every inch of ground in order to reach them—an aspirant at once so high-stepping and so ignorant, so plausible, yet so pernicious. We have a conservative horror of this pop-gun, torpedo female; we predict for Fanny Fern's "Leaves" only a fleeting autumnal flutter.

International Copyright
November 28, 1857

Two of my books translated into German. It's all very well to talk about the "compliment," and "the honor," and all that sort of thing—that sounds very well—but I'm not going, in these "Panic" times, to thank anybody for putting their fore-finger and thumb into my pocket, and helping themselves, because they make me a graceful bow while they are doing it. Why don't they do the handsome thing by us authors? Yes—why don't we have an international copyright law? I'm getting interested in the subject. Fudge for the "tariff"—fudge for "filibustering" and "squatter-sovereignty"—and "sub-treasury"—and "fishing grounds"—and "currency," and such trash—why don't those Congress fellows leave off tossing straws, and right us scribblers?

I have no doubt now that Buchanan takes his three meals a day, and digests them, too, all the same, as if those foreigners hadn't their cribbing paws in our literary pockets, year in and year out. It is the unprincipled principle of the thing—it is the cool impudence of it—it is the idea that what's yours *isn't* yours. That a rasping nutmeg-grater can be secured by a patent, and a rasping book can't.

I won't stand it.

I'll take a hat, and go round and collect the "ayes" and "no-es." I'll draw up a petition, and get more signatures to it than I ever had enemies, and that's pledging myself for considerable. I'll go to Washington—I'll bother Buchanan within an inch of his bachelor life—I'll be a perfect incubus—I'll waylay him in the Capitol—I'll waylay him in the White-House, and I'll beset him in his "Kitchen Cabinet," as they call it. The widow who wearied out the judge shall be a fool to me. I'll not only "continually come," but I'll never go. I'll be a standing rebuke and an everlasting reproach to those pussy-cat male authors, who sit still to have their literary faces slapped. I solemnly declare that, from this day, I will never shake hands with another man who will not swear on his cigar-case to make Washington too hot for any President who won't bestir himself in this matter. And you needn't think that it is all because I take a narrow-little-contracted-Bostonian-look-out-for-number-one-view of this matter. I'm prospectively considering future female-authors "long since unborn," who will profit by it, and hand my honored name down to their blessed grandfathers and grandmothers.

But softly—women never get anything by clamoring for it—I'll be 'umble—I'll be wily—I'll turn petticoat diplomatist—I'll get acquainted with all the "Members"—(It will hurt me to do it,) but I'll even smile sweetly at the South! I'll shake velvet hands, and exchange velvet words with every point of the compass. "Hard Shells" and "Soft Shells" shall be alike to me. "Democrats" and "Republicans," "Know-Nothings" and "foreigners"—I'll embrace them all in my india-rubber affections.

If anything *could* tie my tongue on this subject, I'll tell you what it would be—it is a short word, but full of meaning:

Dickens!

Think how abominably and inextricably we Americans are in his debt; not to mention other good literary fellows, male and female. Think how many hearth-stones he has gladdened, how many sinking hearts he has cheered; how the universal voice of humanity sends every day, across the sea after him, the heart-felt God bless you! Shame that he has had from us nothing more substantial!

It is all very well to say—Oh, he is well enough off pecuniarily; authors shouldn't be mercenary. Just as well might you refuse to pay your landlord his rent, because he owned other houses than the one he allowed you to live in. Justice—my friends—justice; and three cheers for Lord Napier, who is pledged for us authors.[12] Does his lordship want statistics? I am ready to toss into his lap eleven English editions of Fern books, and not a pound to show for it, though I should like very well to give his countrymen a pound! If he has the feelings of a husband, of a father, of a lord, and of what is more, a *man*—let him use his British pocket-handkerchief at this filching of Fern Leaves from "the May-flower."

I ask the noble lord to consider the pens I've worn out, the ink I've consumed, the foolscap I've wasted, and the tears that have blistered it and I ask him—Lord Napier,—whose title I snap my republican fingers at, and whose lovely little boys I should like to kiss if he can look me—Fanny—in the eye, without winking, and say that I've not fairly earned for myself, and my descendants, that quit-claim from future pen and ink—which John Bull ought to sign with a bag of sovereigns, this day, A. D., 1857? and, what's more, I should like, with Mr. Fern's permission, or without it, as the case may be, to hold him—Lord Napier—by the official button till he sees that I get it.

A Rainy Day
February 20, 1858

Rain—rain—rain. Soot and chimney-sweeps! Everything dingy and doleful—gloomy and gummy—sticky, and solemn, and sad. I shall go mad. Everybody's nose is as red as a lobster, and the mud is ankle deep. *New York* mud! Ask the laundresses what that is. One might as well dip one's petticoats in a pot of brown paint. I'll go out though, in spite of it; but how about the umbrella? for it will take both my hands, till the cramp seizes them, to hold my clothes out of the puddles; and as to walking under an umbrella held by a man! Try it once. When he is not giving you all the drippings from the points of the whalebones, he is catching those points in the ribbon on your bonnet; and when he is not doing that, he is holding it so far back that the rain drives slap in your face; and when he is not doing that, he is holding it so far down over your nose that it would take a seer to find out your latitude and longitude. Ask any woman if it isn't a gospel fact, not to mention the puddles he plants his boots in for the edification of your stockings.

Go without an umbrella. Yes, and get a stiff neck for my folly. I won't. I'll not go out at all. I'll sit with my nose flattened against the window-pane, watching those miserable gray clouds, that came on purpose to drive me—Ah, here come a batch of letters, the gods grant there may be something pleasant, for I'm just at the last-drop-in-the-bucket pinch. I'm cross enough to eat my grandmother, and she deserves it, for if it hadn't been for her I shouldn't have been here.

Let's see now. "Mrs. Robert Bonner, alias Fanny Fern." I wonder how Mr. Bonner's wife will relish that? I wonder what will be the predominant expression of Mr. Fern's physiognomy when he sees it? I wonder if a woman, whose husband is a small man, can be taken up for *big*-amy?

Here's another.

"FANNY FERN:—Madam—Please send your autograph *by return of mail.*

JOHN STOKES."

Cool, that!

And here's a manuscript which I am requested to read through, hand to Mr. Bonner, and request him to publish and pay for, as the writer wants money.

Now, if I could ensure this, I would be most happy to do so; but when an editor's acceptance of a MS. depends not upon *my* handing it to him, but upon its merit, and the kind of merit adapted to his uses; and, more than all, when that editor absolutely declines even giving a glance at any new contributions, as he is neck deep in them already, of what avail are my good wishes?

And here's another from a dear little girl whom I never saw, way off in the prairies, who wants me to write another "Play-Day Book" for her. It is written in a little crooked, childish hand; mamma evidently dotting the i's and crossing the t's. She has more sense than half the adults, for at the close she says, *I stop now because I have nothing to say.* Naive little "Fanny!" I wish the world was two-thirds children, and the other third babies. It is the grown people and the rain that put me out of tune. I should be a seraphim else. The little ones always humanize me—combed or uncombed, dirty or clean, I can always see their folded wings. Well might He "take a little child and set it in their midst."

A Leaf for Paul Pry
June 19, 1858

There may be some authoresses who like to be stared at: I am not going to contest that point; there may be some who are gratified, when they enter a ferry-boat or car, to have somebody nudge everybody in the ribs, and whisper loud enough to be heard from Maine to California—Look! that's Dolly Daffodil, the authoress. There may be some who like, when they sit down in an omnibus, to have a lady (?) or gentleman (?) opposite make the same remark, with the following additions: Light hair, hasn't she?—wavy?—tall?

dressed in black?—wonder what's her fancy for always wearing black?—how do you like her mantilla?—funny that she always wears a straw bonnet—and various other edifying remarks of the same nature. This may be very civil. I don't wish to say it is not. There may be some authoresses who like, when they go to church, to have the people in the next pew dislocate their necks in the attempt to ascertain what Dolly Daffodil looks like; whether she holds her hymn-book upside down, or down side up, or is guilty of the hetere-dox-ity of not following the hymn at all, as laid down in the programme. It is a great help to devotion to be told in church, within an inch of your nose, that you are fine-looking, or the contrary; and it may be pleasant for some authoresses, after services are over, to have the people in the pew so absorbed taking an inventory of their chin, eyes, nose, and dress, that they quite forget to let them go home to dinner. I don't wish to find fault with these little Sunday diversions—not at all. It may be very pleasant for them at the opera to have a gentleman turn round, at a whisper from his neighbor, with a *very* audible "you don't say so?"—and resting his arm on the back of the seat before them, take a double-barreled stare straight into their faces, and then remark with regard to the gentleman who accompanies them—"husband, I suppose?" and then to see his wiseacre informant nod an oracular assent when said gentleman is only a friend of your husband's. It may be fun for Dolly Daffodil to sit behind a couple who fancy they have discovered Dolly Daffodil, the authoress, on the opposite side of the house, in the person of a lady dressed within an inch of her life. It may be fun to hear them, after exhausting the bogus authoress through an opera-glass, wonder how her husband likes to see her dressed so extravagantly, and how long her publishers can afford to supply such a wardrobe as *that*; and how funny it is, after all, that books will buy diamonds. It may be funny for Dolly Daffodil's tall daughter, who happens to have hair like her mother's, to be mistaken for Dolly Daffodil, and ogled and commented upon, till the poor thing is as red as a pulpit-cushion. I don't wish to say it isn't, this is a free country, a *very* free country. It may be agreeable for some authoresses to stand like a prize ox, or a trotting horse, or a milliner's lay-figure, to have their physical points discussed; to hear, time after time, the dimensions of their hips, ankles, shoulders, and waist. They may think New York is the central point of good manners, and good breeding in these respects; I don't deny it. New York, herself, may think that, because an authoress don't pucker up her mouth to call the *leg* of a table the *limb* of a table, that it therefore follows she may not have modesty enough to object to being stared out of countenance, or informed that she is an authoress at every street-corner; and it may be an indelible mark of a lady, or a gentleman, to do this, in those loud, *musical* tones which this population has acquired by trying, from their Knickerbocker cradles, to out-yell the deafening din of omnibusses. I don't say it isn't. I don't complain—not at all. As the big blacksmith said, when his wife whipped him—"It does her a great deal of good, and, after all, it don't hurt me any."

A Sketch for Paul Pry
March 26, 1859

A lady from a distance writes to know "how I look, as she has read very contradictory reports in the papers, as to black eyes and blue, blonde hair and raven, short stature and tall, thinness and thickness of figure, till she is quite unable to form an opinion" on this *very* important subject.

As misery loves company, it may be some satisfaction to you, my dear Madam, to know that many people, with much better opportunities of judging, have fallen into most ludicrous mistakes while pursuing this branch of knowledge; taking a minute inventory of some woman, quite innocent of ink-tipped fingers, with a zeal worthy of a New York correspondent for some country paper; hence the discrepancies in the accounts you complain of. Having a strong sympathy for such misguided sons of Adam, I proceed, both in mercy to them and in answer to your letter, to sketch myself and my personal habits so accurately, that hereafter there need be no mistake on a point of such *vital interest*. Listen:

Imagine a thin, angular, stooping figure, blear-eyed, gray-haired, unable to walk without the aid of a stick, unless, indeed, some friendly arm is near. A testy, sour, ferocious old creature, who never laughs herself, and is therefore unwilling anybody else should laugh; who fancies only wiry dogs and vicious horses, and keeps a nest of snakes in her boudoir, that she may amuse herself by terrifying her visitors; who wears long dresses to conceal the loss of her foot, which occurred in an attempt to kick a child who sneezed, just as she was trying to catch an idea; who has twelve children and five grand-children—any mention of the latter being sufficient to set her into the most insane fury—and who are consequently boarded in the country, and never alluded to by those who wish to stand high in her esteem. Imagine her dress to be generally of bright yellow, with pink trimmings, or sea-green looped with sky-blue ribbons. Imagine her so fond of seeing herself reproduced in Daguerrean galleries, that she actually persecutes every owner of one, and every artist she knows, to sketch her.

She rises about twelve o'clock every forenoon, and breakfasts on her favorite dish of fried onions. She then writes for three hours, paying an organ-grinder to execute "Pop Goes the Weazel" under her window the while. Then she admits a hair-dresser to braid her gray locks, after which she rolls herself in huge shawls, to conceal the extreme thinness of her figure, and strikes an attitude on the parlor sofa to receive visitors, which she prefers to be of the *female* persuasion. At six she dines, drinking large quantities of "brown stout." After that she is lifted into a carriage, and proceeds to the opera or the theater, or wherever she can display herself to the best advantage. Her age is undoubtedly seventy, though she confesses only to sixty-nine. As to *Mr.* Fern, he is a corpulent gentleman of sixty—red-faced, bald-headed, just now employed, body and soul, in getting out a patent machine for packing herrings, which has been received with great favor at Washington, and in which he has been greatly assisted by his wife's mechanical turn of mind.

Both Mr. and Mrs. Fern are very hospitable. They are famous for their "literary soirees," at which the principal recommendation is great latitude in length of hair and *ears*. A list of "hotel arrivals" is left daily at their door, and a runner constantly employed to secure the most favorable specimens of this class. If the title of "Lord" be prefixed to the new arrival, the runner receives an extra fee at their hands for prompt intelligence, and the first chance at him. You will be pleased to observe, my dear Madam, that notwithstanding the many claims society has upon their valuable time, this fascinating couple still contrive to push as fast as possible, that valuable patent for packing herrings, to which I have alluded, though I cannot *yet* name the exact day on which it will be at the service of the public. Any further information which may be desired by you or any body else on that, or any other personal topic connected with them, will be most delightedly given by your obliged friend,

FANNY FERN.

Pleasures of Authorship
February 23, 1861

How few persons who read a book ever think of the labor necessary to produce it. The amount of thinking and planning, before pen touches paper;—the most felicitous key-note for the commencement;—that found, the hours upon hours, in which bending over the MS., sometimes in joy, sometimes in sadness, sometimes in weariness, page after page grows under the aching fingers, till finis is added. Then—the reading over for erasions, interlineations, and additions; then the moment when it passes from your reluctant, yet willing hands, into those of the publishers and printers. Then—oh horror! the purgatorial proofs, and crucifying punctuation; concerning which last, I will maintain every author's independent right to do as he or she pleases, spite of all arbitrary "rules." Pencil in hand, with glaring eyes you pounce upon every syllable, lest some typographical error escape you for the eyes of him whose most pious ejaculation is, "oh that mine enemy would write a book!" Then the first copy! when what is writ, being writ, and stereotyped—there you are—spite of misrepresenting errors—to be handed over to the microscopic analysis of a cool world, who stick a pin through your heart, and impale you for the museum of the naturalist. Oh the drops of perspiration which stand on your brow, when you find yourself made to say just what you never *did* say; when quotation marks are omitted, and insignificant words are italicised, and your chronology and geography, spite of your careful re-reading, are at fault, and the mischief is to pay generally, and no laudanum handy. Then come those jackals the critics; some of whom reading the title-page, middle chapter, and last sentence, fill out a non-committal review—formula—ready made and provided—for all occasions, and suited to all subjects. Others again wait, before deciding, for the verdict of some Sir Oracle, who hits or misses, just as his breakfast agrees or disagrees with him on that day. Others again so overload you with praise, that every person of common sense immediately concludes the book *must* be a humbug. Another abuses you without stint or limit, for some private grudge against yourself or some one of the same name, it matters not which. Of course, if you are an old stager you never read a notice at all, after you have thus ascertained how much criticism is worth, and what it amounts to;—not though some of your dear five hundred friends who think it is "shameful" take special pains to bring you an adverse review. You've been behind the scenes, and seen the ropes, and pulleys, and blue lights; it's no use trying to disturb your equanimity in *that* state of things. But if you are a woman, and some ungentlemanly critic reviews not your *book* but *you*, that is another matter; of course, in such a case, you put your pluckiest male friend on the track, and tell him to order his funeral.

Some day you see the other side. A letter comes to you; then another, and another, till mayhap, if you are lucky, you have done counting them; full of love and appreciation, of what you know, better than any body can tell you, is very faulty; but in which, nevertheless, are some of your warmest heart-throbs. It may be a man, or woman, or child, whose spiritual eyes gaze into yours, whose warm hand-grasp reaches you over miles and seas far away, and claims you for a dear though unseen friend; blessing you for some word of yours that has come like a cordial, when heart and soul grew faint, to make life's paths easy to the tired feet. Ah! then your tears fall as you say, *this repays me for all my toil, this is better than a diploma from any college.*

What of the *pecuniary* returns? Oh sure enough; well—if no idiotic accident happens on publication day, if your publisher is not short of "paper" or "copies" at the critical moment when jolly "orders" are coming in, or if he don't "fail" just then, or his store take fire, very likely you'll make a dollar or two. *I* did.

Answers to My Own Correspondents
March 2, 1861

LUCIA:—I am sorry that in your innocence you should have placed any dependence upon the statements of "a New York Correspondent." It is a pity to pull down any of the fine air-castles they are in the habit of building; still it is my duty to inform you that these gentry often describe, with the greatest minuteness, authors and authoresses whom they have never seen, manufacturing, at the same time, little personal histories concerning these celebrities, valuable only as ingenious specimen—"bricks, made without straw." It matters little to the writers whether nature has furnished the authoress about whom they romance with black eyes or blue, brown hair or flaxen; whether nature made her a six-foot grenadier, or a symmetrical pocket edition of womanhood; the description answers all the same for the provincial paper for which it was intended, and these Ananias and Sapphira gentry find that a spicy lie pays as well as the truth—at least till they are found out. No, Madam; notwithstanding the statements of your valuable "New York Correspondent" for the—, I have no "daughters married"; I never "wear a black stocking on one foot and a white one on the other, at the same time, to attract attention"; I never "rode on the top of an omnibus"; I don't "smoke cigarettes or chew opium"; I have no personal knowledge concerning the "mud-scow," "handcart," "cooking stove," and "hotel" that you have his authority for saying have been severally "named for me." I am not "married to Mr. Bonner," who has a most estimable wife of his own. I never "delivered an address in public"; and with regard to "the amount I have made by my pen," you and the special "New York Correspondent" are quite at liberty to speculate about it, without any assistance from me.

As to my "religious creed," the first article in it is, "Thou shalt not bear false witness against thy neighbor."

Unscrupulous Authors
April 20, 1861

There comes a time when the period for promiscuous reading is over, and you take up a volume fastidiously, as you choose a friend, and only when you know the author's name to be good endorsement for the time consumed in the perusal of his book. After having given yourself up to him to do what he will with you, to make you laugh or to make you cry; to make you glad or make you sorry; to make you at peace with your fellows, or to make you turn away disgusted from them;—after all this, for him to lift you up in the seventh heaven, only to drop you flop into a new made grave, is unkind, to say the least. If it were *necessary*, you could forgive it; if, in the last flagrant instance of this kind, the writer could not just as well have cured the melancholy of a young girl by love and sympathy, as to have killed her off merely because she had become troublesome, and he didn't know what else to do with her, one might overlook it. Parents who bring interesting children into the world only to strangle them, when one is used to their pretty ways, stand a chance to be introduced to the gallows for taking such a liberty—why not authors? In a stupid book, of course, one don't care who dies; the author may outrage the probabilities to his heart's content; nobody loses a wink of sleep by it, except some green boarding-school girl, who, heaven help her, ought to be bottling up her tears for her own sorrows, which she will be safe enough to have whenever she outgrows pinafores, and becomes a woman. As I said, stupid authors may do what they like with their heroines, and stupid people may cry over their fate, if their handkerchiefs are handy, and it may be very well for a "literary doctor" to kill off young people in his books from sheer force of habit; we are not going to cry about it, but next time he writes a story, we protest against his introducing us to interesting people, merely to use them for a thread to string medical and theological theories upon. Nor are we about to give the culprit the gratuitous benefit of an advertisement by naming him.[13] What we want to know is, if it is not high time authors had done with these "Yelverton"[14] consciences, and taken a little humanity into consideration, while making their "plots"? We are tired, too, of the piled-up horrors with which some novelists bait for readers. Anybody can introduce a ghost or a bloody head; it takes *genius*, and that of the very highest order, to make what are called "common-place" events and persons interesting. Therefore, when we hear a person say of a book which has enchained thousands, "the plot is nothing, I don't see how or why it is so popular," we simply set him or her down for a goose. We could name writers, who, without a thrilling "plot," can invest chapter after chapter with such a fascination, that your soul, like an instrument in the hands of a skillful player, makes echo as they will. It were well if such authors considered their terrible responsibility for good or ill.

Literary Beginners
March 26, 1864

It is a difficult thing to tell the truth sometimes. Now here is a letter, containing an article by which the writer hopes to make money; and of which my "candid opinion is asked, as soon as convenient."

Now in the first place, the article is most illegibly written; an objection sufficient to condemn it at once, with a hurried Editor—and all Editors are hurried—beside having always a bushel basket full of MSS. already in hand to look over. In the second place, the spelling is wofully at fault. In the third place, the punctuation is altogether missing. In the fourth place, if all these things were amended, the article itself is tame, common-place, and badly expressed. Now that is my "candid opinion" of it.

Still, I am not verdant enough to believe that the writer wished my "candid opinion" were it so condemnatory as this; and should I give it, there is great danger it would be misconstrued. The author in his wounded self-love might say, that, being a writer myself, I was not disposed to be impartial. Or he might go farther and say that I had probably forgotten the time when *I* commenced writing, and longed for an appreciative or encouraging word myself. Now this would pain me very much; it would also be very unjust; because when I began to write I called that person my best and truest friend who dared tell me when I was at fault in such matters. I have now in my remembrance a stranger, who often wrote me, regarding my articles, as they appeared from time to time; who criticized them unsparingly; finding fault in the plainest Saxon when he could not approve or praise. I thanked him then, I do so now; and was gratified at the singular interest he manifested in one unknown to him. I have never seen him all these years of my literary effort; but I know him to have been more truly my friend than they who would flatter me into believing better of what talent I may possess than it really merits.

This is the way I felt about friendly though unfavorable criticism. The question is, have *I* sufficient courage to risk being misunderstood, should *I*, in this instance, speak honestly and plainly. Or shall I write a very polite, non-committal answer, meaning anything, or nothing. Or shall I praise it unqualifiedly, and recommend the writer to persevere in a vocation in which I am sure he is certain to be doomed to disappointment; and all for the sake of being thought a generous, genial, kindly, sympathetic sort of person.

Which shall I do?

The writer would not like to come down off his pedestal, and hear that he must begin at the foot of the ladder, and, first of all, learn to spell correctly, before he can write. And that after words must come thoughts; and that after thoughts must come the felicitous expression of thoughts. And that, after all that, he can then look about for a market for the same.

This, you see, is a tedious process to one who wants not only immediate but *large* pecuniary results; and evidently considers himself entitled to them, notwithstanding his deference to your "candid opinion."

But what a pleasure, when the person appealed to, can conscientiously say to a writer, that he has not *over* but *under*-rated his gifts! What a pleasure if one's opinion can be of any value to him; to be able to speak encouragingly of the present and hopefully for the future. And surely, he who has himself waded through this initiatory "Slough of Despond," and, by one chance in a thousand, landed safely on the other side, should be the last to beckon, or lure into it, those whose careless steps, struggle they ever so blindly, may never find sure or permanent foothold.

"What did I do, after all, about *that letter?*" Well, if you insist upon cornering me, it lies unanswered on my desk, this minute: a staring monument of the moral cowardice of

FANNY FERN.

Who Shall Decide When Doctors Disagree
October 26, 1867

Here lie two letters on my desk, from strangers, regarding a late article of mine in the *Ledger*. One warmly endorses the sentiments therein expressed, and calls upon "God to bless me" for their expression. The other dissents entirely, and commends me to the notice of a *far different Power*, for disseminating such wrong-headed notions. Thank you both! I am used to both styles of epistles. There's nothing I contend for more than individuality of opinion; this would be a stupid world enough if we all thought, felt, and acted after one universal programme; every body must see things from their own stand-point and through their own spectacles; and, provided they use civil language, should "have the floor" in turn to air their ideas. It might be well to suggest that, in commenting on a newspaper article, care should be taken that it be first thoroughly read, that the writer's meaning be not misinterpreted; if this were done in many cases, the foundation for an adverse opinion would be quite knocked from under. Authors must expect the penalties as well as the rewards of their labors; but one of the most trying is to be accused of sentiments and feelings which they hold in utter abhorrence. Still, he would make small progress on a journey, who should stop to hurl a stone at every barking creature at his heels; therefore, in such cases, let patience have her perfect work, and let the victim keep steadily moving on, with an eye fixed upon the goal in the distance. But when you have unintentionally wounded a gentle spirit, which grieves all the more because it conscientiously believes that you have done harm, ah! then, none would be sorrier than the present writer; none would go farther to soothe the hurt; none would try harder to agree in opinion, consistently with self-respect. But if every writer stopped to consider whether his readers would be pleased, or the contrary, with his sentiments, instead of busying himself with the subject on hand for the moment, it would be like the clouding in of the sun on a clear morning. Everything would be reduced to one colorless level. The bright tints taken away, made brighter by the sometime shadows, could give a landscape tame enough, spiritless enough, to engender hypochondria. Surely the world of today is more liberal than this. Surely it is learning "to agree to differ." Surely it knows by this time that a good life, is of more importance than creeds or beliefs. Surely in this year of our Lord, 1867, the days of the Inquisition are past both for editors and writers, and the watch-word of today—and, thank God, for tomorrow, and the day after—is progress, not paralysis.

Having said this, I consider that I have cleared the deck for action, as far as my own ship is concerned. A stray shot won't frighten or discourage me; on the contrary, it only makes me step round the livelier, to see that my guns are in working order. Then, again, any one who wishes to hail me, and haul alongside in a friendly manner, shall be always certain of a kind salute from

FANNY FERN.

Punishments and Rewards of Authors
March 2, 1872

The epistles which public persons receive, if published, would not be credible. Begging letters are a matter of course; often in the highwayman style of—"hand over and deliver." I had one recently from a perfect stranger, who wished a cool hundred or so, and mapped out the circuitous way in which it was to be sent, so that "his folks needn't know it," with a belief in my spooniness, which an acquaintance with me would scarcely have warranted. Following close on the heels of this, came another from a woman, whose ideas of my spare time and common-sense were about equally balanced. This stranger of the female persuasion, being hard-up for amusement, wished "a long, racy letter from me, such as I alone could write, with no religion in it, because she got enough of that from the minister's wife." It is unnecessary to add that both these missives found a home in my waste-paper basket. Autograph letters I do not object to, as they keep me in postage stamps, and my little "Bright Eyes" in cards to draw dogs and horses upon.

A friend of mine has been delivered from manuscripts sent for perusal, with the modest accompanying request to find a publisher for the same, by stating her price to be $200. She has received no request of the kind since this announcement.

These are some of the annoyances of authors; but, verily, they have their rewards too. Here comes a letter from my native State, Maine, with a box of wood mosses and berries to place round the roots of my house-plants; and as an expression of affection from a stranger who knows from my writings how well I love such things. She says, in closing, that she hopes that myself and Mr. Beecher will continue to write for the *New York Ledger* so long as she lives to read it. Mr. Beecher may step up and take his half of this sugar-plum, since he has announced himself a champion of "candy."

Then before me on my desk is a smiling baby face sent by its parents, who are strangers to me, if those can be strangers whose hearts warm toward each other; sent me, they add, "not for a silver cup, but because some chance words of mine touched their hearts, and so this little one was named Fanny Fern."

She smiles down upon me whether my sky be cloudy or clear, and in the light of that smile I will try to write worthily; for "their angels do always behold the face of my Father."

II

"Mr. Chairman, I rise to say, that there are no faults of sex; that there exist only faults of individuals"

On Society's Rules and Roles for Men and Women

Witty, satirical, scathing, unapologetically bold—Fern's commentary about gender roles was legendary. Her weekly *Ledger* column was an unprecedented platform for a woman in the public sphere, and she routinely used it to question her readers' assumptions about the roles of men and women in society. In many cases, Fern responded directly to the sources of patriarchal conditioning; she often skewered domestic advice book passages that instructed women on their subservience to men or affirmed men's power and superiority over women. At other times, she approached her topic as a journalist, responding to a current news story that revealed gender-based biases, hypocrisy, or double standards in the world around her. Whether in the form of humorous observations or searing social criticism, Fern's pieces about gender roles were calculated to enlighten, provoke, and, oftentimes, entertain her readers. She flipped the script on norms and stereotypes they took for granted: men were capable of vanity, conceit, and frivolity; women were capable of artistic and intellectual genius and had a right to earn a living. She also protested gendered norms that impacted women's health, such as restrictive women's clothing and secondhand smoke from men's cigars. While feminist-minded readers—both in Fern's time and today—would find much to relish in the author's outspoken criticism of the patriarchy, Fern's voice defies easy categorization. She balanced out her comments about men with the occasional diatribe against members of her own sex, particularly for any stereotypical behavior she found petty or annoying. Overall, though, she preferred to put her powerful platform to the service of exposing sexist inequities, many of which will continue to resonate with readers today.

Sober Husbands
From Fern Leaves from Fanny's Port-Folio, Second Series, *1854*

"If your husband looks grave, let him alone; don't disturb or annoy him."

Oh, pshaw! Were I married, the soberer my husband looked, the more fun I'd rattle about his ears. *Don't disturb him!* I guess so! I'd salt his coffee—and pepper his tea—and sugar his beef-steak—and tread on his toes—and hide his newspaper—and sew up his pockets—and put pins in his slippers—and dip his cigars in water,—and I wouldn't stop for the great Mogul, till I had shortened his long face to my liking. Certainly, he'd "get vexed"; there wouldn't be any fun in teasing him if he didn't; and that would give his melancholy blood a good, healthful start; and his eyes would snap and sparkle, and he'd say, "Fanny, will you be quiet or not?" and I should laugh, and pull his whiskers, and say decidedly, "*Not!*" and then I should tell him he hadn't the slightest idea how handsome he looked when he was vexed, and then he would pretend not to hear the compliment—but would pull up his dickey, and take a sly peep in the glass (for all that!) and then he'd begin to grow amiable, and get off his stilts, and be just as agreeable all the rest of the evening *as if he wasn't my husband*; and all because I didn't follow that stupid bit of advice "to let him alone." Just as if *I* didn't know! Just imagine me, Fanny, sitting down on a cricket in the corner, with my forefinger in my mouth, looking out the sides of my eyes, and waiting till that man got ready to speak to me! You can see at once it would be—be—. Well, the amount of it is, *I shouldn't do it!*

Hungry Husbands
From Fern Leaves from Fanny's Port-Folio, Second Series, *1854*

"The hand that can make a pie is a continual feast to the husband that marries its owner."[1]

Well, it is a humiliating reflection, that the straightest road to a man's heart is through his palate. He is never so amiable as when he has discussed a roast turkey. Then's your time, "Esther," for "half his kingdom," in the shape of a new bonnet, cap, shawl, or dress. He's too complacent to dispute the matter. Strike while the iron is hot; petition for a trip to Niagara, Saratoga, the Mammoth Cave, the White Mountains, or to London, Rome, or Paris. Should he demur about it, the next day cook him another turkey, and pack your trunk while he is eating it.

There's nothing on earth so savage—except a bear robbed of her cubs—as a hungry husband. It is as much as your life is worth to sneeze, till dinner is on the table, and his knife and fork are in vigorous play. Tommy will get his ears boxed, the ottoman will be kicked into the corner, your work-box be turned bottom upwards, and the poker and tongs will beat a tattoo on that grate that will be a caution to dilatory cooks.

After the first six mouthfuls you may venture to say your soul is your own; his eyes will lose their ferocity, his brow its furrows, and he will very likely recollect to help you to a cold potato! Never mind—*eat it*. You might have to swallow a worse pill—for instance, should he offer to kiss you!

Well, learn a lesson from it—keep him well fed and languid—live yourself on a low diet, and cultivate your thinking powers; and you'll be as spry as a cricket, and hop over all the objections and remonstrances that his dead-and-alive energies can muster. Yes, feed him well, and he will stay contentedly in his cage, like a gorged anaconda. If he were my husband, wouldn't I make him heaps of *pison* things! Bless me! I've made a mistake in the spelling; it should have been *pies and things*!

Feminine Waiters at Hotels
From Fern Leaves from Fanny's Port-Folio, Second Series, *1854*

"Some of our leading hotel-keepers are considering the policy of employing female waiters."

Good news for you, poor pale-faced sempstresses! Throw your thimbles at the heads of your penurious employers; put on your neatest and *plainest* dress; see that your feet and fingers are immaculate, and then rush *en masse* for the situation, ousting every white jacket in Yankeedom. Stipulate with your employers, for leave to carry in the pocket of your French apron, a pistol loaded with cranberry sauce, to plaster up the mouth of the first coxcomb who considers it necessary to preface his request for an omelette, with "*My dear*." It is my opinion that one such hint will be sufficient; if not, you can vary the order of exercises, by anointing him with a "hasty plate of soup" at dinner.

Always make a moustache wait twice as long as you do a man who wears a clean, presentable lip. Should he undertake to expedite your slippers by "a fee," tell him that hotel bills are *generally* settled at the clerk's office, except by *very* verdant travelers.

Should you see a woman at the table, digging down to the bottom of the salt cellar, as if the top stratum were too plebeian; or ordering ninety-nine messes (turning aside from each with affected airs of disgust,) or rolling up the whites of her eyes, declaring that she never sat down to a dinner-table before minus "finger glasses," you may be sure that her aristocratic blood is nourished, *at home*, on herrings and brown bread. When a masculine comes in with a white vest, flashy neck-tie, extraordinary looking plaid trousers, several yards of gold chain festooned over his vest, and a mammoth seal ring on his little finger, you may be sure that his tailor and his laundress are both on the anxious seat; and whenever you see travelers of *either* sex peregrinating the country in their "best bib and tucker," you can set them down for unmitigated "snobs," for high-bred people can't afford to be so extravagant!

I dare say you'll get sick of so much pretension and humbug. Never mind; it is better than to be stitching yourselves into a consumption over six-penny shirts; you'll have your fun out of it. This would be a horridly stupid world, if every body were sensible. I thank my stars every day, for the share of fools a kind Providence sends in my way.

The Last Bachelor Hours of Tom Pax
January 19, 1856

To-morrow, at eleven, then, I am to be married! I feel like a mouse conscious of coming cheese. Is it usual for bachelors to feel this way, or am I a peculiar institution? I trust the parson, being himself a married man, will be discreet enough to make a *short* prayer after the ceremony. Good gracious, my watch has stopped! no it hasn't, either; I should like to put the hands forward a little. What to do with myself till the time comes, that's the question. It is useless to go over to Mary's—she is knee-deep in dressmaker's traps. I never could see, when one dress is sufficient to be married in, the need women have to multiply them to such an indefinite extent. Think of postponing a man's happiness in such circumstances, that one more flounce may be added to a dress! Phew! how stifled this room is! I'll throw up the window; there now—there goes a pane of glass; who cares? I think I will shave; no I won't—I should be sure to cut my chin—how my hand trembles. I wonder what Mary is thinking about? bless her little soul. Well, for the life of me I don't know what to do with myself. Suppose I write down

Tom Pax's Last Will and Testament

In the name of Cupid, Amen.—I, Tom Pax, being of sound mind, and in immediate prospect of matrimony (praised be Providence for the same), and being desirous of settling my worldly affairs while I have the strength and capacity to do so, I do, with my own hand, write, make, and publish this, my last Will and Testament:

And in the first place, and principally, I commit my heart to the keeping of my adorable Mary, and my body to the parson, to be delivered over at the discretion of my groomsmen, to the aforesaid Mary; and as to such worldly goods as a kind Providence hath seen fit to intrust me with, I dispose of the same in the following manner (I also empower my executors to sell and dispose of my real estate, consisting of empty demijohns, old hats, and cigar boxes, and invest the proceeds in stocks or otherwise, to manage as they may think best; all of which is left to their discretion):

I give and bequeath to Tom Harris, my accomplice in single blessedness, my porcelain punch-bowl, white cotton night-cap, and large leathern chair, in whose arms I first renounced bachelordom and all its evil works.

I give and bequeath to the flames the yellow-covered novels and plays formerly used to alleviate my bachelor pangs, and whose attractions fade away before the scorching sun of my prospective happiness, like a snow wreath between a pair of brass andirons.

I give and bequeath to Bridget Donahue, the chambermaid of this lodging-house (to be applied to stuffing a pin-cushion), the locks of female hair, black, chestnut, brown, and tow-color, to be found in my great coat breast pocket.

I give and bequeath to my washwoman, Sally Mudge, my buttonless shirts, stringless dickeys, gossamer-ventilator stockings, and unmended gloves.

I give and bequeath to Denis M'Fudge, my bootblack, my half box of unsmoked Havanas, which are a nuisance in my hymeneal nostrils.

I give and bequeath to my benighted and unconverted bachelor friend, Sam Scott, my miserable and sinful prejudices against the blessed institution of matrimony, and may Cupid, of his infinite loving-kindness, take pity on his petrified heart.

In witness whereof, I, Tom Pax, the Testator, hereunto set my hand and seal, as my last Will and Testament, done this twelfth day of January, in the year of our Lord one thousand eight hundred and fifty-six.

Tom Pax. [L.S.]

Witness,

Fanny Fern.[2]

Tom Pax's Conjugal Soliloquy
February 9, 1856

Mrs. Pax is an authoress. I knew it when I married her. I liked the idea. I had not tried it then. I had not a clear idea what it was to have one's wife belong to the public. I thought marriage was marriage, brains not excepted. I was mistaken. Mrs. Pax is very kind: I don't wish to say that she is not. Very obliging: I would not have you think the contrary; but when I put my arm round Mrs. Pax's waist, and say, "Mary, I love you," she smiles in an absent, moonlight-kind of a way, and says, "Yes, to-day is Wednesday, is it not? I must write an article for 'The Weekly Monopolizer' to-day." That dampens my ardor; but presently I say again, being naturally affectionate, "Mary, I love you"; she replies (still abstractedly), "Thank you, how do you think it will do to call my next article for 'The Weekly Monopolizer,' 'The Stray Waif?'"

Mrs. Pax sews on all my shirt-buttons with the greatest good humor; I would not have you think she does not; but with her thoughts still on "The Weekly Monopolizer," she sews them on the flaps, instead of the wristbands. This is inconvenient; still Mrs. Pax is kindness itself; I make no complaint.

I am very fond of walking. After dinner I say to Mrs. Pax, "Mary, let us take a walk." She says, "Yes, certainly, I must go down town to read the proof of my article for 'The Monopolizer.'" So, I go down town with

Mrs. Pax. After tea I say, "Mary, let us go to the theater to-night"; she says, "I would be very happy to go, but the atmosphere is so bad there, the gas always escapes, and my head must be clear to-morrow, you know, for I have to write the last chapter of my forthcoming work, 'Prairie Life.'" So I stay at home with Mrs. Pax, and as I sit down by her on the sofa, and as nobody comes in, I think that this, after all, is better, (though I must say my wife looks well at the Opera, and I like to take her there). I put my arm around Mrs. Pax. It is a habit I have. In comes the servant; and brings a handful of letters for her by mail, directed to "Julia Jesamine" (that's my wife's *nom-de-plume*). I remove my arm from her waist, because she says "they are probably business letters which require immediate notice." She sits down at the table, and breaks the seals. Four of them are from fellows who want "her autograph." *Mrs. Pax's* autograph! The fifth is from a gentleman who, delighted with her last book, which he says "mirrored his own soul" (how do you suppose Mrs. Pax found out how to "mirror *his* soul?") requests "permission to correspond with the charming authoress." "Charming!" my wife! "his soul!" Mrs. Pax! The sixth is from a gentleman who desires "the loan of five hundred dollars, as he has been unfortunate in business, and has heard that her works have been very remunerative." Five hundred dollars for John Smith, from my wife! The seventh letter is from a man at the West, offering her her own price to deliver a lecture before the Pigtown Young Men's Institute. *I like that!*

Mrs. Pax opens her writing desk; it is one I gave her; takes some delicate buff note-paper; I gave her that, too; dips her gold pen (my gift) into the inkstand, and writes—writes till eleven o'clock. Eleven! and I, her husband, Tom Pax, sit there and wait for her.

The next morning when I awake, I say, "Mary dear?" She says, "Hush! don't speak, I've just got a capital subject to write about for 'The Weekly Monopolizer.'" Not that I am *complaining* of Mrs. Pax, not at all; not that I don't like my wife to be an authoress: I do. To be sure I can't say that I knew *exactly* what it involved. I did not know, for instance, that the Press in speaking of her by her *nom-de-plume* would call her "Our Julia," but I would not have you think I object to her being literary. On the contrary, I am not sure that I do not rather like it; but I ask the Editor of "The Weekly Monopolizer," as a man—as a Christian—as a husband—if he thinks it right—if it is doing as he would be done by—to monopolize my wife's thoughts as early as five o'clock in the morning? I merely ask for information. I trust I have no resentful feelings toward the animal.

Summer Travel
July 12, 1856

Take a journey at this elevation of the thermometer! Not I. Think of the breakfastless start before daybreak—think of a twelve hours' ride on the sunny side of the cars, in the neighborhood of some persistent talker, rattling untranslatable jargon into your aching ears; think of a hurried repast, in some barbarous half-way house; amid a heterogeneous assortment of men, women, and children, beef, pork, and mutton; minus forks, minus spoons, minus castor, minus come-atable waiters, and four shillings and indigestion to pay. Think of a "collision"—disemboweled trunks, and a wooden leg; think of an arrival at a crowded hotel; jammed, jaded, dusty, and dolorous; think of your closetless sentry-box of a room, infested by mosquitoes and Red Rovers; bed too narrow, window too small, candle too short, all the world and his wife a-bed, and the geography of the house an unexplained riddle. Think of your unrefreshing, vapor-bath sleep; think of the next morning, as seated on a dusty trunk, with your hair drooping about your ears, through which the whistle of the cars, and the jiggle-joggle of the brakeman, are still resounding; you try to remember, with your hand on your bewildered forehead, whether your breakfast robe is in the yellow trunk, or the black trunk, and if in either, whether it is at the top, bottom, or in the middle of the same, where your muslins and laces were deposited, what on earth you did with your dressing comb, and where amid your luggage, your toilet slippers may be possibly located. Think of a summons to breakfast at this interesting moment, the sun meanwhile streaming in through the blind chinks, with volcanic power. Think of all that, I say.

Now if I could travel *incog.* in masculine attire, no dresses to look after, no muslins to rumple, no bonnet to soil, no tresses to keep smooth, with only a hat and things, a neck-tie or two, a change of—of shirts—nothing but a moustache to twist into a horn when the dinner bell rings; just a dip into a wash-basin, a clean dicky, a jump into a pair of—trousers, and above all, liberty to go where I liked, without being stared at or questioned; a seat in a chair on its hind-legs, on a breezy door-step, a seat on the stairs in a wide hall, "taking notes"; a peep everywhere I chose, by lordly right of my pantaloons; nobody nudging somebody, to inquire why Miss Spinks the authoress wore her hair in curls instead of plaits; or making the astounding discovery that it was hips, not hoops, that made her dress stand out—that now, would be worth talking about: I'll do it.

But stop—I should have to cut my hair short—I should have to shave every morning, or at any rate call for hot water and go through the motions; men would jostle rudely past me, just as if they never had said such pretty things to me in flounces; I should be obliged, just as I had secured a nice seat in the cars, to get up, and give it to some imperious woman, who would not even say "thank you"; I should have to look on with hungry eyes till "the ladies" were all served at table; I should have to pick up their fans, and reticules, and handkerchiefs whenever they chose to drop them; I should have to give up the rocking-chairs, arm-chairs, and sofas for their use, and be called "a brute" at that; I should have to rush out of the cars, with five minutes' grace, at some stopping place, to get a glass of milk, for some "crying baby," with a contracted swallowing apparatus, and be pursued for life by the curses of its owner, because the whistle sounded while his two shilling tumbler was yet in the voracious baby's tight grip. No—no—I'll stay a woman, and what's more, I'll stay at home.

Moral Molasses; or, Too Sweet by Half
October 4, 1856

The most thorough emetic I know of, is in the shape of "Guide to Young Wives," and kindred books; as if one rule could, by any possibility, apply to all persons; as if every man living did not require different management; (bless me, I did not intend to use that torpedo word, but it is out now); as if, when things go wrong, a wife had only to fly up stairs, read a chapter in the "Young Wife's Guide," supposed to be suited to her complaint, and then go down stairs and apply the worthless plaster to the matrimonial sore. Pshaw! as well might a doctor send a peck of pills into a hospital, to be distributed by the hands of the nurse, to any and every male patient brought there, without regard to complaints or constitutional tendencies. I have no patience with such matrimonial nostrums.

"Always meet your husband with a smile." That is one of them. Suppose we put the boot on the other foot, and require the men to come grinning home? no matter how many of their notes may have been protested; no matter how, like Beelzebub, their business partner may have tormented them; no matter how badly elections go;—when they do it, may I be there to see! Nor should they. Passing over the everlasting monotony of that everlasting "Guide Book" smile, let us consider, brethren (sisters not admitted), what matrimony was intended for. As I look at it, as much to share each other's sorrows, as to share each other's joys; neither of the twain to shoulder wholly the one or the other. Those of you, brethren, who agree with me in this lucid view of the subject, please to signify it by rising.

'Tis a vote.

Well then, do people in moments of perplexity generally grin? Is it not asking too much of female, and a confounded sight too much of male nature, to do it when a man's store burns down, and there is no insurance? or when a misguided and infatuated baby stuffs beans up its nose, while its mamma is putting new cuffs on her husband's coat, hearing Katy say her lesson, and telling the cook about dinner? And when this sorely afflicted couple meet, would it not be best to make a clean breast of their troubles, sympathize together over them, have a nice matrimonial cry on each other's shoulders, and wind up with a first-class kiss?

'Tis a vote.

Well then—to the mischief with your grinning over a volcano;—erupt, and have done with it! so shall you love each other more for your very sorrows; so shall you avoid hypocrisy and kindred bedevilments, and pull evenly in the matrimonial harness. I speak as unto *wise* men.

Lastly, brethren, what I particularly admire, is the indirect compliment to your sex, which this absurd rule I have quoted implies; the devotion, magnanimity, fortitude, and courage, it gives *you* fair-weather sailors credit for! But what is the use of talking about it? These guide books are mainly written by sentimental old maids; who, had they ever been within kissing distance of a beard, would not so abominably have wasted pen, ink, and paper; or, by some old bachelor, tip-toeing on the outskirts of the promised land, without a single clear idea of its resources and requirements, or courage enough to settle there if he had.

A Gauntlet for the Men
February 21, 1857

I maintain it: all the heroism of the present day is to be found among women. I say it to your beards. I am sick of such remarks as these: "Poor fellow! he was unfortunate in business, and so he took to drinking"; or—"poor fellow! he had a bad wife, and lost all heart." What does a *woman* do who is unfortunate in business, I would like to know? Why—she tries again, of course, and keeps on trying to the end of the chapter, notwithstanding the pitiful remuneration man bestows upon her labor—notwithstanding his oft-repeated attempts to cheat her out of it when she has earned it! What does a woman do, who has a bad, improvident husband? Works all the harder, to be sure, to make up his deficiencies to her household; works day and night—smiles when her heart and back are both breaking—speaks hopeful words when her very soul is dying within her; denies herself the needed morsel to increase her children's portion, and crushed neither by the iron grip of poverty, nor allured by the Judas-smile of temptation, hopefully puts her trust in Him who feedeth the sparrows.

She—"the weaker sex?" Out on your pusillanimous manhood! "Took to drinking because he was unhappy!" Bless—his—big—Spartan—soul! How I admire him! Couldn't live a minute without he had every thing to his mind; never had the slightest idea of walking round an obstacle, or jumping over it; never practiced that sort of philosophical gymnastics—couldn't grit his teeth at fate, and defy it to do its worst, because they chattered so;—poor fellow! Wanted buttered toast, and had to eat dry bread; liked "2:40," and had to go a-foot;[3] fond of wine, and had to drink Croton;[4] couldn't smoke, though his stove-pipe did; rushed out of the world, and left his wife and children to battle with the fate that his coward soul was afraid to meet. Brave, magnanimous fellow!

Again—we are constantly hearing that the extravagance of women debars young men from the bliss of matrimony. Poor things! they can't select a wife *from out* the frivolous circle of fashion; there are no refined, well-educated, lady-like, practical girls and women, whom any man, with a man's soul, might be proud to call wife, nobly struggling for an honest maintenance as writers, governesses, teachers, sempstresses, and milliners. They never read such an advertisement as this in the papers:

> "Wanted, by a young girl, a situation as governess. She can teach the English branches, French and Italian; and is willing to accept a small remuneration, to secure a respectable home."

Fudge! None so blind as they who *won't* see. The truth is, most of the young men of the present day are selfish to the backbone. "Poor," too—very poor!—never go to Shelby's or Delmonico's for a nice little game supper, washed down with champagne at $2 a bottle; never smoke dozens of cigars a day, at six cents a piece; never invite—*themselves* to go to concerts, the opera, or the theater! Wish they could afford to get married, but can't, at least not till, as they elegantly express it, "they meet a pretty girl who has the tin."[5]

Lady Doctors
April 11, 1857

And so the female doctors are prospering and getting practice. I am sure I am heartily glad of it, for several reasons; one of which is, that it is an honest and honorable deliverance from the everlasting, non-remunerating, consumptive-provoking, monotonous needle. Another is, that it is a more excellent way of support, than by the mercenary and un-retraceable road, through the church-door to the altar, into which so many non-reliant women are driven. Having said this I feel at liberty to remark that we all have our little fancies, and one of mine is, that a hat is a pleasanter object of contemplation in a sick-room than a bonnet. I think, too, that my wrist reposes more comfortably in a big hand than a little one, and if my mouth is to be inspected, I prefer submitting it to a beard than to a flounce. Still—this may be a narrow prejudice, I dare say it is, but like most of my prejudices, I am afraid no amount of fire will burn it out of me.

A female doctor. Great Aesculapius! Before swallowing her pills (of which she would be the first!), I should want to make sure, that I had never come between her and a lover, or a new bonnet, or been the innocent recipient of a gracious smile from her husband. If I desired her undivided attention to my case, I should first remove the looking-glass, and if a consultation seemed advisable, I should wish to arm myself with a grid-iron, or a darning-needle, or some other appropriate weapon, before expressing such a wish. If my female doctor recommended a blister on my head, I should strongly doubt its necessity if my hair happened to be handsome, also the expediency of a scar-defacing plaster for my neck, if it happened to be plump and white. Still, these may be little prejudices; very like they are; but this I will say: before the breath is taken out of me by any female doctor, that while I am in my senses I will never exchange my gentlemanly, soft-voiced, soft-stepping, experienced, intelligent, handsome doctor, for all the female M. D.'s who ever carved up dead bodies or live characters—or tore each other's caps.

On Voices and Beards
April 3, 1858

I once believed in voices as indicative of character; it makes me laugh now to think of it. I was cured of it by a fellow who looked born to express physically "the dignity of human nature." I believe that is the fashionable phrase. Dignity! there's where the laugh comes in; dignity—in a leviathan of muscle and flesh, crawling lazily out of bed at twelve, M., to live the rest of the day by borrowing of anybody who could be bamboozled into believing that honesty, honor and manliness were represented in his deep, rich, sympathetic voice—his stock in trade, which it would be next to impossible to associate with cowardice or dishonor! Yes, cowardice! I say any man is a coward who throws the yoke of labor which the Almighty intended *him* to carry, upon the shoulders of his weaker brother, or sister, or mother, and saunters lazily through the world, demanding, unblushingly, *their* wages, whether in the shape of clothes, food, or money.

The dollars that fellow has borrowed on that voice, the drinks he has swallowed on the strength of it, not to mention the strength of the drinks! the oysters he has eaten by virtue of it, and the rides and invitations he has got!—all by those frank, hearty, jolly, musical tones, which it would puzzle a Shylock to resist. No, I believe no more in voices. Stay! yes, there's one specimen which never deceives, or, rather, which does nothing else. Did you never meet with the purr-y, mincing, die-of-a-rose-leaf female voice? Speak for a coffin for your reputation when you come in contact with that. Look out for a plague spot on your hand when the owner of that voice touches it. Treachery and deceit lurk in its oily, mellifluous whine. The owner of that voice would faint to mention the word leg; but look under her pillow and see the titles of the books she stealthily reads! The owner of that voice might sit for a female Joseph, but if Truth should seize the pencil, Potiphar's wife would glow on the canvas. The owner of that voice never disputes your opinion—oh, no; she acquiesces sweetly, and even deferentially: wait till your back is turned, and hear how much her vituperative tongue will leave of you!

Though I have done believing in voices, with the above exception, my faith remains unshaken in faces. As to heads, I take phrenology mild; but I defy anybody constantly to school the eye and mouth so that they shall tell no tales out of school. The beard movement, which on other accounts I hail, has somewhat overgrown my observations. Every man—(not that there are not some handsome fellows, heaven be blessed for their faces, delightful whether shaved or unshaved)—every man, I say, who has a weak, character-less mouth, or imperfect teeth, hastens to hide them behind a beard; and straightway the imposter goeth on his way rejoicing; perhaps sitteth down to write an article on the vanity of women, and their cupidical, toilette-ical, humbugging devices. Hollow cheeks take refuge under slantwise whiskers; narrow faces broaden themselves with the same; and he is indeed a bold man, or reckless, who does not endeavor to obliterate the traces of this fast age by a hirsute mask.

Catch these fellows once, and shave them—good gracious what dev-il-opments we should have! Verily, my brethren, vanity abideth not wholly with crinoline.

A Chapter for the Brethren
May 22, 1858

Do *gentlemen* ever—spit—in the presence of women? I see plenty of *men* who do it—whose coats, hats, boots, gloves and linen, are as unexception-able as I wish their manners were; but do *gentlemen* ever do it? that's what I want to know. I am not taking Chesterfield for my model; that hoary old sinner, who spent all his life polishing his head, and who could coolly sit down with one foot in the grave, to teach his son how to debauch women, and even taunt him with the modesty, which, thank God, the young man could not at once throw overboard as worthless cargo, even at the bidding of that accomplished old villain his father; I hate the hollow-hearted, dip-lomatic, surface-politeness he inculcates, and after which so many of his own corrupt stamp have patterned, and do pattern.[6] I hate, too, when I set down in the cars opposite a nice, loveable looking man, whom it is quite a pleasure to look at, to have those feelings changed at once into intense disgust by his spitting over my shoulder out of the window, or in the straw at my feet; (oh that straw, which I never bury my gaiter-boot in, without a shuddering horror)! The offender's luxuriant whiskers, which but a moment before were quite captivating, now look like an old shoe-brush; his eyes are very common orbs; his mouth, heaven forbid a woman's should ever come in contact with it after such a bar-room indecency; he might talk like a seraph, and I should be as deaf as if he asked me what Mr. Bonner pays me for my articles.

I can't help it. It gives me a mental as well as a physical nausea; it is a disgusting disrespect to every woman present; and I see no more reason why men, more than they, should contract such a habit. Good sirs—Hand-some sirs—Well-coated, Well-booted, Well-pantalooned—Otherwise love-able sirs—Will you desist?

It is such a pity you won't; you do so many good and gallant things; and that is why I take the pains to improve your manners, though I know at this moment you are inwardly saying words which a minister wouldn't approve! You sometimes bring the tears into my eyes, by cheerfully giving up your seat when you are very tired, to some poor, old, unattractive woman; or some over-burdened mother, with an infant in her arms, look-ing wistfully round for a seat; or as good-naturedly you crush in your hat and dislocate your neck, while you hand up some poor girl's omnibus fare, and then carefully count her change for her, to see that it is all right; or when returning weary and footsore from the city at night, laden with parcels, you stop at the ferry to buy a bouquet, to carry home to your wife; though the girl who sells them is *not* pretty, and though you may lose one boat by it.

These are sweet and good actions, which often beautify your rugged manhood as does the climbing clematis the sturdy oak around which it twines its fragrant blossoms. They make my heart throb with a sweet, strange pleasure, though I may see but for a passing moment in a whole life-time the man who performs them, though I know no more of his name, or history, than he does that he has given me pleasure, and why.

"Are women perfect?" Not at all; we, or rather *they*, don't—(I solemnly declare *I* do)—thank you for your little civilities; we—I mean *they*—take much more than their fair share of room in cars and omnibusses; and talk any quantity of weary nonsense then and there in your hearing about fringe, and lace, and buttons, and basques. They smother you with patchouli, musk, jockey club, etc., which is almost as nauseating as the dead tobacco smoke in your clothes and hair. *They* seem to think you ought to be everlastingly obliged to them for letting you get up in a crowded church and give them your seat, while you stand on one leg during the entire service; (N. B. You are not so much to be pitied when Henry Ward Beecher preaches.)[7] *They* ought to be ashamed of themselves for doing these uncivil, unladylike, and inexcusable things; but, good sirs, I pray you, don't reward us who *are* civil, who *do* thank you, who want to like you, by—spitting upon us.

Hear! Hear!
June 12, 1858

Mr. Chairman, I rise to say, that there are no faults of sex; that there exist only faults of individuals. Prove it? Do not men say that "woman never proves anything, she only asserts?" Very well. I *"assert,"* then, that men are just as fond of gossiping as women; one talks about the laces and shawls of her neighbor Mrs. Smith, how many times she has been married, and to whom; the other gets up scandal quite as virulent concerning political opponents, or business rivals. Women are no fonder of dress than men, only that men have the grace to do their prinking in the house; as everybody who has ever had the eye-range of hotel-windows, and knows what a work of time it is for them to locate a breast-pin, or a set of studs, or to tie a cravat, or to wriggle into a new coat, can testify. Women are no vainer than men; the ugliest man alive always believes himself capable of attracting the prettiest woman. A walk in Broadway with one's eyes open will convince any skeptic of this. Women are no fonder of coquetting than men, only that the latter hide it under a thousand dignified, humbugging names. Men are no more tolerant of a rival than women. The flattered beauty, with a sweet smile, presents her rival with a pomade, which, she assures her, will add lustre to her beautiful ringlets; but which, in fact, causes them all to drop off. Artists, when a new debutant makes a successful hit with a picture, do not refuse it a place in their public exhibition; but they take care to hang it in so bad a light, or to surround it with such unharmonious tints, that it shall be completely neutralized.

Lady friends, it is said, when vexed with each other, betray one another's secrets; how is it with politicians when they turn their coats? Pshaw! it is six of one and half-a-dozen of the other; men are exactly like women about all these things, only a little more so! For hundreds of years they have been peppering our sex, and we have been fools enough to bear it, with such proverbs as this—"when a woman will, she will, and when she won't, she won't, and there's an end of it"; as if we all did not know, though it has been as much as our necks were worth to say it, that one might as well try to pry up the Alps with a cambric needle, as to move a man's will when he plants his lordly foot down. Hitherto women, silently accepting this fact, have been content, where they could not contend, to *Delilah* them out of it; but the day has gone by for such baby play. Women have the floor now, and the pen, too, Mr. Public; and you may take your seat. Wriggle in it you may; turn aside the great earnest questions of the day about woman's rights, in the flippant school-boy tone of the "New York Times," if you will; these questions, in which every husband, father and brother, who *truly* respects our sex, should take a manly interest;—remember, they have yet to be met and settled. "Free Love" may bring discredit on them, by intruding its nauseous doctrine in their midst, and with a bland smile and winning speech, hold out freedom to woman with one hand, while with the other he is riveting, *and knows that he is riveting for his own selfish, sensual pleasure*, her chains—tenfold tighter with the other.[8] These tares must needs grow up with the wheat; still is the wheat there, silently ripening unto a harvest that we may never see, but which we may be well content to sow for other reapers.

Gimcrack Furniture
December 18, 1858

Ever since I came to New York, I have been hunting for that impossibility, a practical, convenient, sensible *lady's* writing-desk. Of course it is easy enough to find, in any furniture warehouse, any quantity of rosewood, and look-ing-glass, and silk-curtain affairs, with any quantity of tiny, useless drawers and "pigeon-holes," and cunning little places for inkstands, and pen-knives, and cameo wafers, and a cunning little shelf to draw out, just big enough to rest the lace sleeve ruffles of your right hand upon, while you write a cunning little note, on one of your cunning little initial-pink-note-papers, to some cunning little moustache of your acquaintance. That's not exactly the thing to write a book upon; to stow away a hecatomb of correspondence in; to hide whole reams of writing paper in; to rest an inkstand upon which holds more than a thimble-full; to include a shelf to draw out which will support my arm up to the elbow, and as much of my at times weary side as I feel inclined to lean upon it. This being the case, my only alternative was a great nasty man's business writing-desk; I mean a great man's nasty business writing-desk; no, I don't—I mean a *man's great, nasty, business writing-desk*; a cumbrous, lumbering, ungraceful, elephantine, disenchanting affair, with a big hole underneath to put a pair of trousers through.

Because I sniff at a useless thing, must I needs have an ugly one? Isn't there, in this year of our Lord 1858, a cabinet maker extant who can combine utility with beauty? or must I needs wait for the millennium, when everything is to lie down together and have everything it wants?

I will declare that there is no medium in the furniture line, between handsome but useless things, and those which are homely, but practical. Look at a lady's work-box—all rosewood, satin, and *the inevitable look-ing-glass*, with scissors that won't cut, bodkin made only to look at, and thimble so fragile that the first time you use a needle it perforates through the top to your finger, and all the other arrangements ditto. I am getting sick of it. I hate a sham in anything, down to an editor who thinks to make a woman pocket an insult by calling her "fascinating." The *"Times"* are evidently out of joint.

A Hint for Shopping Husbands
March 19, 1859

I never witnessed an execution; but I saw a man the other day, (married he surely was, for there was a button off his shirt-bosom,) trying to select a lace collar from out a dainty cobweb heap, sufficiently perplexing even to a practised female eye. The clumsy way he poised the gauzy things on his fore-finger, with his head askew, trying to comprehend their respective merits! The long, weary sigh he drew, as the shopman handed him new specimens. The look of relief with which he heard *me* inquire for lace collars, saying, as plain as looks could say, Ah, now, thank Heaven, I shall have a woman's view of the subject! The *disinterested* manner in which, with this view, he pushed a stool forward for me to sit down, to watch upon which collar my eye fell complacently, all the while turning over *his* heap in the same idiotic way. Oh, it was funny! Of course I kept him on the anxious seat a little while, persistently holding my tongue, the better to enjoy his dilemma. Didn't he fidget? Men are such impatient wretches; didn't I know that, too?

At length, fearful he might rush out for strychnine, I spake. I descanted upon shape, and texture, and pattern and upon the probability of their "doing up well," to all of which my rueful knight listened like a criminal who scents a reprieve. Then I made my selection; then he chose two exactly like mine, before you could wink, and with a sublime gratitude, refused to let the shopman consider the bill that was fluttering in his gloved fingers, "till he had made change for the lady." We understood each other, for there are cases in which words are superfluous. No doubt his wife thought his taste in collars was excellent.

"Oh, the Extravagance of Women!"
July 16, 1859

"Fifty" and "one hundred dollars" for gentlemen's straw hats! Good—I am delighted, gentlemen! I saw the hideous things in the window, and not being very expert at figures read the price fifty *cents!*

"Dear at that," said I, innocently, to Mr. Fern. "Fifty *dollars*," he replied, with dignity; and as I spoke a happy man strutted down the street with "fifty dollars" on his head. Heavens, how ugly that hat was! I have one at home that I occasionally wear—with what else belongs thereto—when I go out rainy evenings, which cost but half a dollar, and looks millions prettier. Fifty and one hundred dollars for a gentleman's hat! "Oh, these *women*, how they ruin husbands, and brothers, and fathers by their extravagance!" "If *women* would *only* give up their vanities and affectations," as I heard a minister exclaim last night—(it wasn't H. W. B.[9]—he knows better)—but never mind who it was. I had a great mind to get up, and tell him about those hats. I trust now we shall have an end of all this tirade about "women's follies," at least from those who live in glass houses. I shall mark every man who wears a "fifty" or "one hundred dollar" hat; you may depend on that.

Why Rosa Bonheur Don't Marry
December 31, 1859

Rosa Bonheur,[10] the well-known artist, made this memorable answer when asked why she did not marry. "I am not fit for a wife—art is my mistress." Adding quickly, for she had a woman's warm heart, "Let us change the subject—it is too painful." When Rosa said the words, "not fit for a wife," of course she spoke after the manner of men; but *why* should *not* Rosa be fit for a wife merely because she is a beautiful artist? Are there no men in the world who are unselfish enough to rejoice that woman has more than that one resource—*love*? They, who have a thousand? They who hold that a man should come and go at his pleasure, without reference to his wife, without a question being asked by her, much less any token of dissent, and, funnier than all, without losing a particle of her love in consequence. They who can come home to their meals two hours after the time they were prepared for them, or not at all; sleep in the house or out, as the fancy suits; and expect her to sit by the hearth nursing her patience, and cultivating a smiling expression of countenance to greet them on their return; although she may need quite as much, if not more than they, that relaxation at the day's close, which *they* claim as their necessary and especial prerogative? They whose shirt-buttons must on no account be hazarded, though her health and even reason may? Ah, Rosa knew the majority of men well, and therefore chose wisely. "Art" might not, indeed satisfy her heart, but neither would it by slow torture break it. From the soft eyes of the dumb creatures she loved came at least no threatening glances; she could lay her curly head upon their shaggy coats without fearing a repulse. We trust that millennium may some day arrive, *when men will be just to women.* When *"love"*—so often, alas! but a broken reed—will not be *the only* staff with which she with her sensitive organization shall be allowed to walk life's toilsome journey. When men will be willing that she, like themselves, shall have some resource, beside the grave or a mad-house, if that fail. We have few men who are willing, but we want a *tie* vote.

Lijah Loodle was once in search of a wife—under difficulties. Lijah had a horror of "a knowing woman," for reasons which were obvious. Lijah, like many of his sex, labored under the delusion that a fool was easy to manage. He liked those seraphic creatures, with skim-milk eyes, pink cheeks, claws all cased in velvet—looking as angelic as a cat over a saucer of predestined cream. Somebody hinted to Lijah a fear that he might sometimes want *ideas*, as well as pink cheeks. Lijah's reply was mannish and characteristic. "Oh, for society I shall go out of the house, you know." And so he did;—for the pink cheeks soon became an old story; the seraphic smirk horribly wearisome; and the "meekness," which had so enchanted him, and which was to be the talisman of his conjugal peace, had settled into a mulish obstinacy, compared with which a thunder-gust of passion from a panther-woman would have been a veritable god-send. Moral. Let not a man sniff at a woman because she knoweth too much, lest he find himself worse off with one who knoweth too little.

Male-Mischief
February 25, 1860

"Satan finds some mischief still
For idle hands to do."

It is perfectly astonishing the "muss" (to use a New-Yorkism) which a male pair of hands can make in your room in the short space of five minutes. You have put every thing in that dainty order, without which you could not for the life of you accomplish any work. There is not particle of dust on any thing, in sight, or out of sight—which last is quite as important. All your little pet things are in the right location; pictures plumb on the wall, work-box and ink-stand tidy and within hail. Mr. Smith comes in. He wants "a bit of string." Mr. Smith is always wanting a bit of string. Mr. Smith says kindly (good fellow) "don't get up dear, I'll find it." That's just what you are afraid of, but it won't do to say so; so you sit still and perspire, while Mr. Smith looks for his "bit of string." First, he throws open the door of the wrong closet, and knocks down all your silk dresses, which he catches up with irreverent haste, and hangs in a heap on the first peg. Then he says (innocently), "o—h—I went to the wrong closet, didn't I?" Then he proceeds to the right closet and finds the "bit of string." In taking it down he catches it on the neck of a phial. Down it comes smash—with the contents on the floor. Mr. Smith says "d-estruction!" in which remark you fully coincide. Then Mr. Smith wants a pair of scissors to cut his "bit of string"; so he goes to your work-box, which he upsets, scattering needles, literally at "sixes and sevens," all over the floor, mixed with bodkins, spools, tape, and torment only knows what. He gathers them up at one fell swoop, and ladles them back into the box, in a manner peculiarly and eminently masculine; and asks if—the—hinge—of—the—lid—of—that—box—was—

broken—before, or if *he* did it. As if the rascal didn't know! But of course you tell the old fib, that it had been loose for some time, and that it was no manner of consequence; all the while devoutly hoping that this might be the last mischance. Not a bit of it. "He thinks he will take a little brandy to set him right"; so he uncorks the bottle on the spotless white toilet-cover of your bureau, spills the brandy all over it, powders the sugar on the covers of a nice book, and lays the sticky spoon on a nice lace collar that has just been "done up." Then he uncorks your cologne-bottle to anoint his smoky whiskers, and sets down the bottle, leaving the cork out. Then he takes up your gold bracelet and tries it on his wrist, "to see if it will fit." The "*fit*" need I say, is *not* in the bracelet—the fastening of which he breaks. Then he throws up the window, "to see what sort of a day it is"; and over goes a vase of flowers, which you have been arranging with all the skill you were mistress of, to display the perfection of each blossom. He looks at the vase, and says, "miserable thing! it was always ricketty; I must buy you a better one dear," which you devoutly hope he will do, though a long acquaintance with that gentleman's habits does not authorize you in it. Then Mr. Smith goes to the glass and takes a solemn survey of his beard. Did you ever notice the difference between a man's and a woman's way of looking in the glass? It is wonderfully characteristic! The woman perks her head on one side saucily and well pleased like a bird; man strides in a lordly dignified way up to it as if it were a very *petty* thing for him to do, but meantime he'd like to catch that glass saying that he is not a fine-looking fellow! Well—Mr. Smith takes a solemn survey of his beard, which he fancies "needs clipping," and takes your sharpest and best pair of scissors, for the wiry operation; the stray under-brush meanwhile falling wheresoever it best pleases the laws of gravitation to send it. The Mr. Smith, says, "really, dear, this is such a pleasant room, one hates to leave it, but—alas! business—business."

"*Business!*" I should think so—business enough, to put that room to rights, for the next three hours!

Books of "Advice to Women"
March 17, 1860

I should like to see one sensible and consequently *just* book of "advice to women." The grain of wheat occasionally found in such volumes, scarcely compensates for the intolerable quantity of chaff one must wade through to reach it. It is inexpressibly disgusting, the selfish, one-sided spirit which would put woman through a course of *seraph-training*, for the better endurance of petty fire-side brutalities from the other sex, for which they should be taken by the collar by the seraph's brother, (if indeed she be lucky enough to have one who is endowed with the requisite spirit to do it). Ignoring—these advisers—every necessity of woman's nature, making her as truly a mirror to reflect *his* thoughts, *his* opinions, narrow as they often are, as if God had endowed her with no individuality, no brain to think, and no heart to feel.

In one of those immaculate Tommy-Good-child, be-virtuous-and-you'll-be-happy books of advice, the writer devoting a chapter to young men, recommends them always to marry women *superior* to themselves. While we admit that it would not be a difficult task for some young men to pick out women "superior" to themselves, before whom they might be audacious enough to bend the knee, we cannot but admire this one-sided philosophy for the fire-side improvement of mental inferiority, and physical awkwardness. We congratulate this "superior woman" upon her pleasing task more especially, as this large-hearted and long-headed adviser holds out to her the encouragement, that her husband even at that fearful odds at the goal, will come out ahead of her in the race, because she—being in all probability cradle-tied—will undoubtedly forever remain at the same mental standpoint at which marriage found her, and—let *me* add—*took her in.*

We give this as a fair specimen of the anti-generous spirit in which "books of advice to women" are written. I won't even qualify it by saying "generally." Goodness knows by whom. Sometimes, perhaps, by a theorizing old bachelor, on whose crusty toes some married lady has trodden, by taking possession of the heart of "his friend Tom," every corner of which he thought was foreordained, with his, to ossifying bachelor-fellowship; sometimes, perhaps, by some disappointed but still quenchable old maid, who paints meek female Moses-es—, in the forlorn hope that some stalwart pair of corduroys, may seek the original in *her.* Sometimes, perhaps, who knows,—by some dyspeptic minister, made so to the shame of his parish, by a small salary and overwork, who, with the usual parochial complement of nine small infants, is driven to that last resource of the wretched—"a book of advice to women," in which is concentrated all the bitterness engendered by a penurious parish, for a series of crucifying years.

"Books of advice to women!" It is as if some storekeeper should cut out and make a quantity of silk dresses with hooks and eyes all ready to snap round customers. One won't meet at the belt;—another is short in the skirt; another drags on the ground; another compresses the chest to suffocation; till my man of speculation finally makes up his mind, that it would have been best to let every woman take her own measure, instead of wriggling through life in *habits* of his choosing, without regard to the way the Almighty put her together.

Pencilings by the Way
March 31, 1860

I don't like to admit it, but there are two things a woman can't do. 1st. She *can't sharpen a lead pencil.* Give her one and see. Mark how jaggedly she hacks away every particle of wood from the lead, leaving an unsupported spike of the latter, which breaks—immediately you try to use it. You can almost forgive the male creature his compassionate contempt, as chucking her under the chin, he twitches it from her awkward little paw, and rounds, and tapers it off in the most ravishing manner, for durable use.

Last week a philanthropist (need I say a *male* philanthropist) knowing my weakness, presented me with a two-cent-sharp-pointed-lead-pencil. My dreams that night were peaceful. I awoke like a strong-minded woman to run a race. I sat down to my desk. I might have known it. "I never loved a tree or flower," etc. Some fiend in human shape, had "borrowed" it. Oh the misery that may be contained in that word "borrowed." When you are in a hurry; when the "devil" is waiting in the basement, stamping his feet to get back to the printing office; when you've nothing but a miserable little-"chunky"-old-worn-out-stub of an inch long lead pencil to make your "stet"-s and "d"-s. Shade of Ben Franklin! *shall* I, before I "shuffle off this mortal coil"—though I don't know what *that* is,—ever own another two-cent-sharp-pointed-lead-pencil?

I have said that there were two things a woman can't do. I have mentioned one. I wish to hear no argument on *that point*, because when I once make up my mind, "all the king's men" can't change it. Well—then—Secondly: A woman can't do up a bundle. She takes a whole newspaper to wrap up a paper of pins, and a coil of rope to tie it, and it comes undone at that. When I go shopping, which it is sometimes my hard lot to do, I look on with the fascinated gaze of a bird in the neighborhood of a magnetic serpent, to watch clerks do up bundles. How the paper falls into just the right creases; how deftly they turn it over, and tuck it under, and tie it up, and then throw it down on the counter, as if they had done the most common-place thing in the world, instead of a deed which might—and faith—*does!* task the ingenuity of "angels." It is perfectly astonishing! It repays me for all my botheration in matching this color, and deciding on that, in hearing them call a piece of tape "a *chaste* article," and for sitting on those revolving stools fastened down so near the counter, that it takes a peculiarly constructed shopper to stay on one of them.

Thirdly—I might allude to the fact that women cannot carry an umbrella; or rather to the very peculiar manner in which they perform that duty; but I won't. I scorn to turn traitor to a sex who, whatever may be their faults,—are always loyal to each other.—So I shall not say, as I might otherwise have said, that when they unfurl the parachute alluded to, they put it right down over their noses,—take the middle of the sidewalk, raking off men's hats and women's bonnets, as they go, and walking right into the breakfast of some unfortunate wight, with that total disregard of the consequent *gasp*, which to be understood must be *felt*, as the offender cocks up one corner of the parachute, and looks defiantly at the victim who has had the effrontery to come into the world and hazard the whalebone and handle of *her* "umberil!" No, I won't speak of any thing of the kind; beside, has not a celebrated writer remarked, that when dear "woman is cross it is only because she is *sick*." Let us hope he is right. We all know that is not the cause of a MAN'S crossness. *Give him his favorite dish, and you may dine off him afterward—if you want to.*

Guilty or Not Guilty
April 7, 1860

I have received a letter from one of the voting sex, informing me, that I, whose word is law and gospel with the ladies, am doing my best to prejudice them against a sex, "the greater number of whom he confesses to be, all that I have represented them, and deserving of the severest censure." That this influence I am not only exerting through the columns of the ever popular LEDGER on ladies in this, but also in other countries; and not only that, but I have the faculty of making any man believe that black is white, or the contrary. In view of this dreadful state of things, the writer earnestly implores me to consider my ways, and also to inform him what, from my standpoint, "constitutes a gentleman."

In the first place, I beg leave to stand from under the awful responsibility of influencing crinoline[11] either in this or any other country. Have I not written till pen and patience have given out, on their many shortcomings, without the slightest amendment on their part? Do they not continue to trail showy silks and velvets through ferry-boats and omnibusses? Do they not crowd men out of their seats in cars? Do they regard my oft-repeated request that they smile graciously upon those who rise and offer them their seats?

Do they not carry home a parcel of candy to their puny children everytime they go out? Do they not expose their children's naked calves to the biting wind, because "it is the fashion?" Do they not carry small children to places of public amusement which do not close till hours after they *should* have been snugly tucked in bed? Do they not let their young daughters stay in heated school-rooms, day after day, from nine o'clock till three, while they themselves loll comfortably in their arm chairs, regardless of their daughters' bent spines, aching heads, and consequent and inevitable disgust of grammar and geography. Do not short, little dumplings of women wear the biggest hoops, and broadest flounces, and highest pit-a-pat heels, and sallow women continue to wear lilac and pea-green, and rosy women bright scarlet and yellow; although I have more than once hinted it to be my royal pleasure, that there should be a reform in these particulars? Do they care a boot-lacing whether I like these things or the contrary? By the rood—*No.*

My second offence is that I can make any man believe that black is white, or the contrary. Ah—*now he talks!* With my hand on my mouth, I can only murmur—"Guilty!"

As to "my idea of what constitutes a gentleman," I am not going to walk into a trap so maliciously sprung for me. For all that, I will say, there are sometimes moments of disgust in the presence of the other sex, when I have my little thoughts. I have found "Fox's book of Martyrs," a quieting volume on such occasions, also a little rhyme beginning "I would not live alway!"[12]

A Hue and Cry from the Other Side of the House
May 5, 1860

At last the *women* have taken to tobacco. A contemporary tells us that the New York women practice snuff-dipping after the following fashion: "Each lady has her bottle, and swab-stick, or box and mop, from, and by which, she conveys the filthy dust to her lips; one can scarcely repress a shudder of disgust." Oh, I dare say not, now that the boot is on the *other* foot! For a long while women have not been able to repress *their* disgust, when forced to swallow, in crowded thoroughfares, continuous puffs of tobac-co-smoke from men who would instantly take fire at any imputation upon their gentlemanliness. For a long while, to the "disgust" of the ladies, nice, sweet-atmosphered parlors have been defiled by male visitors fresh from a prolonged meerschaum debauch; and even to the hospitalities of the table, have they brought this poison, although quite aware of its disagreeableness to the hostess, who has kindly catered for their appetites. It won't hurt these smokers now, to take *their* turn at "shuddering." It won't hurt them to take a cup of tea from snuffy fingers, or inhale a snuffy breath, or gaze at a discolored mouth, as the ladies have so often been forced to do. If they "shudder" long enough to reform, perhaps the women may discontinue what they probably commenced only in self-defence.

Sometimes one's husband is tobacco-infatuated. His wife who loves him, and to whose faults she is lenient, bears it patiently while she deplores it, especially, when he carefully endeavors to obliterate all traces of it, as far as possible before approaching her; but I never could see why her indul-gence should be extended to a male visitor, who aware of her dislike to tobacco-smoke, is quite careless or indifferent about introducing it to her parlor or table. I, for one, do not believe in the chivalry which evaporates in *fine speeches* to women. And when men deplore that neither ruined health, self-respect, nor love for husband or children, can give a *woman* addicted to this practice sufficient resolution to abstain, I ask, how the "weaker ves-sel" should be expected to do that, which men themselves are confessedly impotent to effect. The amount of it is, the less they say on this subject the better, at least while they continue to make their *own children's nurseries* foul with tobacco-smoke, for it is a hallucination of the smoker, that with his last whiff passes off all offence to the most fastidious nose, or delicate lungs!

The *women* "dip!" Well, why should the cleanliness and decency all be on one side? Why, too, when Betty is obstreperous, and help is scarce, and often good for nothing when obtained, and family cares accumulate without end, and are expected to be taken as a matter of course, and the stereotyped "smile" which guides for women recommend, is not possible, even when the father of nine bumptious children is known for a dead certainty to be approaching; why, instead of meeting these cares day after day, like—a *woman*, should not this harassed wife take a quiet "dip" into Lethe,[13]—*man* fashion?

"Desperate diseases require desperate remedies." (I've been thumped on the knuckles for not writing that properly in my copy-book, so I remembered it.) Viewing the subject in the light of that school-day-proverb, allow me to say that I, for one, can almost rejoice that New York women have taken to "dipping."

Male-Gossips
July 28, 1860

A female gossip is bad enough in all conscience; but a male-gossip is, by all odds, the more detestable of the two; spending his time in collecting, from street-corners, saloons, and business places, all the parentheses of small talk, to scatter broadcast wherever there is a field to sow mischief. The male-gossip is always a coward; while he pursues this sneaking occupation, and weaves these bits and ends of "they-say-so's" into his conversation, interlarded with crocodile deprecation of all forms of sin, (all of which were white beside this pet vice of his,) he never omits leaving a loop-hole, through which he can make safe and crawling egress in case of difficulty. *The toe of a boot* is the best thing with which "to point the moral and adorn the tale" of this venomous animal.

What Constitutes a Handsome Man
March 16, 1861

Well—in the first place, there must be enough of him; or, failing in that, but, come to think of it he *mustn't* fail in that, because there can be no beauty without health, or at least, according to my way of thinking. In the second place, he must have a beard; whiskers—as the gods please, but a beard I insist upon, else one might as well look at a girl. Let his voice have a dash of Niagara, with the music of a baby's laugh in it. Let his smile be like the breaking forth of the sunshine on a spring morning. As to his figure, it should be strong enough to contend with a man, and slight enough to tremble in the presence of the woman he loves. Of course, if he is a well made man, it follows that he must be graceful, on the principle that perfect machinery always moves harmoniously, therefore you and himself and the milk pitcher, are safe elbow neighbors at the tea-table. *This* style of handsome man would no more think of carrying a cane, than he would use a parasol to keep the sun out of his eyes. He can wear gloves, or warm his hands in his breast pockets, as he pleases. He can even commit the suicidal-beauty-act of turning his outside coat-collar up over his ears of a stormy day, with perfect impunity;—*the tailor didn't make him*, and as to his hatter, if he depended on this handsome man's patronage of the "latest spring style," I fear he would die of hope deferred; and yet—by Apollo! what a bow he makes, and what an expressive adieu he can wave with his hand! For all this he is not conceited—for he hath *brains*.

But your conventional "handsome man," of the barber's-window-wax-figure-head-pattern; with a pet lock in the middle of his forehead, an apple-sized head, and a raspberry moustache with six hairs in it; a pink spot on its cheek, and a little dot of a "goatee" on its cunning little chin; with pretty blinking little studs in its shirt-bosom, and a neck-tie that looks as if he would faint were it tumbled, I'd as lief look at a poodle. I always feel a desire to nip it up with a pair of sugar-tongs, drop it gently into a bowl of cream, and strew pink rose-leaves over its little remains.

Finally, my readers, when *soul* magnetises *soul*, the question of beauty is a dead letter. *Whom one loves is always handsome*; the world's arbitrary rules notwithstanding; therefore when you say "what *can* the handsome Mr. Smith see to admire in that stick of a Miss Jones?" or "what *can* the pretty Miss T. see to like in that homely Mr. Johns?" you simply talk nonsense—as you generally do, on such subjects. Still the parson gets his fees, and the census goes on all the same.

A Stone for a Glass House
April 27, 1861

Dandyism, like the measles, should be gone through in early life. On a fine, handsome boy of sixteen or eighteen it sits gracefully, and offends no one. After that, we look to see him in earnest, about something *besides* bright neck-ties and cream-colored kids—well enough for a Broadway gambler, lounging on a sunny corner, but, according to our female ideas, eschewed by men of brains. It may be a weakness, but a pair of light gloves on a *man*, except on some festive occasion, immediately inclines our nose skyward; dark gloves, Messieurs, if you please, and—as you love us—no glitter of watch-chain or shirt-fixin's. *Then*—though you may be no Solomon—we know you sometimes think. In this connection, would it be too much to ask, what madness has seized the male population of New York, to array themselves, like so many footmen, in those long, petticoat-y coats which now caress their heels, making day hideous. Talk of "female servility to fashion," when short, dumpy men allow their tailors to swallow them up in these swaddling clothes, by which even the tallest man escapes utter ugliness, "so as by fire!" We regaled our eyes a whole block, the other day, with the sight of a gentleman who had the moral courage to go out and face fashion in a bran-new-short-bob-tailed coat. Goodness, how refreshing! No man in these footman-like coats is allowed a waist—the two defining back waist-buttons being placed where a sitting position might be supposed to render them uncomfortable. In short, no monstrosity of female fashion was ever uglier. Now, in our view, consistency demands that the other sex should be dumb—from this time—henceforth—and forevermore—upon the "compulsory vagaries of female fashion." As to "female extravagance"—contemplate forty-five dollars for a man's coat; sixty dollars for a dozen shirts; twelve dollars for a vest; fourteen for a pair of pants; twelve dollars a dozen for gloves, each pair to be worn but once; and three hundred dollars for a watch; all expended by unhappy young men, who *would be glad to be married, were not the women of the present day so extravagant!*"

I am disposed to be lenient on the boot-question—for if I have a weakness, which is a matter of doubt among those who know me best! it is for a row of nicely-fitting gaiter-boots all my own, and paid for. I know it is a weakness *to pay for them*, but that is a provincial relict of my down-east birth-place in Portland-Maine; where the girls are as sound as the timber, and the men are primitively honest.

A Bit of Injustice
June 8, 1861

As a general thing there are few people who speak approbatively of a woman who has a smart business talent or capability. No matter how isolated or destitute her condition, the majority would consider it more "feminine" would she unobtrusively gather up her thimble, and, retiring into some out-of-the-way-place, gradually scoop out her coffin with it, than to develop that smart turn for business which would lift her at once out of her troubles; and which, in a man so situated, would be applauded as exceedingly praiseworthy. The most curious part of it is, that they who are loudest in their abhorrence of this "unfeminine" trait, are they who are the most intolerant of dependent female relatives. "Anywhere, out of the world," would be their reply, if applied to by the latter for a straw for the drowning. "Do something for yourself," is their advice in general terms; but, above all, you are to do it quietly, unobtrusively; in other words, die as soon as you like on sixpence a day, but don't trouble *us*! Of such cold-blooded comfort, in sight of a new-made grave, might well be born "the *smart business woman.*" And, in truth, so it often is. Hands that never toiled before, grow rough with labor; eyes that have been tearless for long, happy years, drop agony over the slow lagging hours; feet that have been tenderly led and cared for stumble as best they may in the new, rough path of self-denial. But out of this bitterness groweth sweetness. *No crust so tough as the grudged bread of dependence.* Blessed the "smart business woman" who, in a self-sustained crisis like this, after having through much tribulation reached the goal, is able to look back on the weary track and see the sweet flower of faith and trust in her kind still blooming.

Lady Letter-Writers
June 15, 1861

We believe it is generally admitted that a woman of even average acquirements can write a better letter than a man. We think there are two good reasons for this. First, they are not above narrating the *little* things which bring up a person or a scene more vividly to the mind than any thing else. They write *naturally*, as they talk; while a man takes his pen too often in the mood in which he would mount a platform to address his "fellow-citizens," using big words, and stiltified language. Hence a man's letters are for the most part stiff and uninteresting. Commend us to a woman's letter when information about home matters, or any other matters, is really needed. In making these remarks, we do not forget a sentimental class of female letter writers; they are the exceptions, and any one who has patience, may read their wordy, idea-less effusions. We cannot. Still every one of us must remember when absent, letters from some female member of the family, which were worth more than all that the collected male intellect of the household could furnish. You, and you, and you—have them now we dare say, stained by time and perhaps tears, yet still precious above rubies.

Tell Us
August 31, 1861

We wish some Solomon would settle the question, What is a *gentleman?* Does a gentleman smoke in the street? Does a gentleman spit in a lady's presence? Does a gentleman keep his hat upon his head in her presence either in a store or parlor? Does he put his feet upon her sofas or chairs? Does he say rude things under cover of "a joke"? Does he ever converse before her on subjects known to be painful to ladies, and which can be as well avoided? Does he annoy respectable ladies by rudely staring at them, or following them in the streets? Does he stand gaping on the church steps to see them pass in and out? We fear, if these questions and many others that might be asked, are to be answered in the negative, the ranks of "gentlemen" in New York would be marvellously thinned out.

An Offer
March 22, 1862

Tom Jones would like to be married. Tom does not quite relish the idea of a connubial idiot; and yet, for many reasons unnecessary to state, he does not desire a wife who knows much. He would like one who will be always on tiptoe to await his coming, and yet be perfectly satisfied, and good-humored, if after all her preparations, culinary and otherwise, he may conclude at all times, or at any time, to prefer other society to hers. He also desires his wife to be possessed of principle enough for both, because in his own case, principle would interfere with many of his little arrangements. He would like her always to be very nicely dressed, although his own boots and coats are innocent of a brush from year's end to year's end. He wishes her to speak low, and not speak much; because he has a great deal to say himself, and when he has roared it out, like the liberal, great Dr. Johnson, "he wishes the subject ended!" Tom wishes his wife possessed of military instincts, so that she may discipline her household; after that is done, he wishes to turn the key on these military instincts, lest they might be of use in some emergency necessary to her personal happiness. Tom wants a wife who loves, more than she reasons, because he intends himself to pursue quite a contrary policy. Tom would like a wife who adjusts everything with a smile; although he may use his boots for other purposes than that of locomotion. She must have a pretty face, an easy temper, and an intellect the size of which would allow him to consider his own colossal. Any young lady very weak in the head, and strong in the nerves, and quite destitute of any disgusting little selfishnesses, may consider herself eligible, provided she has money; none others need apply.

Tit for Tat-Tling
March 29, 1862

We hope nothing more will be said by men about the inability of a woman to keep a secret. Since our good President, in order to keep the *national* secrets, is obliged to take possession of the telegraph wires, and keep them from the editors, who, like a parcel of old women, keep hinting about what they *could* tell, in such a transparent way, that their promise *not to tell* is a dead letter; to say nothing of the editor of the Fly Trap walking into the editor of the Daily Net, with the denunciatory force of two or three dictionaries, for being so editorially lucky as to get a bit of news, genuine or otherwise, to tell before *he* got a chance at it. Gentlemen, the less you say in future about "women not keeping secrets" the better.

Which?
May 24, 1862

It is said that one woman never speaks in praise of another without annexing a depreciatory "but." As I have before remarked on similar charges, this fault has no particular sex. What man ever thought that other man handsome or talented, whom a *lady friend* praised? He is a good fellow, certainly, *but* not much force to him; or he would be fine-looking *"but"* for his nose, feet or hands! Then everybody knows the overwhelming love of rival politicians and generals for each other, while the good fellowship between rival musicians and artists was long since matter of history. In fine, there is as much human nature in a hat as in a bonnet, and it needs a magnifying glass to see the difference in favor of one or the other.

Back Track on the Platform
March 30, 1872

Every written or spoken sentence, *not* calculated to benefit mankind, carries with it, I verily believe, its own antidote in the shape of narrowness, and bigotry.

This comforting thought occurred to me on leaving a lecture hall the other evening, where the speaker, in saying some very good things, had mentioned all female employments, save housekeeping, especially those of writing and lecturing, with utter contempt, averring that the education and training of children were the only things worthy their notice. He did not stop to explain what was to become of all the old maids and single women generally; or whether they might be excused for earning an honest support by pen and ink, or even stepping upon the platform, when they had no "home," and consequently no "home duties" to attend to; and whether, if the lecture they should deliver were as narrow and illogical as his own, the patient public might not, as in his case, be willing to *pay* and *listen*. Also, while insisting upon every woman being a mother, and desiring nothing beyond her nursery walls, not even her own intellectual progression, to qualify her to meet the questioning *youth*, as well as the dependent *infancy* of her children, I heard not one syllable from him upon the home duty devolving on the *father* and *the husband*, as to his share in their government and *home* education, which, in my opinion, is more important than that of school; nor of the cultivation of his companionable qualities, to assist in making home pleasant. Not a word did he say on this head, no more than as if these things were not binding equally on him as on the wife. As if that *could* be "home," in any true sense, where *both* did not know and practise these duties. He told us it was "of course more pleasant for women to be like the noisy cascade, and to mount the platform, than to imitate the gentle, silent rivulet, and stay quietly at home out of the public eye." As the lecturer had a home himself, and was a husband and father, and not particularly in need of any emolument from lecturing, it occurred to me that the propriety of his own absence from the "gentle rivulet" of home duties might admit of a doubt. It could not be possible that he who could map out a wife's home duty by such strict latitude and longitude, should himself have wearied of their tameness, and "mounted the platform to keep in the public eye?"

What nonsense even a male lecturer may utter! said I, as I left his presence. As if there were no women, good and earnest as well as gifted, who neglected no duties while mounting the platform, but who honored it with their womanly, dignified presence, and made every large-souled, large-brained man who listened to them rejoice that they were there.

This "vine and oak" style of talk is getting monotonous.[14] There is more "oak" to the women of to-day than there was to those of the past. Else how could the great army of drunken, incompetent, unpractical, idle husbands be supported as they are by wives, who can't stop to be "gentle, silent rivulets," but have to "keep in the public eye" as business women? Our lecturer didn't mention this little fact—not he!

III

"These are bold words;
but they are needed words"

On Women's Rights

Being a famous columnist during the formative years of the women's suffrage campaign in the US, Fanny Fern had a significant platform for her perspective on the *Woman Question*. Aside from her writing about gender codes more generally, she produced many pieces that make pointed arguments in favor of women's rights. Much of Fern's feminist commentary addresses the importance of women's financial independence and intellectual and artistic potential, as well as the need for social and legal reform to protect the rights of married women—all areas that reflect her own past struggles. She supported the campaign for women's suffrage in unequivocal terms, even while she acknowledged that she was disappointing the conservatives in her audience. Fern's witty and satirical approach anticipates later eras of feminist humor, including the 1915 collection of satirical poetry *Are Women People? A Book of Rhymes for Suffrage Times*, by *New York Tribune* contributor Alice Duer Miller. A typical example of Fern's satirical style of pointing out sexist practices in her society is her call, in "Women on the Platform," for reporters to share the details of a male lecturer's attire, as they do automatically in the case of "lady speakers":

> When John Jones or Senator Rouser frees his mind in public, we are left in painful ignorance of the color and fit of his pants, coat, necktie and vest—and worse still, the shape of his boots. This seems to me a great omission. How can we possibly judge

of his oratorical powers, of the strength or weakness of his logic, or of his fitness in any way to mount the platform, when these important points are left unsolved to our feeble feminine imaginations?

That, along with many other double standards she exposes, will still resonate with readers today.

The Weaker Vessel
From Fern Leaves from Fanny's Port-Folio, *1853*

"Time after time you must have known women decide questions on the instant, with unerring accuracy, which you had been poring over for hours, perhaps, with no other result than to find yourself getting deeper in the tangled noose of difficulties. A witty French writer says, 'When a man has toiled step by step, up a flight of stairs, he will be sure to find a woman at the top.'"[1]

My dear Monsieur, that's Gospel truth; but only a gallant Frenchman like you would own it. "Jonathan" would whittle, and John Bull would eat roast-beef, till jack-knife and digestion gave out, before they would step into that confession-box. You are a gentleman, and a scholar, if you do live on fricasseed kittens and frog-soup. I'll tell you what it is, Monsieur,—between you and I and your snuff-box,—when an American woman gets to the top of that mental staircase, she is obliged to appear entirely unconscious of it, or it would be "disputed territory" quicker than a report of your musket. You may have heard of a place this side of the "big pond," called "Bunker Hill";—if you haven't, John Bull knows all about it. Well, all the husbands over here have signed the "Declaration of Independence,"—that's all,—and the way they won't surrender to flesh and blood, or even to one of their own "ribs," would be edifying to your French ears. Consequently, my dear Monsieur, what can't be had by force, must be won by stratagem. So we sit on "that top stair," and laugh in our sleeves at them,—all the time demurely deferring to their opinion. Just so long as they have no suspicion of bit, bridle, or mistress, they can be led by the nose. It is only very fresh ones, Monsieur, who keep the reins in sight. You won't be astonished to hear, in such cases, that there is great rearing, and plunging, and curveting, without even the reward of "throwing dust in the eyes" of the animal driven. I think you will agree with me, that it is a great mistake to contend with one of the "lords of creation." A little finesse, Monsieur;—you understand!—walk round the bump of antagonism, and pat the bump of self-conceit. That's the way we do it.

Remember me to "my uncle's" nephew; and tell him he is about as near the mental state of "Napoleon," as Tom Thumb is to the Colossus of Rhodes! Bon jour!

Has a Mother a Right to Her Children?
April 4, 1857

Most unquestionably, law or no law. Let us begin at the beginning. Let us take into consideration the physical prostration of mind and body endured by mothers antecedent to the birth of their offspring; their extreme nervousness and restlessness, without the ability for locomotion; the great nameless horror which hangs over those who, for the first time, are called upon to endure agonies that no man living would have fortitude to bear more than once, even at their shortest period of duration; and which, to those who have passed through it, is intensified by the vivid recollection (the only verse in the Bible which I call in question being this—"She remembereth no more her pains, for joy that a man-child is born into the world"). Granted that the mother's life is spared through this terrible ordeal, she rises from her sick-bed, after weeks of prostration, with the precious burden in her arms which she carried so long and so patiently beneath her heart. Oh, the continuous, tireless watching necessary to preserve the life and limbs of this fragile little thing! At a time, too, of all times, when the mother most needs relaxation and repose. It is known only to those who have passed through it. Its reward is with Him who seeth in secret.

I speak now only of *good* mothers; mothers who deserve the high and holy name. Mothers who in their unselfish devotion look not at their capacity to endure, but the duties allotted to them (would that husbands and fathers did not so often leave it to the tombstone to call their attention to the former). Mothers, whose fragile hands keep the domestic treadmill in as unerring motion as if no new care was superadded in the feeble wail of the new-born infant. Mothers whose work is literally *never* done; who sleep with one eye open, entrusting to no careless hireling the precious little life. Mothers who can scarce secure to themselves five minutes of the morning hours free from interruption, to ask God's help that a feeble, tired woman may hold evenly the scales of domestic justice amid the conflicting elements of human needs and human frailties. Now I ask you—shall any human law, for any conceivable reason, wrest the child of such a mother from her frenzied clasp?

Shall any human law give into a man's hand, though that man be the child's own father, the sole right to its direction and disposal? Has not she, who suffered, martyr-like, these crucifying pains—these wearisome days and sleepless nights, *earned* this her sweet reward?

Shall any virtuous woman, who is in the full possession of her mental faculties, how poor soever she may be, be *beggared* by robbing her of that which has been, and, thank God! will be, the salvation of many a down-trodden wife?

A Word on the Other Side
October 24, 1857

Heaven give our sex patience to read such trash as the following: "If irritation should occur, a woman must expect to hear from her husband a strength and vehemence of language far more than the occasion requires."[2]

Now, with my arms a-kimbo, I ask, *why* a woman should "expect" it? Is it because her husband claims to be her intellectual superior? Is it because he is his wife's natural protector? Is it because an unblest marriage lot is more tolerable to her susceptible organization and monotonous life, than to his hardier nature relieved by out-door occupations? Is it because the thousand diversions which society winks at and excuses in his case, are stamped in hers as guilty and unhallowed? Is it because maternity has never gasped out in his hearing its sacred agony? Is it because no future wife is to mourn in that man's imitative boy his father's low standard of a husband's duty?

Oh, away with such one-sided moralizing; that the law provides no escape from a brutal husband, who is breaking his wife's heart, unless he also attempts breaking her head, should be, and, I thank God, is, by every magnanimous and honorable man—and, alas, there are all too few—a wife's strongest defence. I have no patience with those who would reduce woman to a mere machine, to be twitched this way and twitched that, and jarred, and unharmonized at the dogged will of a stupid brute. (This does not sound pretty, I know; but when a woman is irritated, men "must expect to hear a strength and vehemence of language far more than the occasion requires!") I have no patience with those who preach one code of morality for the wife, and another for the husband. If the marriage vow allows him to absence himself from his home under cover of the darkness, scorning to give account of himself, it also allows it in her. There is no sex designated in the fifth commandment. "*Thou* shalt not," and "*thou*," and "*thou!*" There is no excuse that I have ever yet heard offered for a man's violation of it, that should not answer equally for his wife. What is right for him is just as right for her. It is right for neither. The weakness of their cause who plead for license in this sin, was never better shown than in a defence lately set up in this city, viz. that, "without houses of infamy, our wives and daughters would not be safe."

Oh, most shallow reasoner, *how safe* are our "wives and daughters" with them? Let our medical men, versed in the secrets of family history, answer! Let weeping wives who mourn over little graves tell you!

But while women submit to have their wifely honor insulted, and their lives jeopardized by the legalized or un-legalized brutality of husbands, just so long they will have to suffer it, and I was going to say, just so long they *ought*. Let not those women who have too little self-respect to take their lives in their hands, and say to a dissolute husband, this you can never give, and this you shall not therefore take away—whine about "their lot." "But the children?" Aye—the children—shame that the law should come between them and a good mother! Still—better let her leave them, than remain to bring into the world their puny brothers and sisters. Does she shrink from the toil of self support? What toil, let me ask, could be more hopeless, more endless, *more degrading* than that from which she turns away?

There are all phases of misery. A case has recently come under my notice, of a wife rendered feeble by the frequently occurring cares and pains of maternity, whose husband penuriously refuses to obtain medical advice or household help, when her tottering step and trembling hands tell more eloquently than words of mine could do, her total unfitness for family duties. And this when he has a good business—when, as a mere matter of policy, it were dollars in his short-sighted pocket to hoard well her strength, who, in the pitying language of Him who will most surely avenge her cause, "hath done what she could."

Now I ask *you*, and *you*, and *you*, if this woman should lay down her life on the altar of that man's selfishness? I ask you if he is not her murderer, as truly, but not as mercifully, as if our most righteous, woman-protecting law saw him place the glittering knife at her throat? I ask you if she has not as God-given a right to her life, as he has to his? I ask you if, through fear of the world, she should stay there to die? I ask you if that world could be sterner, its eye colder, its heart flintier, its voice harsher, than that from which she turns—all honor to her self-sacrificing nature, *sorrowing* away?

Perhaps you ask, would I have a woman, for every trifling cause, "leave her husband and family?" Most emphatically, *No*. But there are aggravated cases for which the law provides no remedy—from which it affords no protection; and that hundreds of suffering women bear their chains because they have not courage to face a scandal-loving world, to whom it matters not a pin that their every nerve is quivering with suppressed agony, is no proof to the contrary of what I assert. What I say is this: in such cases, let a woman who *has the self-sustaining power* quietly take her fate in her own hands, and right herself. Of course she will be misjudged and abused. *It is for her to choose whether she can better bear this at hands from which she has a rightful claim for love and protection, or from a nine-days-wonder-loving public.* These are bold words; but they are needed words—words whose full import I have well considered, and from the responsibility of which I do not shrink.

"Where Have I Been, and What Have I Seen?"
December 19, 1857

Well—in the first place, I have been to see Miss Hosmer's statue of "Beatrice Cenci," and I hope all who read this will go, too.[3] Now, if you look for an artistic description of it, you must look somewhere else; there are plenty of walking dictionaries who will prate to you about the "pose" of the figure, etc., as they look through their cold, scientific spectacles. I shall simply say that to my eye it is so surpassingly lovely, I could almost weep that no breath of life will ever warm it into love. If there is a fault in those undulating limbs, and in that sweet, sad, child-like face, I thank the gods my eye was too dull to perceive it; and I thank the gods, too, that the young sculptress has had the courage to assert herself to be what nature intended her to be—a genius—even at the risk of being called unfeminine, eccentric, and unwomanly. "Unwomanly?" because crotchet-stitching and worsted foolery could not satisfy her soul! Unwomanly? because she galloped over the country on horseback, in search of health and pleasure, instead of drawing on her primrose kids, and making a lay-figure of herself, to exhibit the fashions, by dawdling about the streets. Well, *let* her be unwomanly, then, I say; I wish there were more women bitten with the same complaint; let her be "eccentric," if nature made her so, so long as she outrages only the feelings of those conservative old ladies of both sexes, who would destroy individuality by running all our sex in the same mold of artificial nonentity—who are shocked if a woman calls things by their right names—who are such double-distilled fools, that they cannot see that a frank, natural, hearty, honest woman may be safely trusted, when your Miss Nancies would be found kissing behind the door.[4] Show me a cut-and-dried "proper" person of either sex, and I will show you one whose evil inclinations wait only upon opportunity. Show me a long face, and I'll invariably show you an arrant hypocrite. Show me a woman who rests the tips of her prudish fingers on a man's coat sleeve when she takes his arm, and I will show you a woman who will run away with him the first chance she gets, be he married or single.

"What have I seen?" I have seen the portrait of "Rosa Bonheur;"[5] with the short, dark hair pushed back, man-fashion, from an open, fine, spirited, and not unhandsome face; with the delicate white hand which I acknowledge feeling a most masculine inclination to "propose" for, resting upon the arm of—(dear Miss Nancies of both sexes, pray forgive me, I must say it;) resting on the arm of a tremendous great bull; which it was actually refreshing to see after the kidded dandies we had just left in Broadway. "And this is Rosa Bonheur," said I. Well, Miss Rosa, it is my opinion that you are sufficient unto yourself, and would consider a husband only in the light of an incumbrance. I am very sure that a woman who can paint such animals as yours, would have to wait till a race of men has sprung up, very different from those unchivalric wretches who stand in this warm gallery *with their hats on*, in the presence of so many ladies, not to mention your talented self. "Ah, my dear," said an old gentleman to whom I made this last remark, "the good old stock has nearly run out; you musn't expect it, my dear." And so I don't—but if men only knew how to be gallant without being effeminate, how to be manly and yet to be tender, *wouldn't* we adore them? But, good gracious, they don't; and so I am glad that a new order of woman is arising like the Bonheurs and Hosmers, who are evidently sufficient unto themselves, both as it regards love and bread and butter; in the meantime, there are plenty of monosyllabic dolls left for those men who, being of small mental stature themselves, are desirous of finding a wife who will "look up to them."

Is Not Woman Capable of It?
December 26, 1857

Charles Read, the popular novelist, says that "woman is incapable of a long-protracted mental struggle."[6]

Who refuses to accept the divorce which her husband's "State-prison" uniform holds out to her, and keeps his children and her heart warm for him, until what time, with her arm round his neck, she can defy the scornful finger of that society he has outraged?

Who toils patiently on, though a husband who has deserted her, and does nothing toward her support, is allowed by law to return whenever he is short of funds, and appropriate her earnings?

Who goes to the police court with bruised flesh, to beg off the husband who has broken his cane over her back, with the husband-comforting plea *"that he was not himself" when he did it.*

Who keeps a tavern, all but the sign, for the diplomatic husband, who, when he has a public or private axe to grind, is lavish of the hospitality which he expects the mother of his numerous children to see punctiliously carried out, under penalty of his Jove-like displeasure, and who reads the harassed woman a lecture on "the necessity of economy," when the bills consequent upon this out-lay come flocking in?

Who eats, uncomplainingly, mutton chops at home with the children, while their father dines at his club-house up-town, and otherwise luxuriates?

Who forces a smile when he perpetrates the very common, very delicate, and very agreeable joke of asking some lady, in her presence, if she will agree to be Mrs. Smith No. 2?

Who only sighs a little at the ghost of past happiness, when he nearly breaks his conjugal neck trying to pick up some lady's pocket-handkerchief, while *her* married hands unassisted put on the heavy cloak or shawl?

Who, when she has kept awake with the baby all night, replenishes his cup of coffee for the third time, before she has had time to swallow a mouthful? And who, just as she is at last ready to begin her long-needed, but now cold, breakfast, is requested to tell her husband, as he buttons his overcoat comfortably over his, whether the coal, wood, butter, sugar, tea, flour, potatoes, are "out" and what is to be the programme for that day's dinner?

And who, after all this, patiently answers the incredible question of "how she spent the dollar he gave her yesterday?" which was expected to find Tommy's shoes, Susan's geography, James's grammar, Mary's aprons, the baby's bibs, and a new sugar bowl and milk pitcher, which Biddy, bad luck to her, had broken?

And lastly, if woman is incapable of long-protracted mental struggles, who are these female sculptors and artists, and astronomers and authoresses, who are, every day and hour, refuting this audacious assertion of Mr. Read's?—who, if he knows anything, must know that woman's forte is in long-protracted struggles with pain, bodily and mental—with discouragements, disappointments and misery, which men either drown in wine and dissipation, or end with a pistol shot.

And Mr. Read, *is* it true, as they say, that although woman *is* such a mental goose, you stole your "Never too late to Mend" from the "Claudia" of Madame George Sand, and your "White Lies," now publishing in the London Journal, word for word, line for line, from Madame Emile de Girardin's last famous work, "La Joie Fait Peur?"[7]

And why is it, Mr. Read, that those men who are always depreciating the quality of woman's brain, are always the first to pilfer its products, and pass them off for their own?

Please step up to the captain's office and settle *that*, Mr. Read.

Lady-Skating
March 20, 1858

Future generations will probably be born with a back-bone; ladies have taken to skating! The saints be praised! no more crooking over "registers" in skin-drying parlors, with pallid faces and throbbing heads. Fashion for once has done the female world a good turn, and we grasp her hand for it, in the name of those timid souls who never dare venture away from her royal apron-strings, and in the name of countless cradles yet to come. Think of it! Emancipation for narrow-chested mothers, and their dead-and-alive, nipped-up, sentimental, snail-creeping daughters, whom nobody but the undertaker ever contemplates with satisfaction. The gods be praised!

Of course Cupid will lurk in those skate-straps; of course manly fingers will tremble, not altogether with cold, as they adjust them round nice ankles. As if I didn't know; as if female skating never was in fashion before 1858; as if there was not once a nice pond where—but that's a digression.

As I was going to say, the times are certainly improving. I am not referring now to the "N. Y. Times." I was thinking of New England, where a *minister* was lately discovered *skating!* Imagine the pious horror of his "constituents." Imagine what a surfeit of starch and buckram he must have been bursting with, before he dared break through the ice. No more Puritan babies named after *him*. No more donation parties, and black surplices, and embroidered book-marks, and sets of shirts made by the ticklish fingers of old maids of the parish; no more silver mugs presented to the unholy off-spring of a man who disgraced his calling by using muscles which of course the Lord made only to dry up and wither. Bless him! I wish I had been there to clap him on his clerical back, and buckle his skate-straps. I should believe in the millennium, could I see a whole flock of black coats gliding like emancipated crows over the ice.

I tell you I feel encouraged. The devil has had it his own way long enough, making goodness so sour-visaged and straight-laced as to drive everything that was human into the alluring but withering clasp of vice. Beat him at his own weapons, if you want to thin his ranks. It suits him to a charm to see the saints crawling and sniveling round creation, till everybody feels as if God put us here to torment us, and as if it were a mortal sin in his eyes to be happy, and rebel accordingly. Out upon such a religion! Lift up your church roofs, and give your creeds an airing. Stop boring restless children to death with long services on Sunday, and then capping the climax of their disgust by telling them, with an orac-ular air, that "Heaven is one eternal Sabbath." No wonder they are in no hurry to go there. What right have you to fence it in with such nar-row boundaries? I am sure there's not an angel there that would consider your

"Hark from the tombs a doleful sound"

any accession to their choir. The sincerest Christians I ever knew were the cheerfulest, the lovingest. I hate that stilt-ified, dismal, unchristian religion, which sniffs nothing but dead carcasses in a world full of life and brightness and beauty, and all for our seeing and enjoying within innocent and proper limits, of which you, by reason of your biliousness, can be no judge. I deplore its blighting effects on the young bounding natures which cannot, and will not, and ought not to believe it acceptable to God. "O sing unto the Lord a *new* song. Sing unto the Lord *all the earth.*"

"What Is My Opinion about Woman Voting?"
May 29, 1858

All my life I have taken the liberty to say what I think, and I am not going to stop now. Though I have not written on this subject, I have done some thinking, and the result will not be satisfactory to the conservative;

for I hold up both hands for a woman's ballot-box. It implies, in my humble opinion, nothing derogatory to the loveliest feminine traits; no greater exposure than women are every day meeting, in various ways, with the full approbation of husbands, fathers, and brothers, or through their indifference. Every summer they are taken to watering-places by these their protectors, where they are jostled and elbowed in full *(un)*dress, even if they do not waltz with black-legs[8] and morally broken down men of every description. They sit, at such places, at the public table opposite, or by the side of, men who bring thither women whom they would dare bring to no private *respectable* table in the land. And if these wives and mothers intercept in passing the telegraphic glances of such women, enlightening them at once as to their true character, or rather, want of it, and express surprise and disgust at the tainted neighborhood into which their innocent young sisters and daughters have been brought, how seldom is there any other reply from their male protectors than an indifferent "Oh it is none of our business, you know—this is a public-house." Nor are the gentlemen shocked when their wives, sisters, and daughters, are elbowed, jostled, and pushed about in the lobbies of the theater or opera-house, when, for some reason or other, tickets have not been secured before-hand, and so they are kept waiting till the ticket-master has pocketed the price of an evening's squeeze. None of them seem to feel troubled for the sensibilities of their lady-friends, when gentlemen in the next box bandy profane words with the usher respecting a prior right to a seat, and perhaps bandy fists, as well as words. Women may go into business streets, to wholesale stores, in quest of a good bargain, without jeopardising the family pudding, and it is all right; nay, they may travel hundreds of miles alone—nights included—and that when they are neither old nor ugly—"and pray is it not perfectly safe for an *American* woman to do so?" is the indignant male rejoinder, with an extra cock of the republican nose; they may go to the coal-yard, and wood-yard, and the butcher's and grocer's, without any objection being raised by the men—*not they!* anywhere but to the ballot-box—that would be unfeminine and indelicate.

Now, one might say that their reason for this tender regard for our toes, crinoline, and reputation (and how many of them in this last respect regard every woman as a sister, I should be afraid to ask), is—that yielding this point would place in our hands a weapon of power which they are very unwilling we should wield; that in many ways they would be necessitated to contemplate their "P's and Q's" with regard to us in a much more diplomatic, unselfish, and careful manner. For instance, if the democratic Mrs. B. came into the cars, just before election, and the democratic Mr.

C. was up for a candidate, the latter—as he valued her vote—had better not keep his seat while she was standing; no—though he might have a "rocking-horse" for his boy under one arm, and a barrel of flour under the other. However, male politicians have always kept such clean hands that one would think a woman for very shame could never be influenced by such petty personal motives!

Seriously—is it not an acknowledged fact that a virtuous woman's presence has a refining effect? and surely, where more than at the ballot-box is this influence needed? Men have shown us what they can make it, and certainly by no possibility could it be worse, even if woman had a finger in it. Our scholars and poets have refrained from voting, jointly fearing their tender sensibilities and tender coat-tails. Let them no longer unpatriotically ignore the future of their country, but join the women in a decent ballot-box.

I should dislike to apply the term coward to these talented men, who sit in their libraries burying that "talent," so far as Government is concerned, while ruffians, who can neither read nor write, are choosing their children's rulers by the help of bad rum. In Heaven's name, if they will not wake up themselves to what is due from their intelligence and their manhood, at least let them bid God-speed to the day when the mothers of their children may be allowed an intelligent and intelligible voice.

How this will be brought about I do not know; that it is only a question of time I am very sure; and I am just as sure that it will in no wise peril connubial puddings, or connubial babies; and though I have no cherished fancy for hearing women "talk politics," it would certainly be music in this sinner's ears, when compared to the everlasting "he" or "the divine ribbons" and "adorable laces." It is very well for bandboxy men to call Lucy Stone obnoxious names.[9] I have not the pleasure of her personal acquaintance, and I am not sure I should have fought it out with *that* sheriff, but I have read, and do endorse, her publicly expressed views on Woman voting, and rejoice that such men as Brady, Curtis, Chapin and others, are standing manfully by her side on this vexed question.

"Independence"
July 30, 1859

"Fourth of July." Well—I don't feel patriotic. Perhaps I might if they would stop that deafening racket. Washington was very well, if he *couldn't* spell, and

I'm glad we are all free; but as a woman—I shouldn't know it, didn't some orator tell me. Can I go out of an evening without a hat at my side?[10] Can I go out with one on my head without danger of a station-house? Can I clap my hands at some public speaker when I am nearly bursting with delight? Can I signify the contrary when my hair stands on end with vexation? Can I stand up in the cars "like a gentleman" without being immediately invited "to sit down?" Can I get into an omnibus without having my six-pence taken from my hand and given to the driver? Can I cross Broadway without having a police-man tackled to my helpless elbow? Can I go to see anything *pleasant,* like an execution or a dissection? Can I drive that splendid "Lantern," distancing—like his owner—all competitors?[11] Can I have the nomination for "Governor of Vermont," like our other contributor, John G. Saxe?[12] Can I be a Senator, that I may hurry up that millennial, International Copyright Law? Can I *even* be "President?" Bah—you know I can't. *"Free!"* Humph!

Was She a Heroine, or a Criminal?
October 8, 1859

The law, and popular opinion, veto women's wearing male apparel. The law, and popular opinion, often strain at a gnat and swallow a camel. Whether they do so in this particular case or not, we shall not shock conservatism by discussing. But on reading the little incident we are about to relate, we confess we had our thoughts.

A short time since, in enlightened England, a woman in Monmouth-shire was charged with this heinous crime. She wore seaman's clothes, and in appearance, gait, and gestures, seemed every inch a sailor. For the last ten years it was proven that she had worn this costume successfully, and devoted herself to hard and incessant toil. In various capacities she had voyaged to Quebec, Bombay, and other distant places, and at times shipped in coasters, never shrinking from her share of duty, but loading and unloading with the crew. On one occasion, it is said, she carried between the vessel and the shore, in a day, no less than seventy sacks of flour, while at the winch her courage never flagged, her strength never failed. During two of the ten years spoken of, she worked as a laborer on the railway to Exeter. Her last voyage was from Truro, as an able-bodied seaman, at eleven dollars a month. Arriving at length at Newport, her sex was by some means suspected, and she was arrested. It then appeared that she was a married woman; and had undergone these incredible hardships to support a husband, who by a misfortune was forever disabled from doing it himself.

Thus, this heroic creature, self-exiled for ten years, for so noble a purpose, conducting herself with perfect propriety the while, was dragged before a magistrate by the police, like a criminal, questioned, reprimanded, and finally, upon being dismissed under the injunction "never to do so again," *was obliged to take refuge in an omnibus to avoid being immediately mobbed.* Now I ask, had this woman supported herself, or her husband, or both, in her own proper attire, tinselled with the wages of shame, would the same discriminating law, through its magistrates, have considered it their business to interfere?

Glorious nineteenth century!

Again; not long since, a certain merchant dismissed all his men-clerks and substituted young women. After a fair trial, he affirmed that they discharged their duty much more to his satisfaction, in every respect, than the young men; never went on "sprees," or got drunk; never purloined; were punctual at their posts, attentive and complaisant to customers; after making this admission, he added, with a chuckle of satisfaction, "*and then, I get them for one-third less wages!*"

And yet, hands of horror are raised, and uplifted eyes turned inside out, that a woman should exist so impious as to wish "she had been born a man." Was there ever a *man* who would honestly say he would willingly have been *a woman?* I have asked the question of every man I know, and never yet received other than a negative answer.

Shall Women Vote?
June 30, 1860

The principal objection made by conservatives to their doing so, is on the score of their being thrown into rowdy company of both sexes. Admitting this necessity (though, by the way, I don't do it! because if incompetent men-voters are ruled out, it would follow incompetent women should be also), I cannot sufficiently admire the objection; when a good-looking woman, wife or sister, whom husbands and brothers allow, without a demur, to walk our public thoroughfares unattended, can scarcely do it without being jostled, and ogled at street corners, by squads of gamblers, and often times followed whole blocks, and even spoken to by well-dressed villains; when these ladies often have their toes and elbows nudged by them in omnibusses and cars, or an impertinent hand dropped on their shoulder or waist as if by accident. When two ladies, though leaning on the arm of a gentleman, cannot return from the Opera late at night, to a ferry-boat, without being insulted by the wretched of their own sex, or the rascals who make them such. I admire that, when a husband thinks it quite the thing for his wife to explore all sorts of localities, in search of articles needed for family consumption, because "he has not time to attend to it." I like that, when he coolly permits his wife and daughters to waltz at public places, with the chance male acquaintance of a week or a day. I admire that, when his serenity is undisturbed, though Tom, Dick and Harry, tear the crinoline from their backs, in the struggle to secure seats for an hour's enjoyment of the latest nine-day, New York wonder.

Pshaw! all such talk is humbug, as the men themselves very well know. We are always "dear—delicate fragile creatures," who should be immediately gagged with this sugar plum whenever we talk about that of which it is their interest to keep us ignorant. It won't do, gentlemen; the sugar-plum game is well nigh "played out." *Women will assuredly vote some day*; meanwhile the majority of them will "keep up a considerable of a thinking." The whole truth about the male creatures' dislike to it, is embodied in a remark of "Mr. Tulliver's," in a late admirable work. This gentleman, with more honesty than is usual with the sex, having admitted that from out a bunch of sisters, he selected his milk-and-water-wife *"because he was not going to be told the right of things by his own fire-side!"*[3] I take particular pleasure in passing this sentiment round, because editors who have quoted largely and approvingly from this book, somehow or other, have never seemed to see *this* passage!

On the Fence
November 9, 1861

A public writer who hampers his thoughts or his pen, with the futile hope of offending nobody, had better take to some line of business where pusillanimity is considered a virtue. I, for one, have not yet learned the hair-splitting art of admiring a man, or a set of men, individually, and asking pardon for the painful necessity of hating them geographically. I don't understand making believe knock a man, or a set of men, down with one hand, while patting them affectionately on the back with the other. In short, "neutrality," which seems to be the word-embodiment of Judas Iscariot-ism, is not in my dictionary. My boundary line has no zigzag in it. I know a sheep from a goat; a lamb from a wolf; and am not afraid to call both by their right names, though I'm not a man. What *is* a man anyhow? For, by the holy prophet, I am nonplussed now-a-days for an answer. It would seem, in some instances, to be a creature who bows and cringes to the basest, and humbly begs pardon for coming into the world at all, unless it come in a coach and six.

Now I was born. That was not my fault. What is worse I was born a woman, which was an aggravation of the insult, only to be computed by a sufferer, and that *not a fellow*-sufferer! But now I *am* here, under such discouraging circumstances, I will, at least, take a woman's privilege, and say what I like. Why not? A woman is not eligible to any office. I can't be president. I can't have a foreign diplomacy. I am not a politician to tread tiptoe over the map of the United (?) States. It stands to reason, then, I needn't be bowing and cringing to the four points of the compass, for fear I shall be laid on the shelf or turned out of office. Thank goodness that, though I'm sunk low enough to be a woman, I'm not "a man," with an India rubber creed and an elastic-spring-knee, to bend to everybody who cracks the whip-lash of interest or policy over my head! There, if this is not a feminine oration, you may live to the age of Methuselah before you'll hear one more so.

A Public Evil
February 1, 1862

There are a set of fellows, calling themselves "gentlemen," who infest our city omnibusses for the purpose of annoying ladies. Sometimes by persistently touching ladies' feet with their great boots, notwithstanding the efforts of the ladies to keep them out of their way. Sometimes by dropping a hand carelessly on a lady's shoulder, under pretence of resting the arm on the window-sill. Sometimes by sitting offensively near, when there is plenty of room upon the seat. What can a dignified lady do in a case like this when she is among utter strangers? She is too timid to wish to draw attention to herself by complaining, and perhaps afraid also that she may not be properly understood if she should. What *is* she to do? Why—pull the strap and leave the omnibus, at great inconvenience to herself often, leaving this well-dressed rascal in possession of the field. It would be well if some of these ladies had nerve enough to expose these fellows to the gentlemen passengers occasionally, and have them ejected from public conveyances, as they should be. It is because they *know* ladies are too timid to do this that they still continue their disgusting annoyances to them.

The Women of 1867
August 10, 1867

A woman who wrote, used to be considered a sort of monstrosity. At this day it is difficult to find one who does not write, or has not written, or who has not, at least, a strong desire to do so. Gridirons and darning-needles are getting monotonous. A part of their time the women of today are content to devote to their consideration when necessary; but you will rarely find one—at least among women who *think*—who does not silently rebel against allowing them a monopoly.

What? you inquire, would you encourage, in the present overcrowded state of the literary market, any more women scribblers? Stop a bit. It does not follow that she should wish or seek to give to the world what she has written. I look around and see innumerable women, to whose barren, loveless life this would be improvement and solace, and I say to them, write! Write, if it will make that life brighter, or happier, or less monotonous. Write! it will be a safe outlet for thoughts and feelings, that maybe the nearest friend you have has never dreamed had place in your heart and brain. You should have read the letters I have received; you should have talked with the women I have talked with; in short, you should have walked this earth with your eyes open, instead of shut, as far as its women are concerned, to endorse this advice. Nor do I qualify what I have said on account of social position, or age, or even education. It is not *safe* for the women of 1867 to shut down so much that cries out for sympathy and expression, because life is such a maelstrom of business or folly, or both, that those to whom they have bound themselves, body and soul, recognize only the needs of the former. *Let them write if they will.* One of these days, when that diary is found, when the hand that penned it shall be dust, with what amazement and remorse will many a husband, or father, exclaim: I never knew my wife, or my child, till this moment; all these years she has sat by my hearth, and slumbered by my side, and I have been a *stranger* to her. And you sit there, and you read sentence after sentence, and recall the day, the month, the week, when she moved calmly, and *you* thought happily, or, at least, *contentedly*, about the house, all the while her heart was aching, when a kind word from *you*, or even a touch of your hand upon her head, as you passed out to business, or pleasure, would have cheered her, oh *so* much! When have you sat down by her side after the day's work for both was over, and talked with her just a few moments of something besides the price of groceries, and the number of shoes Tommy had kicked out, all of which, proper and necessary in their place, need not of necessity form the stable of conversation between a married pair; had you done this; had you recognized that she had a *soul* as well as yourself, how much sunshine you might have thrown over her colorless life.

"Perhaps, sir," you reply; "but I have left my wife far behind in the region of thought. It would only distress her to do this!" How do you know that? And if it were so, are you *content* to leave her—the mother of your children—so far behind? *Ought* you to do it? Should you not, by raising the self-respect you have well nigh crushed by your indifference and neglect, extend a manly hand to her help? *I* think so. The pink cheeks which first won you may have faded, but remember that it was *in your service*, when you quietly accept the fact that "you have left your wife far behind you in mental improvement." Oh! it is pitiable this growing apart of man and wife, for lack of a little generous consideration and magnanimity! It is pitiable to see a husband without a thought that he might and *should* occasionally, have given his wife a lift out of the petty, harrowing details of her woman's life, turn from her, in company, to address his conversation to some woman who, happier than she, has had time and opportunity for mental culture. You do not see, sir—you *will* not see—you do not desire to see, how her cheek flushes, and her eye moistens, and her heart sinks like lead as you thus wound her self-respect. You think her "cross and ill-natured," if when, the next morning, you converse with her on the price of butter, she answers you listlessly and with a total want of interest in the treadmill-subject.

I say to such women: Write! Rescue a part of each week at least for reading, and putting down on paper, for your own private benefit, your thoughts and feelings. Not for the *world's* eye, unless you choose, but to lift yourselves out from the dead-level of your lives; to keep off inanition; to lessen the number who are yearly added to our lunatic asylums from the ranks of misappreciated, unhappy womanhood, narrowed by lives made up of details. Fight it! oppose it, for your own sakes and your children's! Do not be *mentally* annihilated by it. It is all very well to sneer at this and raise the old cry of "a woman's sphere being home"—which, by the way, you hear oftenest from men whose home is only a place to feed and sleep in. You might as well say that a man's sphere is his shop or his counting-room.

How many of them, think you, would be contented, year in and year out, to eat, drink, and sleep as well as to transact business there, and *never desire* or *take*, at all costs, some let-up from its monotonous grind? How many would like to forego the walk to and from the place of business? forego the opportunities for conversation, which chance thus throws in their way, with other men bent on the same or other errands? Have, literally, *no* variety in their lives? Oh, if you could be a woman but one year and try it! A woman—but not necessarily a butterfly—not necessarily a machine, which, once wound up by the marriage ceremony, is expected to click on with undeviating monotony till Death stops the hands.

Woman's Qualification to Vote
May 23, 1868

One of the sapient advisers of women, so numerous at the present day, ridicules the idea of a woman's voting till she has learned to be "moderate" in following the fashions; moderate in her household expenses; moderate in her way of dressing her hair; moderate in the length of her party-robes, and in the shortness of her walking costume. Till woman has attained this desirable moderation, he declares her totally unfit for the ballot.

Granted—for the sake of the argument, granted; but as it is a poor rule that won't work both ways, suppose we determine a man's fitness for the ballot by the same rule. Let not his short-tailed coats refuse to be sat upon by the fat owner thereof. Let not his pantaloons be so tight that he cannot stoop without danger. Let not his overcoat flap against his heels, because a new-fangled custom demands an extra inch or two. Let not the crown of his hat pierce the skies, or be so ridiculously shallow as to convey the idea that it belongs to his little son. Let him smoke "moderately." Let him drink "moderately." Let him drive "moderately." Let him stock-gamble "moderately." Let him stay out at night "moderately." Let him, in short, prepare himself by a severe training in the virtue of "moderation" for the privilege of casting a vote.

Why, there is not a man in the land who wouldn't sniff at the idea! and yet, I suppose, it never occurred to the writer of this advice to women that he was uttering impertinent nonsense, or that the rules he laid down were quite as well suited to his own sex as to ours.

Every day, I see gentlemen who are as much walking advertisements of their tailor's last exaggerated fashion, as any foolish woman could be of her dressmaker's newly-fledged insanity. If Bismarck be the rage, or Metternich green,[14] their neckties and gloves slavishly follow Fashion's behest. Hats, coats, trousers are long-tail or short, tight or loose, as she bids; and that whether legs are straight or crooked, whether the outline is round or angular, whether the owner looks like an interrogation-point or a tub on two legs. At least he is in the fashion—that manly thought consoles him.

If "moderation" in smoking were the test of fitness for the ballot-box, how many men do you think would be able to vote?

Oh, pshaw! Advice to women will go in at one ear and out at the other, while male advisers are such egregious fools. The silliest woman who ever cleaned the streets with her silken robe, or exhibited thick ankles in a short one, or froze her ears in January in a saucer of a bonnet, knows that she can find a parallel for all her nonsense in the male side of the question. Men inhabit too many glass-houses for them, at present, to hurl missiles of that sort at their fair neighbors. Reform *yourselves*, gentlemen. *You* who are so much mightier, and stronger, and more competent, by *your own showing*, show us, poor weak "grown-up-children," how to behave pretty!

Woman's Millennium
From Ginger-Snaps, *1870*

HURRAH for Massachusetts! Read this:

> "Chief Justice Bigelow, of Massachusetts, made short work with a divorce case which came before him at Springfield a day or two ago. It was an application of a wife for a divorce from her husband, on the ground of extreme cruelty. It coming up in testimony that the woman had been beaten and otherwise ill-used by her husband, the Judge at once decided the case in her favor, taking occasion to remark that in case of any violence by a husband to the wife, he should not hear all the points before deciding in favor of the latter. The woman might forgive cruelty toward herself, but the court would not."[15]

Now *that's* what I call a righteous decision. Let all the wives with bruised shoulders, and arms, and backs, and eyes, (bruised *hearts* are too common to talk about!) emigrate forthwith to this enlightened State. Here's a man who is *just* to a woman. Think of the rarity of the thing! Compliments, and flattery, and gifts we can all have, till we get to be old women, and some of us afterwards; but *justice,* Messieurs! ah! that's quite another thing. Female eyes have grown dim looking for *that,* all through the ages. Men start up from their tobacco-torpor nowadays and ask, angrily, what means this present restlessness of American women? This wide and deep-spread discontent, which heaves to and fro, developing itself in a thousand different forms? *My* grandmother was contented enough. *My* aunt never looked beyond her own family. Are you quite sure of the first, and does the latter deserve praise or blame for the pin-measure view of the world to which she, the God-appointed instructor and guide of future men and women, chooses to limit herself? Has she a *right* to launch them on the turbulent ocean of life, with only one poor miserable broken oar to paddle their way? Such women are not praiseworthy; no more than they who, busying themselves in public affairs, leave their children to "come up" as chance or accident dictates. Are you quite sure, too, that because only lately this "wail of discontent" has reached your ear, that it has not been stifled under thousands of tombstones? Ah, well I remember when too young to know what life *meant for a woman*, hearing one who I have since learned had suffered and forgiven much, murmur to herself as she wearily laid her head upon her pillow, "God be thanked for sleep and forgetfulness!" and yet not one who saw her smiling face, or heard her cheerful voice, or was charmed with her intelligent conversation, ever dreamed that she was not "a contented wife," as the phrase runs.

And just in this connection I would quote a remark which, for its truth, should be inscribed on the *pipe* (for there he would oftenest meet it) of every man in the land.

"Only so far as a man is happily *married to himself* is he fit for married life, and family life in general. Unless he has 'cleared himself up,' as the Germans say, he can at best but enter into ambiguous relations to another. When a man is discordant in himself, he makes all that he comes in contact with discordant."

Now, candidly I ask you, oughtn't that remark to be in the Holy Scriptures? Perhaps you ask if the same is not true of women? I am not such an idiot as to deny that, either; but what I marvel at is this—that it should be such a perfectly natural and eminently righteous thing for a man to halloo to high heaven that his mate is not to his mind, after he has compassed heaven and earth to get her, and such a crime for a woman to be "discontented and restless under similar circumstances."

Nevertheless, I think woman's millennium is to come out of all this unquiet and chaos. Here's a remark made at a royal-literary-fund-dinner in

England,—as true as I live, in *England*, and in London at that,—and by Charles Kingsley at that,[16]—in response to a toast:

"As for imaginative literature," he said, "if the world continued to go on as it was proceeding, *ladies* must be called upon to fulfil this duty. Where would they find among men such poets as Mrs. Rossetti, Mrs. Jean Ingelow, or Miss A. Procter? Or who could write such works of prose fiction as the authors of 'John Halifax' or 'Romola'? In former times *men* only dealt with literature, but the more delicate the weapon became, the more delicate were the hands which wielded it. If he could give any advice to young men how they might escape the trials and troubles that might beset their path in the literary profession—how escape Whitecross Street prison and the workhouse—it would be by marrying a literary lady, and setting himself down to the humble and chivalrous duty of reviewing his wife's books."

The picture of that sublime bit of majesty, a British husband, performing such a feat, is so impossible to contemplate, that I must stop, that my readers and myself may take breath.

I am inclined to believe that there are a great many kinds of women, both in England and America. This idea seems to be lost sight of, by the writers of both nations, who have lately undertaken to describe the feminine element, under such titles as "the Girl of the Period," or "The Woman of the Time";[17] presenting to our view monstrosities, which no doubt exist, but which are no more to be taken specimens of the whole, than is the Bearded Woman, or the Mammoth Fat Girl.

New York, for instance, is not wholly given over to the feminine devil. Angels walk our streets, discernible to eyes that *wish* to see. Noble, thoughtful, earnest women; sick of shams and pretence; striving each so far as in her lies, to abate both, and to diminish the amount of physical and moral suffering. Then, I never go into the country for a few weeks' summer holiday, that I do not find large-hearted, large-brained women, stowed away among the green hills, in little cottages, which are glorified inside and outside by their presence; women who, amid the press of house and garden work, find time for mental culture; whose little book-shelves hold well-read copies of our best authors. Women—sound physically, mentally, morally; women, whom the *Man of the Period*, who most surely exists, has never found. Now and then, some man, fit to be her mate, in his rambles in the sweet summer time, is struck as I am by these gems hidden amid the green hills, and appropriates them for his own. But for the most part, the more sensible a man is, the bigger the fool he marries. This is especially true of biographers![18] What a wrong, then, to the great army of sensible, earnest women in either country to pick out a butterfly as the national type. Because a few men in New York and London and Paris wear corsets, and dye their whiskers and hair, and pad out their hollow cheeks and shrunken calves, it does not follow that Victor Hugo, and John Bright, and the great army of brave men who won our late victory, are all popinjays. For every female fool I will find you a male mate. So when the inventory of the former is taken, the roll-call of the latter might as well be voiced. Are women so "fond of gossip"? Pray, what is the staple of after-dinner conversation when the wine comes on and the women go off? Do women "lavish money on personal adornment"? How many men are there who would be willing to tell on what, and on whom, their money was worse than lavished? Do women "leave their nursery altogether to hirelings"? How many corresponding men are there, whose own children under their own roofs, are almost entire strangers to their club-frequenting fathers? And yet what good, noble men are to be seen for the looking? Faithful to their trusts, faithful to themselves, unmoved by the waves of folly and sin that dash around them, as is the rock of Gibraltar.

I claim that justice be done by these writers on both sides of the water, to both sexes. Fools, like the poor, we shall have always with us; but, thank God, the "just" man and the "just" woman "still live" to redeem the race. Men worthy to be fathers, and large-brained women, who do not even in this degenerate day, disdain to look well after their own households.

Women on the Platform
From Ginger-Snaps, *1870*

"MISS MARIANNA THOMPSON, now a student at the Theological school, received, during her summer vacation two invitations to settle with good societies, each of which offered her twelve hundred dollars per year. Pretty good for a school-girl, I think."

Yes, that is very good; and we trust Miss Thompson will accept one of these (or a better) and do great good to her hearers. And, should some excellent young man ask her to "settle" with him as wife, *at no salary at all*, we advise her to heed that "call" as well.—N. Y. Tribune.

Well, now, Mr. *Tribune*, I don't. I have seen too many women, quite as capable as Miss Thompson of being self-supporting individuals, exhausting the last remnant of their strength in the family, and carefully saving every penny for a husband, who never doled out twenty-five cents, without asking the purpose for which it was needed, and reiterating the stale advice to spend it judiciously. I have seen such women, too proud to complain or remonstrate, turn away with a crimson cheek, and a moist eye, to dicker, and haggle, and contrive for this end, when the husband who gave this advice, had effectually blotted out the word self-denial from his own dictionary.

No, Mr. *Tribune*, I differ from you entirely. I advise no woman to refuse twelve hundred independent dollars a year for good, honest labor, to become such a serf as this. And while we are on this subject, I would like to air the disgust with which I am nauseated, at the idea of any decent, intelligent, self-respecting, capable wife, ever being obliged *to ask* for that which she so laboriously earns, and which is just as much hers by right, as the money that her husband receives from his customers is *his*, instead of his next-door—dry-goods—neighbor's.

No man should thus humiliate a woman; no woman should permit herself to be thus humiliated. I am not now speaking of those foolish women, to whom a ribbon, or a necklace, is dearer than their husband's strength, life, or mercantile honor. I put such women entirely out of the question; only remarking, that if a man marries a fool in the hope of her being pliant, and easily ruled by him, he will find too late that he is mistaken. But that's his affair. Men always have, and always will keep on admiring their own perspicacity in reading female character, when not one in ten knows any more what his wife is spiritually made of, than what sheep furnished the coat for his own back.

Sary Gamp advised her comrade—nurse—to put the mutual bottle on the shelf, and *"look the other way!"*[19]

That's just what I would advise the husbands of intelligent wives to do with regard to the money which they "allow" them, and which one would imagine was rightly theirs, by virtue of risking their lives every Friday to become the mother of twins; by virtue of, when lying faint and weak beside them, giving out orders for the comfort and well-being of the family down-stairs before they are able to get about; by virtue of *never* being able for one moment, day or night, sick or well, to drop, or to shake, off the responsibility which a *good* wife and mother must always feel, whether present or absent from her family.

Oh! treat such a woman generously. Make up your mind what in justice she should receive in the money way, and don't above all things, wait for her to ask you for it, and never, never be mean enough to charge a woman of this kind "to spend it carefully."

I daresay you have done it, and *you*, and *you*; I daresay you are real good fellows too, and *mean* to do what is right. And I know you "love" your wives—i.e., as *men* love—thus—wounding a sensitive spirit, without the least notion you are doing it; thus—charging the tear that follows to a coming toothache or stomach-ache! Great blundering creatures! I sometimes don't know whether to box your ears or hug you. Because the very next minute you will say, or do, some such perfectly lovely thing, that, woman fashion, I exclaim, "Well—well"; but I won't tell you what I do say, because you'll hop right off the stool of repentance, and go to your normal occupation of crowing and bragging.

But, seriously, I do wish you would consider a little this same money question, and when the time comes for payment, don't, as I tell you, open your pocket-book, heave a deep sigh, as you spread a bill on your knee, and give it a despairing glance of love, as you dump it in your wife's outstretched hand. No, sir! follow Sary Gamp's advice: "Put it on the shelf, and look the other way," and don't trouble yourself to tell her to "*make it go as far as she can,*" because she will naturally do that, and there's where you are a fool again. I should think you'd know by this time, that it will go so far *you* won't see it again your natural lifetime. And why shouldn't it? Does she require to know whether you pay fifteen cents apiece for your cigars; whether you couldn't buy a cheaper kind, and how many a day you smoke? Come now, be honest—would *you* like that?

As I have always declined all requests to lecture, or to speak in public, I may be allowed to make a few remarks on the treatment of those who do.

Can anybody tell me why reporters, in making mention of lady speakers, always consider it to be necessary to report, fully and *firstly*, the dresses worn by them? When John Jones or Senator Rouser frees his mind in public, we are left in painful ignorance of the color and fit of his pants, coat, necktie and vest—and worse still, the shape of his boots. This seems to me a great omission. How can we possibly judge of his oratorical powers, of the strength or weakness of his logic, or of his fitness in any way to mount the platform, when these important points are left unsolved to our feeble feminine imaginations? For one, I respectfully request reporters to ease my mind on these subjects—to tell me decidedly whether a dress, or a frock-coat, or a bob-tailed jacket was worn by these masculine orators; whether their pants had a stripe down the side, and whether the dress lapels of their coats were faced with silk, or disappointed the anxious and inquiring eye of the public by presenting only a broadcloth surface. I have looked in vain for any satisfaction on these points.

I propose that the present staff of male reporters should be remodelled, and that some enterprising journal should send to Paris for the man-milliner

Worth,[20] in order that this necessary branch of reportorial business be more minutely and correctly attended to.

Speaking of reporters, I was present the other night at a female-suffrage meeting, where many distinguished men made eloquent speeches in favor thereof. At the reporters' table sat two young lady reporters side by side with the brethren of the same craft. Truly, remarked I to my companion, it is very well to plead for women's rights, but more delicious to me is the sight of those two girls *taking them*! But, rejoined my cautious male friend, you see, Fanny, a woman couldn't go to report a rat-fight, or a prize-fight, or a dog-fight. *But,* replied I, just let the women go "marching on" as they have begun, and there will soon *be* no rat-fights, dog-fights, or prize-fights to report. It will appear from this, that I believe in the woman *that is to be*. I do—although she has as yet had to struggle with both hands tied, and then had her ears boxed for not doing more execution. Cut the string, gentlemen, and see what you shall see! "Pooh! you are afraid" to knock that chip off our shoulder.

How strange it all seems to me, the more I ponder it, that men can't, or don't, or won't see that woman's enlightenment is man's millennium. "My wife don't understand so and so, and it's no use talking to her."—"My wife will have just so many dresses, and don't care for anything else."—"My wife won't look after my children, but leaves them to nurses, she is so fond of pleasure." So it would seem that these Adams and the "wife thou gavest to be with me," even now find their respective and flowery Edens full of thorns, even *without* that serpent, female suffrage, whose slimy trail is so deprecated.

Put *this* in the crown of your hats, gentlemen! *A fool of either sex is the hardest animal to drive that ever required a bit. Better one who jumps a fence now and then, than your sulky, stupid donkey, whose rhinoceros back feels neither pat or goad.*

Clubs for the Working Men
March 16, 1872

I read an article on this subject the other day, which set me thinking. In it was set forth the necessity, after a man's hard day's work, of an evening of rest, away from home, where he should find light and warmth, and boon companionship, other than is to be found in the corner grocery.

Now this is well, were there not a better way, as I believe. I am not about to propose clubs for working-women, because our police reports show every day that they have existed for a long time—thanks to "corner groceries"—and that they are made of any implement that comes handy, and result in bruised flesh and a broken head. This being the case, I cannot see why the working-woman, as well as the working-man, does not need, after a hard day's work, "light, warmth, and boon companionship of an evening, away from home." Nay, all the more, since work, hard as her husband may, it is often in the fresh, open air; or, if not, he has it going and returning, and the boon companionship of his fellow-workmen with it; while she, with "Ginx's last baby"[21] to look after, in some noisome tenement house, stands over the perpetual wash-tub or cooking-stove, with two or three half-grown children hanging to her draggled skirts, never exchanging her unwomanly rags, not even perhaps to mass for a hurried prayer in the church which, God be thanked, is free alike to poor and rich, and which suggests, in its own way, a distant heaven for her.

Thinking over all this, I said why not Germanize this thing? Why not have clubs for working-men and their families, with innocent amusement, minus the drink? Isn't it possible? Or if not, I wish it were, for the poor harassed women's sake. I only see the millennial germ of it; but this I know, that the wives need it more, far more, than their husbands, the wide world over, and in every strata of society; by the pains of motherhood, even in favorable conditions; by her intenser nervous organization; by her indoor confinement and narrowing, petty detail-worries; by the work that ends not at sundown as does his. By the wakeful, unrestful nights, which every mother knows; *this* is the hardest, most wearing kind of work, no matter what may be said of the husband, who has his sleep at least; who demands *that* in every family exigency as his right, and as the foundation of his ability to labor for his family. Ah! what if the wife and mother, with less strength, feebler organization, should make a stand for this? even when, in addition to her other cares, she helps in some outside honest way to support the family?

Does she not, too, need warmth, light, and boon companionship of an evening? While it is true that

"All work and no play
Makes Jack a dull boy,"

remember it is just as true of Jack's wife as it is of Jack, and the founders of "Working-men's Clubs" would do well to put this into their foundation.

IV

"I wish I was mother to the whole of you!"

On Behalf of Children

Concern about the welfare and status of children in society was a frequent theme throughout the entire span of Fanny Fern's writing career. In addition to writing three books for children, she addresses issues related to children's upbringing, education, and rights in her weekly column. The works included here represent Fern's views about childrearing practices and family government, children's education, and general advocacy for children's rights and status in society, sometimes directed at children themselves. An overarching concern in Fern's writing on these subjects is the lack of regard too many adults had for the best interests and basic rights of children. She called out parents who delegated important aspects of their children's care, or who sacrificed the comfort and health of their children to fashion trends or convenience; and she protested the rigid routines of a typical school day, which deprived children of proper exercise, fresh air, and recreation, and placed unrealistic and unhealthy demands on them academically. In her writing for children, she cultivated a personal rapport with her young readers as "Aunt Fanny," creating a space for them to feel seen and valued.

Children's Rights
From Fern Leaves from Fanny's Port-Folio, *1853*

MEN'S rights! Women's rights! I throw down the gauntlet for children's rights! Yes, little pets, Fanny Fern's about "takin' notes," and she'll "print 'em," too, if you don't get your dues. She has seen you seated by a pleasant window, in a railroad car, with your bright eyes dancing with delight, at the prospect of all the pretty things you were going to see, forcibly ejected by some overgrown Napoleon, who fancied your place, and thought, in his wisdom, that children had no taste for anything but sugar-candy. Fanny Fern knew better. She knew that the pretty trees and flowers, and bright blue sky, gave your little souls a thrill of delight, though you could not tell why; and she knew that great big man's soul was a great deal smaller than yours, to sit there and read a stupid political paper, when such a glowing landscape was before him, that he might have feasted his eyes upon. And she longed to wipe away the big tear that you didn't dare to let fall; and she understood how a little girl or boy, that didn't get a ride every day in the year, should not be quite able to swallow that great big lump in the throat, as he or she sat jammed down in a dark, crowded corner of the car, instead of sitting by that pleasant window.

Yes; and Fanny has seen you sometimes, when you've been muffled up to the tip of your little nose in woolen wrappers, in a close, crowded church, nodding your little heads, and keeping time to the sixth-lie and seventh-lie of some pompous theologian, whose preaching would have been high Dutch to you, had you been wide awake.

And she has seen you sitting, like little automatons, in a badly-ventilated school-room, with your nervous little toes at just such an angle, for hours; under the tuition of a Miss Nancy Nipper, who didn't care a rush-light whether your spine was as crooked as the letter S or not, if the Great Mogul Committee, who marched in once a month to make the "grand tour," voted her a "model school-marm."

Yes, and that ain't all. She has seen you sent off to bed, just at the witching hour of candle-light, when some entertaining guest was in the middle of a delightful story, that you, poor, miserable "little pitcher," was doomed never to hear the end of! Yes, and she has seen "the line and plummet" laid to you so rigidly, that you were driven to deceit and evasion; and then seen you punished for the very sin your tormentors helped you to commit. And she has seen your ears boxed just as hard for tearing a hole in your best pinafore, or breaking a China cup, as for telling as big a lie as Ananias and Sapphira did.

And when, by patient labor, you had reared an edifice of tiny blocks,—fairer in its architectural proportions, to your infantile eye, than any palace in ancient Rome,—she has seen it ruthlessly kicked into a shattered ruin, by somebody in the house, whose dinner hadn't digested!

Never mind. I wish I was mother to the whole of you! Such glorious times as we'd have! Reading pretty books, that had no big words in 'em;

going to school, where you could sneeze without getting a rap on the head for not asking leave first; and going to church on the quiet, blessed Sabbath, where the minister—like our dear Saviour—sometimes remembered to "take the little children in his arms, and bless them."

Then, if you asked me a question, I wouldn't pretend not to hear; or lazily tell you I "didn't know," or turn you off with some fabulous evasion, for your memory to chew to a cud till you were old enough to see how you had been fooled. And I 'd never wear such a fashionable gown that you couldn't climb on my lap whenever the fit took you; or refuse to kiss you, for fear you'd ruffle my curls, or my collar, or my temper,—not a bit of it; and then you should pay me with your merry laugh, and your little confiding hand slid ever trustingly in mine.

O, I tell you, my little pets, Fanny is sick of din, and strife, and envy, and uncharitableness!—and she'd rather, by ten thousand, live in a little world full of fresh, guileless, loving little children, than in this great museum full of such dry, dusty, withered hearts.

Children in 1853
From Little Ferns for Fanny's Little Friends, *1854*

I went with a friend, the other day, to look at some "rooms to let." She liked the rooms, and the man who owned them liked she should have them; but when she mentioned she had children—he stepped six paces off—set his teeth together—pulled his waist-coat down with a jerk, and said—"*Never—take—children,—ma'am!*"

Now, I'd like to know if that man was *born* grown up?

I'd like to know if children are to have their necks wrung like so many chickens, if they happen to "*peep*"?

I'd like to know if they haven't just as much right in the world as grown folks?

I begin to feel catamount-y about it!

I'd like to know if boarding-house keepers, (after children have been in a close school-room for five or six hours, feeding on verbs and pronouns,) are to put them off with a "second table," leaving them to stand round in the entries on one leg, smelling the dinner, while grown people (who have lunched at oyster shops and confectioner's saloons) sit two or three hours longer than is necessary at dessert, cracking their nuts and their jokes?

I'd like to know if, when they have a quarter given them to spend, they must *always* receive a bad shilling out of it at the stores, in "change"?

I'd like to know if people in omnibuses are at liberty to take them by the coat collar, lift them out of a nice seat, take it themselves, and then perch them on their sharp knee-bones, to jolt over the pavements?

I have a great mind to pick up all the children, and form a colony on some bright island, where these people, who were made up in a hurry, without hearts, couldn't find us; or if they did, we'd just say to them when they tried to come ashore—*Never take grown-up folks here, sir!* or, we'd treat them to a "second dinner,"—bill of fare, cold potatoes, bad cooking butter, bread full of saleratus, bones without any meat on them, watery soups, and curdled milk—(that is to say, after *we* had picked our nuts long enough to suit us at dessert!) How do you suppose they'd like to change places with "children" that way?

Now here's Aunt Fanny's creed, and you may read it to your mother if you like.

I believe in great round apples and *big* slices of good plain gingerbread for children.

I believe in making their clothes loose enough to enable them to eat it all, and jump round in when they get through.

I believe in not giving away their little property, such as dolls, kites, balls, hoops, and the like, without their leave.

I believe in not promising them a ride, and then forgetting all about it.

I believe in not teasing them for amusement, and then punishing them for being "troublesome."

I believe in not allowing Bridget and Betty to box their ears because the pot boils over, or because their beaux didn't come the evening before.

I believe in sending them to school where there are backs to the benches, and where the schoolma'am has had at least "*one* offer."

I believe no house can be properly furnished with out at least a *dozen* children in it.

I believe little children to be all that is left us of Paradise; and that any housekeeper harboring a person who "don't like them," had better *count up her silver, without loss of time!*

The "Favorite" Child
February 28, 1857

Why will parents use that expression? What right have you to have a *favorite* child? The All-Father maketh his sun to shine alike upon the daisy and the rose. Where would you be, were His care measured by your merits or deserts? Is your child none the less your child, that nature has denied him a fluent tongue, or forgotten her cunning, when, in careless mood, she fashioned his limbs? Because beauty beams not from the eye, is there no intelligence there? Because the rosy flush mantles not the pale cheek, does the blood never tingle at your coldness or neglect? Because the passive arms are not wound about your neck, has the soul no passionate yearnings for parental love? O, how often does God, more merciful than you, passing by the *Josephs* of your household, stoop in his pity and touch those quivering lips with a live coal from off the altar? How often does this neglected one, burst from out the chrysalis in which your criminal coldness has enveloped him, and soaring far above your wildest parental imaginings, compel from your ambition, what he could not gain from your love?

How often does he replenish with liberal hand the coffers which the "favorite child," in the selfishness which you fostered, has drained of their last fraction. "He that is first shall be last, and the last shall be first." Let parents write this on their heart tablets. Let them remember it when they repulse the little clinging arms, or turn a deaf ear to the childish tale of sorrow. Oh, gather up those clinging tendrils of affection with gentlest touch; trample them not with the foot of haste or insensibility rudely in the dust.

"And they, in the darkest of days, shall be
Greenness, and beauty, and strength to thee."

Parent and Child; or, Which Shall Rule
May 9, 1857

"Give me two cents, I say, or I'll kick you!"

I turned to look at the threatener. It was a little fellow about as tall as my sun-shade, stamping defiance at a fine, matronly-looking woman, who must have been his mother, so like were her large black eyes to the gleaming orbs of the boy. "Give me two cents, I say, or I'll kick you," he repeated, tugging fiercely at her silk dress to find the pocket, while every feature in his handsome face was distorted with passion. Surely she will not do it, said I to myself, anxiously awaiting the issue, as I apparently examined some ribbons in a shop-window; surely she will not be so mad, so foolish, so untrue to herself, so untrue to her child, so belie the beautiful picture of healthy maternity, so God-impressed in that finely-developed form and animated face. Oh, if I might speak to her, and beg her not to do it, thought I, as she put her hand in her pocket, and the fierce look died away on the boy's face, and was succeeded by one of triumph; if I might tell her that she is fostering the noisome weeds that will surely choke the flowers—sowing the wind to reap the whirlwind.

"But the boy is so passionate; it is less trouble to grant his request than to deny him." Granting this were so; who gave you a right to weigh your own ease in the balance with your child's soul? Who gave you a right to educate him for a convict's cell, or the gallows? But, thoughtless—weakly indulgent—cruel-kind mother, it is not easier, as you selfishly, short-sightedly reason, to grant his request than to deny it; not easier for him—not easier for you. The appetite for rule grows by what it feeds on. Is he less domineering now than he was yesterday? Will he be less so to-morrow than he is to-day? Certainly not.

"But I have not time to contest every inch of ground with him." Take time then—make time; neglect every thing else, but neglect not that. With every child comes this turning point: *Which shall be the victor—my mother or I?* and it must be met. She is no true mother who dodges or evades it. True—there will be a fierce struggle at first; but be firm as a rock; recede not one inch; there may be two—three—or even more, but the battle once won, as won it shall be if you are a faithful mother, it is won for this world—aye, perhaps for another.

"But I am not at liberty to control him thus; when parents do not pull together in the harness, the reins of government will slacken; when I would restrain and correct him, his father interferes; children are quick-witted, and my boy sees his advantage. What can I do, unsustained and single-handed?" True—true—God help the child then. Better for him had he never been born; better for you both, for so surely as the beard grows upon that little chin, so surely shall he bring your gray hairs with sorrow to the grave; and so surely shall he curse you for your very indulgence, before he is placed in the dishonored one your parental hands are digging for him.

These things need not be—ought not to be. Oh! if parents had but a firm hand to govern, and yet a ready ear for childish sympathy; if they would agree—whatever they might say in private—never to differ in presence of their children, as to their government; if the dissension-breeding "Joseph's coat" were banished from every hearthstone; if there were less weak indulgence and less asceticism; if the bow were neither entirely relaxed, nor strained so tightly that it broke; if there were less out-door dissipation, and more home-pleasures; if parents would not forget that they were once children, nor, on the other hand, forget that their children will be one day parents; if there were less form of Godliness, and more Godliness (for children are Argus-eyed; it is not what you preach, but what you practice), we should then have no beardless skeptics, no dissolute sons, no runaway marriages, no icy barriers between those rocked in the same cradle—nursed at the same breast.

The Child Whom Nobody Can Do Anything With
January 23, 1858

I wonder is it foreordained that there shall be one child in every family whom "nobody can do anything with?" Who tears around the paternal pasture with its heels in the air, looking at rules, as a colt does at fences, as good things to jump over. We all know that the poor thing must be "broken in," and all its graceful curvetings sobered down to a monotonous jog-trot; that it must be taught to bear heavy burdens, and to toil up many a steep ascent at the touch of the spur; but who that has climbed the weary height does not pass the halter round the neck of the pretty creature with a half-sigh, that its happy day of careless freedom should be soon ended?

How it bounds away from you, making you almost glad that your attempt was a failure; how lovingly your eye follows it, as it makes the swift breathless circle, and stops at a safe distance to nod you defiance. Something of all this every loving parent has felt, while trying to reduce to order the child whom "nobody can do anything with."

Geography, grammar and history seem to be put into one ear, only to go out at the other. The multiplication table might as well be written in Arabic, for any idea it conveys, or lodges, if conveyed, in the poor thing's head. Temperate, torrid, and frigid zones may all be of a temperature for all she can remember, and her mother might have been present at the creation of the world, or at the birth of the Author of it, for aught she can chronologically be brought to see.

But look! she is tired of play, and has taken up her pencil to draw; she has had no instruction; but peep over her shoulder and follow her pencil; there is the true artist touch in that little sketch, though she does not know it—a freedom, a boldness which teaching may regulate, never impart. Now she is tired of drawing, and takes up a volume of poems, far beyond the comprehension, one would think, of a child of her years, and though she often miscalls a word, and knows little and cares less about commas and semi-colons, yet not the finest touch of humor or pathos escapes her, and the poet would be lucky, were he always sure of so appreciative a reader. She might tell you that France was bounded south by the Gulf of Mexico, but you yourself could not criticise Dickens or Thackeray with more discrimination.

Down goes the book, and she is on the tips of her toes pirouetting. She has never seen a dancing-school, nor need she; perfectly modeled machinery cannot but move harmoniously; she does not know, as she floats about, that she is an animated poem. Now she is tired of dancing, and she throws herself into an old arm-chair, in an attitude an artist might copy, and commences to sing; she is ignorant of quavers, crotchets and semi-breves, of tenors, baritones and sopranos, and yet you, who have heard them with rapturous encores, stop to listen to her simple melody.

Now she is down in the kitchen playing cook; she turns a beef-steak as if she had been brought up in a restaurant, and washes dishes for fun, as if it had been always sober earnest; singing, dancing, and drawing the cook's portrait at intervals, and all equally well done.

Now send that child to any school in the land, where "Moral Science" is hammered remorselessly and uselessly into curly heads, and she would be pronounced an incorrigible dunce. Idiotically-stupid parrot-girls would ride over her shrinking, sensitive shame-facedness, rough-shod. She would be kept after school, kept in during recess, and have a discouraging list of bad recitation marks as long as Long Island; get a crooked spine, grow ashamed of throwing snow-balls, have a chronic headache, and an incurable disgust of teachers and schools, as well she might.

She is like a wild rose, creeping here, climbing there, blossoming where you least expect it, on some rough stone wall or gnarled trunk, at its own free, graceful will. You may dig it up and transplant it into your formal garden if you like, but you would never know it more for the luxuriant wild-rose, this "child whom nobody can do anything with."

Some who read this may ask, and properly, is such a child never to know the restraint of rule? I would be the last to answer in the negative, nor (and here it seems to me the great agony of outraged childhood comes in) would I have parents or teachers stretch or dwarf children of all sorts, sizes and capacities, on the same narrow Procrustean bed of scholastic or parental rule. No farmer plants his celery and potatoes in the same spot, and expects it to bear good fruit. Some vegetables he shields from the rude touch, the rough wind, the blazing sun; he knows that each requires different and appropriate nurture, according to its capacities. Should they who have the care of the immortal be less wise?

"You have too much imagination, you should try to crush it out," was said many years ago to the writer, in her school days, by one who should have known that "He who seeth the end from the beginning" bestows *no* faculty to be "crushed out"; and who must have seen before now that this very faculty it is which has placed the writer, at this moment, beyond the necessity of singing, like so many of her sex, the weary Song of the Shirt.

To My Little Ledger Friends
April 10, 1858

I want to say a few words to the *little children* who write me such nice letters.

Some of you live in and about New York, some at a great distance from it. I should be very glad, had I time, to write each of you a long letter—indeed, many long letters; but how is this possible if I "make some more books for you," as you all request me to do. One cannot write a book as fast as one can read it through; perhaps you do not think of that. Besides, I must write every week for Mr. Bonner, who does so much to make your firesides cheerful and happy. Then I have a great many other calls upon my time, of which you know nothing. Like your own mamma, I have children. They sometimes say, "Oh, do throw away that tiresome pen, and talk to us." And then I say, "Yes, presently." But still I have to keep on writing. Then, you know, if I only used my head, and never my feet, my head would not last long. I must exercise a great deal every day, else I should fly up the chimney, or through the roof, like a witch. But for all that I don't forget one little girl or boy who ever wrote to me; and although I cannot answer, it always pleases me to hear from you. I want you all to believe this, and write me whenever you feel like it.

A Word for the Children
July 3, 1858

There is not a day of my life in which I am not vexed at the injustice done to children. A Sunday or two since, I went to hear Mr. Beecher preach, that live apostle, who can galvanize the deadest soul that ever Satan paralyzed. In the pew directly in front of me sat a fine little lad, about twelve years old, unobtrusively taking notes of the sermon. By my side sat a man—gentleman, I suppose, he called himself—his coat, pants, boots, and linen were all right as far as I am any judge, and dress seems to be the test now-a-days—who occupied himself in leaning over the front of the pew, and reading what the boy was writing—evidently much to the discomfiture of the latter. I would like to ask why that child's penciled notes should not have been as safe from curious eyes as if he had been an adult? and what right that grown-up man had to bother and annoy him, by impertinently peeping over his shoulder? and of what use it is to preach good manners to children, while nobody thinks it worth while to practise the same toward them? The other day I was sitting in a car, and a nice, well-behaved boy of ten years took his seat and paid his fare. Directly after in came the conductor, and, without a word of comment, coolly took him by the shoulder and stood him on his feet, and then motioned a lady to his vacant seat. Why not *ask* the child, at least? I have often been struck with the ready civility of boys in this respect, in public conveyances—but that is no reason why they should be imposed upon; the lady who took the seat might possibly have thanked a *gentleman* for yielding it to her, but she evidently did not think that good manners required she should thank the boy. Again—what right has a gentleman to take a blushing little girl of twelve or thirteen and seat her on his knee, when he happens to want her place? I have seen timid, bashful girls suffering crucifixion at the smiles called forth by this free and easy act; and sometimes actually turning away their faces to conceal tears of mortification; for there are little female children unspoiled even by the present bold system of childhood annihilation—little violets who seek the shade, and do not care to be handled and pulled about by every passer-by. Again, why will parents, or those who have the charge of children make hypocrites of them by saying, Go kiss such and such a person? A kiss is a holy thing, or should be, and not to be lightly bestowed. At any rate, it never should be compulsorily given. Children have their likes and dislikes, and often much more rationally grounded than those of grown people, though they may not be able to syllable them. I never shall forget a snuffy old lady whom I used to be obliged, when a child, to kiss. I am not at all sure that my unconquerable aversion to every form of tobacco—and even the "Fanny Fern Tobacco" fails to mollify me!—does not date from these repulsive and compulsory kisses. With what a lingering horror I approached her, and with what a shiver of disgust I retreated to scrub my lips with my pinafore, and shake my locks lest peradventure a particle of snuff had lodged there. How I wondered what she would do in Heaven without that snuff-box, for she was a "church member," and my notions of Heaven could by no stretch of liberality admit such a nuisance; and how I inwardly vowed that if I ever grew to be a woman, and if I ever was married, and if I ever had a little girl, all of which were dead certainties in my childish future, I would never make her kiss a person unless she chose to do it, never—never—which article of my pinafore creed I do here publicly endorse with my matronly hand.

Again, what more abominable tyranny than to force a child to eat turnip, or cabbage, or fat meat, or anything else for which they have an unconquerable and unexplainable disgust? It is infamous. I have seen a child actually shudder and turn pale at being obliged to swallow such things. Pray, why should not their wishes in this respect be regarded as much as those of their seniors? Not that a child should eat everything which it craves indiscriminately, but it should never, in my opinion, be forced to swallow what is unpalatable, except in the case of medicine, about which parents tell such fibs—that it "tastes good," and all that—when they should say honestly, "It is very bad indeed, but you know you *must* take it, and the sooner it is over, the better; now be brave and swallow it." I do protest too against forcing big boys to wear long curls down their backs after they are well into jackets, for the gratification of mamma's pride, who "can't bear to cut them off," not even though her boy skulks out of sight of every "fellow" he meets, for fear of being called a "girl-boy"; or making a boy of that age wear an apron, which the "fellows" are quite as apt to twit him about, or anything else which makes him look odd or ridiculous. There is no computing the sufferings of children in these respects. I dare say many who read this will say, "But they should be taught not to mind such things," &c.; that's all very well to say, but suppose you try it yourself;—suppose you were compelled to walk into church on Sunday with a collar that covered your cheeks, and your great-grand-father's coat and vest on; to hear the suppressed titters, and be an object of remark every time you stirred, and you a man who hated notoriety, and felt like knocking every body down who stared at you? How would that suit? Nothing like bringing a case home to yourself. Just sit down and recall your own childhood, and remember the big lumps in your little throat that seemed like to choke you, and the big tears of shame that came rolling down on your jacket, from some such cause, and don't go through the world striding with your grown-up boots on little children. They are not all angels, I know; some of them are malicious, and ugly, and selfish and disagreeable; and whose fault is it—answer me that? Not, one time in ten, the child's. You may be sure of it. God made it right, but there were bunglers who undertook the charge which an angel might shrink from.

A Whisper to Mothers
April 16, 1859

"She is such a strange child—so different from other children," a mother remarked in my hearing, with a sigh of discontent; as if all children should be made after one model; as if one of the greatest charms of life were not individuality; as if one of the dreariest, and weariest, and least improving, and most stagnating things in the world, were not a family or neighborhood which was only a mutual echo and re-echo.

"Different from other children!" Well—*let her be different*; you can't help it if you would—you ought not if you could. It is not your mission, or that of any parent, to crush out this or that faculty or bias which is God-implanted for wise purposes. You are only to modify and direct such by judicious counsel. A child who thinks for itself, prefers waiting upon itself, and is naturally self-sustained, is of course much more trouble than a heavy-headed child, who "stays put" wherever and however you choose to "dump" him down; but it is useless to ask which, with equally good training, will be the most efficient worker in the great life-field. Suppose he *does* question your opinions occasionally, don't be in a hurry to call it "impertinence"; don't be too lazy or too dignified to argue the matter with him; thank God, rather, that his faculties are wide awake and active. Nor does it necessarily follow that such a child must be contumacious or disobedient. Such a nature, however, should be tenderly dealt with. Firm yet *gentle* words—never injustice or harsh usage. You may tell such a child to "hold its tongue" when it corners you in an argument, often without any intentional disrespect, but you cannot prevent its thinking. It should not follow that a young person must, as a matter of course, though they mostly do, adopt the parental religious creed. Some parents I have known unwise enough to insist upon this. A forced faith for the wear and tear of life's trials, is but a broken reed to lean upon. On these subjects talk yourself; let your child talk, and then let him, like yourself, be free to think and choose, when this is done.

Out of twenty violets in a garden, you shall not find any two alike, but this does not displease you. One is a royal purple, another a light lilac color;

one flecked with little bright golden spots, another shaded off with different tints of the same violet color, with a delicacy no artist could improve. You plant them, and let them all grow and develop according to their nature, now and then plucking off a dead leaf, now loosening the earth about the roots, or watering it, or giving it shade or sunshine, as the case may be, but you don't try to erase the delicate tints upon its leaves, and substitute others which you fancy are better. No human fingers could re-create what you would mar—you know that, so you bend over it lovingly, and let it nod to the breeze, and bend pliantly to the shower, or lift its sweet face, when the sun shines out, and through all its various changes you do not sigh for monotony. So, when I see a family of children, I like the mother's blue eyes reproduced, and the father's black eyes. I like the waving, sunny locks, and the light brown, and the raven; I like the peach-blossom skin, and the gipsey olive, all round the same hearth-stone, all rocked in the same cradle. Each is beautiful of its kind; the variety pleases me. Just so I like diversity in regard to temperament and mental faculties. Each have their merits; Heaven forbid they should be rolled up and swathed up like mental mummies, bolt upright, rigid, and fearfully repeated; no collision of mind to strike out new ideas, no progress, no improvement. Surely this is not the age for that.

A Nursery Thought
April 14, 1860

Do you ever think how much work a little child does in a day? How from sunrise to sunset, the little feet patter round—to us—so aimlessly. Climbing up here, kneeling down there, running to another place, but never *still*. Twisting and turning, and rolling and reaching, and doubling, as if testing every bone and muscle for their future uses. It is very curious to watch it. One who does so may well understand the deep breathing of the rosy little sleeper, as with one arm tossed over its curly head, it prepares for the next day's gymnastics. Tireless through the day, till that time comes, as the maternal love which so patiently accommodates itself hour after hour, to its thousand wants and caprices, real or fancied.

A busy creature is a little child. To be looked upon with awe as well as delight, as its clear eye looks trustingly into faces, that to God and man have essayed to wear a mask. As it sits down in its little chair to ponder precociously over the white lie you thought it "funny" to tell it. As rising and leaning on your knee, it says thoughtfully, in a tone which should provoke a tear, not a smile—"I don't believe it." A lovely and yet a fearful thing is that little child.

A Whisper to Mothers
August 25, 1860

Now that the warm weather is upon us, I want to say a word for the children. Hasty slaps, or shakes, "boxed ears," and sly pinches, may be escape-valves for a parent's or teacher's pent-up irritation; but it is neither conducive to prolonged obedience, or improved temper, on the part of the child, who seldom knows *for what* he is punished so rudely, and who finds it quite as difficult to endure the dog-days serenely, as yourselves. At any rate, try bathing the little, flushed face and heated hands and wrists before you strike; that will both give you and the child a chance to *cool*. And, don't selfishly tuck them into bed in the cool of the evening, when an hour's play on the door-step or piazza, or a look at the stars as they peep out, while seated on your knee, would mesmerise the child so gently that they and you will sleep undisturbed when you *do* sleep. The amount of it is, now that the children are *here*, and without being allowed a vote on the subject, the least you can do, in my opinion, is to be considerate and merciful to their little wants.

How to Look at It
May 4, 1861

I am sometimes struck with wonder that grown people should ever have the presumption to rebuke children and young people, or at least, if they do so, should do it otherwise than in a spirit of the profoundest humility. We who *should* stand so rebuked in the presence of our Heavenly Father for so many years of waywardness, impatience, obstinacy, willfulness, and utter disregard of His forbearance, and unremitted loving kindness through it all? How dare we, whose feet are dusty and travel-worn with devious life-paths, leading anywhere *but* to the straight and narrow path of self-denial, arraign so imperiously the bounding footsteps so elastic with exuberant life? How dare we crimson the young check with tearful shame, while our own heads are not bent with the weight of sins palliated and unconfessed? Oh, how many men and women now lost to the world and themselves for all noble and good purposes, were to-day blessing their kind, had judgment in *their* childhood been thus tempered with parental mercy; had but the bitter, angry word died unspoken on the lip, ere it froze the warm stream that would have followed so unquestioningly the divining rod of love; had but the helping hand of parental encouragement been extended, when the dark cloud of misfortune descended on heads all unused to the storm? And so, when I see man or woman warped from their moral symmetry, speaking or writing words steeped in bitterness and defiance, I would fain go back and look at the cradle that was all too narrow for the beautiful proportions, now so twisted, cramped and disfigured. I would fain look at the *babe,* brought, without volition of its own, into contact with hydra-headed evil, and unprovided, by those who should have looked to it, with the proper weapons for self-defence and safety. Alas for the great host of the discouraged, lying wounded and slain by the wayside *for this cause alone!* Alas for the gray-haired man, reeling through the streets, the taunt of every Lilliputian big enough to syllable words of reviling! Alas for the young man counting the lagging hours in his prison cell! Alas for the woman, into whose darkened soul no ray of light ever shines, save the phosphorescent glimmer born of decay! A solemn hour, indeed is that when a babe's first wailing cry is heard in a household.

A Word to Parents
July 27, 1861

There is one thing of which some mothers are guilty, against which I wish to enter my protest; not that there is *but* one; but my present misery is their practice of *waking children and young people in the morning*. I think this should never be done, as nature *alone*, at the earlier stages of existence, should determine the hour of waking. If it is wished that a child, for any reason, should wake earlier, it should be put to bed earlier; but this rousing the half-rested young things to a day of petulance, consequent upon such indiscretion, I believe to be downright cruelty. Nothing is gained by it, what advantage soever may be thought to follow. *A child will always wake when it has had sleep enough,* unless, indeed, it is drugged; and I never look upon the poor, little, yawning things, prematurely and causelessly pulled out of their nests, without a feeling of indignation. That child performs its whole duty, who sleeps, and eats, and plays enough, and minds what it is told. As to a book, it is my belief it should never look into one, until after it is seven years old. Then we should seldom see any big-headed, narrow-chested, fretful children. The time wholly spent in growing vigorously would be amply *atoned* for, if I must at this day use that deprecatory word, by the vigor with which they would learn when put to their books. And, as to whipping or punishing children, it is my belief that, as a general rule, where the child is punished once, the parents *should* be punished six times, as being the guiltier party. Sometimes, on account of their spasmodic government, granting at one time what is refused at another, so that the child never knows what it is to expect; sometimes because the irritating manner of the parent, *causes* the very misdemeanor for which the child is made to suffer; sometimes because the parent feeds the child so improperly that it is next to impossible for it to be otherwise than fractious. And so we might go on multiplying instances without number. As to the children of the poor, and their parents, both are to be pitied. The poor woman in an unhealthy cellar, tied to the wash-tub, with half a dozen rebellious little things clinging to her skirts, looking forward, perhaps, to the return of a drunken husband at night; how can we judge *her* harshly, whose every moment must be spent in toil, even if the hasty word or blow *does* descend, where time for *government*, or reasoning with the clamorous, untamed brood is a thing impossible. But for those parents more happily situated, what excuse can be found broad enough to cover indolence or inefficiency in this regard? Those whose "nay" should *mean* nay, and whose "yea" should be as inviolate as the laws of the Medes and Persians?

I fully believe in making a child mind; and I think no cruelty comparable to that of which injudicious indulgence is guilty, when it introduces to the world a man or woman who is a man or woman only in *stature*, having all a child's unreasonableness, wilfulness and temper, untamed and unchecked, and what is worse, *having no desire* to check or tame it.

I say this advisedly, for, from out the cruelty of parents, terrible as that is, will sometimes grow the self-sustained, self-reliant, useful man or woman; but who shall compute the misery that follows in the wake of the pampered, conceited, petted, arrogant *grown-up child*, acknowledging no law in earth or Heaven but its own imperious will?

Mercy for Children
November 30, 1861

It is a notorious fact that dismal views of theology and of nations and individuals are on record in our libraries, which are known to have proceeded, not from the brain, but the stomach. And yet we do not hear that their authors, although grown to man's estate, have ever been put in the pillory by way of punishment. Can anybody tell, then, why a little child who has been defrauded of its usual amount of sleep, or over-wearied in any way, or over or underfed, should always be put through his paces with the severity of a martinet, without any margin being allowed for infantile hindrances and obstructions? I often think if grown people were punished and reproved as unseasonably and unjustly as children often are, what a howl would be raised in the community; and yet these poor little victims of the governmental straight-jacket, may neither mutter nor peep, though every bone and muscle and nerve have been abominably outraged by ignorance and stupidity.

A child under five years, is never fractious according to our belief, unless it has good and sufficient reason for being so. Parents would do well to satisfy themselves of this, before administering reproof or punishment. The contrary course, is as if one stood by the bedside of a man with a fever, and called him to account for every mistake of his past life, when his head was beating like a trip-hammer, and his pulse on the race-horse order, under the insane supposition, that the censor was producing an excellent moral effect.

The Use of Grandmothers
May 23, 1863

A little boy, who had spilled a pitcher of milk, stood crying, in view of a whipping, over the wreck. A little playmate stepped up to him and said, condolingly:—Why, Bobby, haven't you got a *grandmother*?

If there's not a sermon in *that* text, where shall one find it? Who of us cannot remember this family mediator, always ready with an excuse for broken china, or torn clothes, or tardy lessons, or little white fibs? Who was it had always on hand the convenient stomach-ache, or headache, or toothache, to work on parental tenderness? Whose consoling stick of candy, or paper of sugar-plums, or seed-cake, never gave out; and who always kept strings to play horse with, and could improvise riding whips and tiny kites, and dress rag-babies, and tell stories between daylight and dark to an indefinable amount to ward off the dreaded go-to-bed hour?

Who staid at home, none so happy, with the children while papa and mamma "went pleasuring?" Who straightened out the little waxen limbs for the coffin when papa and mamma were blind with tears? Who gathered up the little useless robes and shoes and toys, and hid them away from torturing sight till heaven's own balm was poured into those aching hearts? "Haven't you got a grandmother?" Alas! if only our grown-up follies and faults might always find as merciful judgment, how many whom harshness and severity have driven to despair and crime, were now to be found useful and happy members of society.

A Chapter for Mothers
May 30, 1863

We do not believe in delegating *absolutely* the care of young children to any person whatsoever. No parent, we think, who is not selfishly careless on this point, will be satisfied to do so. One has only to open one's eyes, in the different Parks in New York, where children and their nurses congregate, to be convinced of this fact. Not long since, I saw a bright little fellow of five years running before me on the gravel-walk, laughing and tossing his little arms above his head, as if he could not sufficiently express his glee at the fresh air and bright sunlight. Suddenly he spied a great treasure; viz.: a small, smooth, round, white stone, and, boy-fashion, picked it up for the pleasure of tossing it down again. Nurse, who was just behind, darted up to him and struck him violently three times on the top of his head, so as to crush his cap completely over his eyes. This done, she jerked him up and down by one arm, till the child's face was white with pain; and all for the simple and natural act of picking up a shiny pebble on the gravel-walk.

I will not say what punishment I would like to have inflicted on this termagant,[1] who went off with her sobbing victim, rubbing his little nose the wrong way, and otherwise aggravating him to the verge of madness; but I will say, to mothers—who are not, of course, always able to go out themselves with their young children—never trust them out of your sight with persons not *proven* to be competent for their office. I am not unaware that there are even *parents* who are sometimes guilty of impatient and angry handling of their own children; and *because* even a parent's love is not always, under weariness of body, proof against these things, would I have those closely watched who have not this controlling motive for patience and justice toward the helpless.

Certainly, under no circumstances should a nurse be allowed to strike a child. Many a healthy child has been injured for life by an angry twitch or blow, and parents have mourned and wondered, and doctors have prescribed, while nurse has kept her own secret. I hope not to be misunderstood here. I know that there are faithful, conscientious persons in this capacity worthy of implicit trust and confidence; but I risk nothing in saying that they are too rare. I am not unaware that a nurse's position is at best a disagreeable and trying one; but this she knew when she accepted this mode of livelihood. I know that there are most foolish and unreasonable mothers; and I know that a child, subject to no government at home, is hard to manage away from home. Still, it remains that it is not to be felled with a blow on the head like an ox, or suspended by one limb in the air, or shook till it is white in the lips, or otherwise brutally treated, by those who have it in charge out of doors.

Were I mayor of New York I would do several things; but, first, I would appoint a special policeman in each Park to report to parents these cases; one of such advanced age and known imperturbability that his judgment would not be affected by the bright eyes and smart ribboned cap of the prettiest nurse-termagant among them.

A Chapter for Parents
August 29, 1863

There is one great defect in the present system of family education. Not that there is only one; but we wish to call attention at present to the practice of obliging the *girls* of a family, in almost every instance in which self-denial is involved, to give way to the boys. "Remember he is your brother," is the appeal to tender little hearts, which, though often swelling under a sense of injustice, naturally give way under this argument. This might be all very well, were the boys also taught reciprocity in this matter, but as this unfortunately is not often the case, a monstrous little tyrant is produced whose overbearing exactions and hourly selfishnesses are disgusting to witness. As years roll on, Augustus's handkerchiefs are hemmed at half a wink from his lordship that he wishes it done, and his breakfast kept hot for him, though he change his breakfast hour as often as the disgusted cook leaves her place; while his sister's faintest intimation of a desire for his escort of an evening is met with a yawn, and an allusion to "the fellows" who are always "expecting him." It is easy to see what delightful ideas of reciprocity in mutual good offices Augustus will carry into the conjugal state, if he ever marries. His bride soon finds this out to her dismay, and half a dozen babies, and her wakeful nights and careworn days, are no excuse for not always placing his clean linen on a chair by his bed when needed, "to save him the trouble of opening his bureau drawers." "Before he was married" his handkerchiefs were always laid in a pile in the north-east corner of his drawer, duly perfumed, and with the exquisite word "*Augustus*" embroidered in the corner.—And *now*! "Before he was married" he was always consulted about the number of plums in his favorite pudding.—And *now*! "Before he was married" he was never bothered to wait upon a woman out of an evening unless he chose.—And *now!* "Before he was married" he had his breakfast any time between seven in the morning and three in the afternoon.—And *now*!

And so the poor weary woman hears the changes rung upon the newly-discovered virtues and perfections of his family, till she heartily wishes he had never left them. It never once occurs meanwhile to this domestic Nero to look at the *other* side of the question. How should it? when all his life at home was one ovation to his vanity and selfishness. "He could never bear contradiction! dear Augustus couldn't"; so he must never be contradicted. His friends must either agree with him or be silent, "because a contrary course always vexed him." Now we beg all mothers, who are thus educating domestic tyrants in their nurseries, to have some regard for the wife of his future, waiting for him somewhere, all unconscious, poor thing! of her fate; even if they have none on his sisters and themselves.

The most interesting story we ever read, was one which did *not* end, as usual, with the marriage of the children of the family, but followed them into homes of their own, where the results of affectionate and at the same time *judicious* home-training manifested themselves in their beautiful, unselfish lives. It would do no harm, if mothers would sometimes ask themselves, when looking at their boys, what sort of *husband* am I educating for somebody? It is very common to think what sort of *wife* a *daughter* may make. Surely the former question, although it so seldom occurring, is no less important.

A Grandmother's Dilemma
June 30, 1866

I wish some philosopher would tell me at what age a child's naughtiness *really* begins. I am led to make this remark because I am subject to the unceasing ridicule of certain persons, who shall be nameless, who sarcastically advise me "to practice what I preach." As if, to begin with, anybody ever did *that*, from Adam's time down. You see before I punish, or cause to be punished, a little child, I want to be sure that it hasn't got the stomach-ache; or is not cutting some tooth; or has not, through the indiscretion, or carelessness or ignorance of those entrusted with it, partaken of some indigestible mess, to cause its "naughtiness," as it is called. Then—I want those people who counsel me to such strict justice with a mere baby, to reflect how many times a day, according to this rule, *they* themselves ought to be "walloped" for impatient, cross words; proceeding, it may be, from teeth, or stomach, or head, or nerves; but just as detrimental as to the results as if they came from meditated, adult naughtiness.

Scruples of conscience, you see—that's it. However, yesterday I said: Perhaps I *am* a little soft in this matter; perhaps it *is* time I began. So I stiffened up to it.

"Tittikins," said I to the cherub in question, "don't throw your hat on the floor; bring it to me, dear."

"I san't," replied Tittikins, who has not yet compassed the letter *h*. "I san't,"—with the most trusting, bewitching little smile, as if I were only getting up a new play for her amusement, and immediately commenced singing to herself:

"Baby bye,
Here's a fly—
Let us watch him,
You and I";

adding, "Didn't I sing that pretty?"

Now I ask you, was I to get up a fight with that dear little happy thing, just to carry my point? I tell you my "government" on that occasion was a miserable failure; I made up my mind, after deep reflection, that if it was not quite patent that a child was really malicious, it was best not to worry it with petty matters; I made up my mind that I would concentrate my strength on the first *lie* it told, and be conveniently blind to lesser peccadilloes. This course is just what I get abused for. But, you see, I stood over a little coffin once, with part of my name on the silver plate; and somehow it always comes between me and this governing business. I think I know what you'll reply to this; and in order that you may have full justification for abusing me, I will own that the other day, when I said to Tittikins, "Now, dear, if you put your hands inside your cup of milk again, I must really punish you," that little three-year-older replied, in the *chirp-est* voice,

"No, you won't! I know better." And one day, when I *really* shut my teeth together, and with a great throb of martyrdom, spanked the back of that dear little hand, she fixed her great, soft, brown, unwinking eyes on me, and said, "I'm brave—I don't mind it!" You can see for yourself that this practical application of the story of the Spartan boy and the fox, which I had told her the day before, was rather unexpected.

Tittikins has no idea of "the rule that won't work both ways." Not long since, she wanted my pen and ink, which, for obvious reasons, I declined giving. She acquiesced, apparently, and went on with her play. Shortly after, I said, "Tittikins, bring me that newspaper, will you?" "No," she replied, with Lilliputian dignity. "If you can't please me, I can't please you." The other day she was making an ear-splitting racket with some brass buttons, in a tin box, when I said, "Can't you play with something else, dear, till I have done writing?" "But I like this best," she replied. "It makes my head ache, though," I said. "You poor dear, you," said Tittikins, patronizingly, as she threw the obnoxious plaything down, and rushed across the room to put her arms around my neck—"you *poor* dear, you, of tourse I won't do it, then."

I have given it up; with shame and confusion of face, I own that child *governs me*. I know her *heart* is all right; I know there's not a grain of *badness* in her; I know she would die to-day, if she hadn't those few flaws to keep her alive. In short, she's *my grandchild*. Isn't that enough?

What Childhood Should Be
October 19, 1867

If it were not too serious a subject for mirth, one might often laugh at the superhuman virtue required by adults, of little children. "Be good," says the autocrat of the family—mother, father, uncle or aunt, as the case may be—"be good." Now being "good" in this instance may mean, that a restless little creature, brimming with pent-up vitality, shall not touch a finger to any article, in a small, confined room, except toys whose magic virtues he long since exhausted, having turned them over, day after day, for weeks, without a solitary word of interest or sympathy having been addressed him in his efforts to extract amusement from the same. At length he cries—cries simply because he is weary and has nothing to do. "Be good," thunders the family autocrat—"be good"; which, translated, means, don't trouble *me*. Now if instead, the autocrat were to take the little creature in his or her lap, in an easy position, so as to rest the little tired limbs, and tell it a story to withdraw its thoughts a while from itself, and give it material out of which to build a little play, which you should presently see him jump down from the lap in glee to rehearse, would it not be vastly more sensible, as well as reasonable?

"Naughtiness," so styled, is oftener than anything else, in young children, want of occupation, confined apartments and insufficient ventilation. The truth is, that "all out doors," as the phrase is, is the only proper apartment for them. *There* is variety; *there* is space; *there* is fresh air. A child brought up wholly in the city, accustomed only to the limitations of a daily walk, is really defrauded of its "childhood"; and, what is more mournful, the theft can never be atoned for in after life. *Nothing* can make up to it, for the gleeful delight of picking shells upon the seashore, or paddling with dimpled feet in the foam of the waves, or plucking handsful of flowers, wheresoever it chooses to stray, or looking at the animal creation, every one of which, from a caterpillar to an ox, is a marvel and a wonder, compared to which a toyshop is of no interest whatever. Simply as an educating process, without regard to health, or pleasure, it is of more value than any other to childhood; we are taking it for granted that such a child is neither fettered by fine clothes, or tyrannized over by a s stupid, ignorant, selfish nurse, who replies to every intelligent query, "Hold your tongue!" or "Don't bother!"

I think that I can always select, from out the grown people I meet, those who, when they came into the world, brought their welcome with them, and over whose infancy heaven's dew and sunshine fell, without stint or limit. What crosses soever in after life they may have been called to bear in a world of mutation, still the eye, at times, brightens, and the worn hands clasp each other, while the eyes seem to be looking back through the far years, as you hear from their lips these slowly-voiced words, "I had such a *happy* childhood!" And now, when the chosen voice, that promised to cherish, is harsh, and stern, and cold, and "duty" is in place of love, and the years move all too slowly and wearily to the coveted grave, there still will remain *this* blessed memory! Perhaps some one scene, stands out in bold relief against all the dark years; some day when the childish grief had reached its climax; and sympathy and love came raining into the little aching heart, healing wheresoever it touched, till smiles chased the tears away, and sobs were turned to kisses. And if, at such a memory and its dark contrast, the agonized cry should escape, "Oh, *mother! mother!*" who shall tell me that eternity has severed such strong heart-strings? What were life worth, if one believed this?

Grandmothers
June 15, 1872

A frivolous old-age! Can there be anything more dreadful? The inability to please, with an unabated desire to do so.

This was all expressed in a remark of a mother to her daughter when her first child was born. "Never teach it to call me grandmother." Oh! how I pity such a woman. Of all the lovely titles in the English language, it seems to me, that of "Grandmother" is the loveliest.

To have one's children's children at our knee: to tell them wonderful tales of their parents' childhood; to come between them and the harm of *too much governing*, which has ruined quite as many children as has too much indulgence; to show your zealous son or daughter, by the light of experience, that it is sometimes wisest not to see a fault, which, if seen, must be immediately corrected; to teach them that rebuke and punishment should both be reserved for great and grave occasions, and that the continual dropping of "scolding" for trifles is destruction to all good government—that for the wearer of a dirty little shoe to forget to wipe it on the door-mat, is not comparable to the offence of telling a lie.

In short, that the surface faults of most children will fall from off them like the calyx from flowers, in the due course of nature, without any of that irritating plucking and pulling which jars the young plant, and harms its healthful growth.

This I contend to be the delightful mission of a sensible grandmother. Grandmother! Who but she knows that there are times when a child can and ought to have a reprieve of an hour from "being put to bed"; and that always, before a child is punished, you should be sure to look and ascertain that its "tongue is not coated,"[2] or that it had no appetite for its breakfast at the breakfast hour, and needs a slice of bread and butter instead of a "whipping."

Grandmother, of all people, knows that in our pellmell rush through life, it is thus that we trample down the little children, of whom the dear loving Saviour said, "Suffer them to come unto me."

How to Put the Children to Bed
From Caper-Sauce, *1872*

Not with a reproof for any of that day's sins of omission or commission. Take any other time *but* bedtime for that. If you ever heard a little creature sighing or sobbing in its sleep, you could never do this. Seal their closing eyelids with a kiss and a blessing. The time will come, all too soon, when they will lay their heads upon their pillows lacking both. Let them then at least have this sweet memory of a happy childhood, of which no future sorrow or trouble can rob them. Give them their rosy *youth*. Nor need this involve wild license. The judicious parent will not so mistake my meaning. If you have ever met the man or the woman whose eyes have suddenly filled when a little child has crept trustingly to its mother's breast, you may have seen one in whose childhood's home "Dignity" and "Severity" stood where Love and Pity should have been. Too much indulgence has ruined thousands of children; too much *Love* not one.

ON SCHOOL REFORM

A Word to Parents and Teachers
March 14, 1857

I have before me a simple but imploring letter from a little child, begging me "to write her a composition." I could number scores of such which I have received. I allude to it for the sake of calling the attention of parents and teachers to this cruel bugbear of childhood, with which I can fully sympathize, although it never had terrors for me. The Multiplication Table was the rock on which I was scholastically wrecked; my total inability to ascertain "if John had ten apples, and Thomas took away three, how many John would have left," having often caused me to wish that all the Johns in creation were—well, never mind that, now. I have learned to like Johns since!

But to return to the subject. Just so long as themes like "The Nature of Evil," or "Hydrostatics," or "Moral Science," and kindred subjects, are given out to poor bewildered children, to bite their nails and grit their teeth over, while the ink dries on the nip of their upheld pens, just so long will "composition day" dawn on them full of terrors. Such themes are bad enough, but when you add the order to write three pages at a mark, you simply invite them to diffuse and unmeaning repetitions, as subversive of good habits of composition as the command is tyrannical, stupid, and ridiculous. You also tempt to duplicity, for a child, cornered in this way, has strong temptations to pass off for its own what is the product of the brains of another; and this of itself, as a matter of principle, should receive serious consideration at the hands of these child-tormentors. A child should never be allowed, much less *compelled* to write words without ideas. Never be guilty of such a piece of stupidity as to return a child's composition to him with the remark, "It is very good, but it is *too short*." If he has said all he has to say, what more would you have? what more can you get but repetition? Tell him to *stop when he gets through if it is at the end of the first line*—a lesson which many an adult has yet to learn.

In the first place, give a child no theme above his comprehension and capacity; or, better still, allow him to make his own selection, and always consider one line, intelligibly and concisely expressed, better than pages of wordy bombast. In this way only can he be taught to write well, sincerely, and fluently. Nature teaches you this: The little bird at first takes but short flights to the nearest twig or tree. Bye and bye, as his strength and confidence grow, they are voluntarily and pleasurably lengthened, till at last you can scarce follow him, as he pierces the clouds. This forcing Nature—pushing the little fledgling rudely out of the nest, can result only in total incapacity, or, at best, but crippled flights. In the name of the children, I enter my earnest protest against it, and beg teachers and parents to think of and remedy this evil.

One More—"Last Word"
October 29, 1859

Why don't I write about the absurdity of cooping up young people for such an unreasonable number of hours in school? My dear sir,—my dear madam, *haven't* I done it? Don't I keep hammering on that subject in public and private, and don't teachers reply—truly—"that parents don't object to the system"; and don't parents reply "that all schools do so?" and meantime, don't young spines crook, and young heads ache, and water-cure establishments flourish, and doctors rub their hands and ride in carriages, and undertakers say "it is an ill-wind that blows nobody any good?" And hasn't that man,—blessed be his memory—who lived long enough to write "Three Hours School a Day,"[3] exhausted the subject? And what, in the name of all the mothers—who care more for the "fit" of their daughters' dresses, than for the strength of their back-bones, can *I* do about it? Can I even prevent their furnishing the children's luncheon-baskets with indigestible dough-nuts, pastry, cake, pickles and candy, to devour at recess? In fact, can I do anything but bite my nails, and wear a hole in the carpet patting my impatient foot, at the troops of pale school-girls I see every day, staggering home under books as heavy inside as outside,—to occupy the time *out* of school, which if spent in vigorous out-door exercise, might possibly atone for that so mis-spent *in* school?

Still—I have no objection to proposing the following questions from Fern's Arithmetic, (not yet in common use in our schools.) 1st. When a young, growing girl is kept in school till her brain, stomach and back-bone give out, how many ideas, after that, is it probable she will retain, even with the most scientific propounding? 2nd. When you have poured into a pitcher all that it is capable of holding, why, in the name of common sense, not *hold up?*

Philanthropy in the Right Direction
March 24, 1860

We begin to think the Millennium is approaching. We lately saw a paragraph in one of our exchanges stating that in a certain public school, the lessons of the pupils had been reduced one-third; and that the result had been proved to be beneficial. *Of course*,—and had they reduced them one-half, it would have been still more so. Good! we said to ourself, after all, perhaps the many pens we have worn out writing on this subject, have not been thrown away—who knows but some little word we may have dropped, had something to do with it?—but no matter for that—so that it is done. Now, how many more schools will follow the example? Teachers may depend upon it that the vigor infused into the remaining lessons will amply compensate for what they now consider a *sacrifice* in the reduction. But parents must wake up to it too; must leave off the insane demand for "another branch of study." An intelligent teacher informed me not long since, of a gentleman who urged this with great warmth, on behalf of a little daughter, who had already quite as many lessons, to say the least, as a little growing creature could stagger under. And it was only at the teacher's earnest request, that he would carefully examine the number and length of the lessons already imposed, in school and out, and the small interval for rest remaining, that he consented to let matters remain as they were! How incredible that parents can force the bud to blossom in this hot-house fashion; only to transplant it to "Greenwood."[4]

We ask again, what intelligent teacher, co-operating with parents, will make the *next* philanthropic move the safety of "The Innocents?"

The Children's Day
June 2, 1860

We are glad to see *Saturday* for the sake of the children. "No school on Saturday" is their first waking thought on that blessed day of reprieve. It does us good to hear their merry shouts in the streets, to watch their gymnastics on fences, to see their indefatigable zeal in disentangling kite-tails from trees and awnings. Pinafores, jackets and trousers of course must suffer; but as just so much money must be spent on every child, it is only a question of choice between dry goods or drugs, shoe leather or pills; let mammas take breath and comfort in this reflection. "No school on Saturday!" If Saturday only came every other day now, or if children only studied three hours a day, which would be better still, how glad we should be. Let those mothers who object to this innovation, seriously ask themselves, whether it is not because *they don't know what to do with their children when out of school*, that they assent so quietly to their daily suicidal imprisonment. If they would reflect, that the time they gain in this way by their absence, must inevitably be made up by their sick-beds, they would be convinced how poor is such short-sighted policy. *Teachers*, of course, can do nothing while parents feel in this way. *The reform must begin at the fireside.*

"No school on Saturday!" If the poor things could be "turned out to grass" in the country till Monday, it would be better still; their lease of life would be lengthened years by the process; there's no doubt of that. If there is anything that gives us unmitigated pleasure, it is a troop of children, tossing their hats in the air for joy at being let out of school. Who blames them for trying lungs and legs to their utmost capabilities of screech and stride? Not that we lack sympathy for the weary teacher, compelled to the impossible task of regulating so much vitality so many consecutive hours, without irreparable injury to it or herself. When parents wake up to *their* duty on this subject, we shall begin to hope; till then, let no one blame the teachers for the sad results of our present system.

Writing "Compositions"
June 9, 1860

I have lately received a letter which it would be well every teacher and parent in the land should read. As I shall not betray the name or residence of the distressed young writer, of whom I have no knowledge except what is communicated by her letter, and as it may call attention to the last-drop-in-the-bucket misery, inflicted upon children already sufficiently over-tasked, who are required to furnish ideas upon a given subject, on which it is utterly impossible their young minds should grasp, I shall make no apology for transcribing it verbatim; calling particular attention to the italicised passages:

"DEAR AUNT FANNY:—You have said you are Auntie to all poor girls in distress. I am in distress, if ever anybody was; and I know that you will be kind to me. Let me tell you about it. I have expected to graduate in about two weeks; but I have no essay to read, and if I don't have one I can't graduate. I would not care so much for that myself, but my father would be so disappointed; and he has made so many sacrifices to keep me at school, that I *can't* disappoint him. Oh! I have worked so hard to keep up with my class, for I am obliged to be absent so much, and now if I can't go through, *I shall die, I know.* I am not afraid of passing examination, for I know I can do that successfully, but I never could write any kind of a decent composition; and now it seems as though it was worse than ever, for *I have tried for four months to write one, but I am further off from it than ever.* I know that you will think me very, *very* dull, and I suppose I am; but, oh! Aunt Fanny, *do, do* pity me. Please, *please* write me one to read—*you* can do it in a very short time. I know that it is a very great favor to ask of you, and I should not dare to do it, but oh! I am almost crazy, and I know by your writings that you will pity and help me. I pray every night that God will help me, and I think He put it into my heart to write to you about it. I have tried everything. Oh dear! I can't write on anything at all. *I have sat up all night, but I am as dull as ever, and I dream about it when I go to sleep.* Oh! Aunt Fanny, do, *do* pity me, and write for me. I will do anything in this wide world for you. Oh, please, do; I will never forget you. You can do anything almost; I will bless you forever. *Oh, I shall die if I don't have one!* Do write me a line, anyway, and direct to———,———. Excuse me for writing so, but I am nearly desperate. *Oh, for the love of God, do write me one in two weeks, or at most three!* I dare not even read over what I have written to you. Oh! Aunt Fanny, don't refuse me."

A better comment than this touching letter, upon the present forcing, hot-house system of education, even I should not desire. Think of
this young girl, goaded to the very verge of insanity by those who *should
know* that they are defeating the very object they are trying to attain by
forcing the young mind to string together to order, and by the page, *words
without ideas.* In my opinion this "composition" business is the greatest
possible nonsense. I believe it to be the baneful root of the inflated style
of writing so prevalent. I believe that there are exercises in English, which
would serve the purpose, millions of times better without driving pupils
mad, and without offering them a premium for deceit, in passing off as
their own, the thoughts of others. Not long since I received a letter from
the principals of a school, enclosing "a composition" to which "a prize"
had just been awarded, and which some person present at the reading
had detected as stolen from one of my books; with a request that I would
look it over and pronounce upon the same. I found it word for word as
I had written it in my book! Perhaps the *moral* effect of this system may
be worth inquiring into, even by those who seem to be utterly insensible
to the wretched spectacle of a young head tossing feverishly, night after
night, on the pillow, under the brooding nightmare of an unwritten "*composition.*" Let careless parents, who are quite as much to blame as teachers,
give this subject a thought.

At Last
November 24, 1860

After so long a time, the scholars in the New York public schools are to
have "no lessons *out* of school." Heaven be praised for that! We flatter
ourselves that the NEW YORK LEDGER has had something to do in this
matter. *Now* we shall look for rosier cheeks and straighter back-bones, since
lessons are left at the school threshold. *Now* the hours between that time
and crossing it again may be healthfully employed in running, jumping and
leaping, as they ought always to have been. *Now* children will not start in
their sleep, and murmur of geography unlearned, and sums in arithmetic
they "*cannot* do." *Now* the little brain will have time for its needful rest,
and the lessons *in* school will be learned with a vigor unknown before. So
again, three cheers for the philanthropy which has effected this much needed
change, in favor of our overtasked children.

Half a Loaf Better Than No Bread
February 22, 1862

I rejoice to see that New York is waking up at last, to the necessity of reducing those tasks for the children that are learned *out* of school. Not that I believe, with the present system of school-hours, that *any* additional task should be imposed after the pupils cross its threshold. *Every instant of the interval, in my opinion, should be devoted to recreation—out-door recreation, too, as far as practicable.* Parents should be aware of the perfect exhaustion of mind and body during the last two agonizing school hours, fully to understand the vital importance of an uninterrupted mental reprieve. I have seen young girls return home in such a hysterical state from mere exhaustion, that they had no appetite for their food, and scarcely strength to lay aside their cloaks and bonnets. And yet there lay a pile of books, from which they were to learn long lessons in such a state as this! And so day after day passed, and heads ached, and spines were being bent out of shape, and digestion became impaired, and these were to be future wives and mothers! I say it is horrible! I had rather a daughter of mine were a perfect dunce, than such a suffering life-invalid.

A Fatal Error
February 11, 1865

"She is *so* fond of study," said a proud, unthinking mother of a bright little child of ten. "All night, in her sleep, she is saying over her arithmetic lessons; and the moment she is out of bed she is teasing for her breakfast, for fear she will be late at school. She will make a bright girl by-and-by," said the mother, smiling. *If she lives*, I replied. Were she my child, she should not see a book, or the inside of a school-room, for a year at least. She should have skates instead of grammar, and a boy's sled instead of geography; and when that unnatural look had gone out of her eyes, and her cheek had a tinge of color, and she relished her breakfast and slept sweetly as a child of her age ought, it would be quite time enough to talk of "school" again. The undertaker does not dig all the graves for little children; school-teachers help, encouraged by such mothers as you, who like to hear a little child of ten years say her arithmetic lessons in her sleep. You may think it a hard thing to say; but it is harder to weep remorseful tears over a little dead child.

Will Parents Take Heed?
From Caper-Sauce, *1872*

On all hands complaints are made of the increasing ill-health of our school-children. Now who is to take this matter in hand? Who is to say there shall be absolutely *no* lessons learned out of school, unless the present duration of school hours shall be shortened? It needs, we think, only that the parents shall themselves *insist* upon this to effect it. Why wait till brain-fever has set in? Why wait till little spines are irretrievably crooked? And of what mortal use is it to keep on pouring anything into a vessel when it is incapable of holding any more, and is only wasted upon the ground?

V

"How I longed to sit down in those little tents, and talk with those heroes of Gettysburg"

Select Commentary about the Civil War

Fanny Fern is not typically remembered as a Civil War author. However, as a famous newspaper contributor with a regular weekly column throughout the entirety of the war, she often addressed the wartime realities that her readers dealt with in their day-to-day lives. Some of the works included here reveal the limitations that Fern faced as a woman writing in the nineteenth century, denied access to the male-dominated spaces and settings of the war and to the political processes surrounding it. Because she could neither cast a vote, nor hold an office, nor serve in the military, nor even thoroughly investigate and report about the war, Fern's commentary about the war often returns to a critique of gender roles in a patriarchal society. Also, in keeping with her typical sympathy for the neglected and underappreciated, Fern records the courage of humble privates, the sacrifices and grief of war widows and families, and the heroic perseverance of disabled veterans. In doing so, she consciously contributed to the shaping of historical narratives in the immediate aftermath of the war.

The Time to Speak
June 1, 1861

When timidity creeps into its hiding place, or measures its stealthy pace under the transparent mask of neutrality, then—God be thanked for the man of bold utterance! He refreshes us like the quick thunder storm, when the air grows too thick for our breath. Death, we know, sometimes follows the clap of the thunder, and the flash of the lightning; but is the bracing air that follows, of no account to gasping millions? The blast of the tempest whirls away the withered branches that have so long interlaced themselves with the arms of healthful vigor; decayed leaves, too, lay strewn around; but when all this rubbish is cleared away, and men walk erect in the sunshine, ah! how free they tread! As in the physical, so in the moral world. There are periods when the air, surcharged with foulness, must be cleared, or our souls strangle. Men grope their way with faint, purposeless steps in unhealthy valleys, nor once lift their eyes to the sublime purity of mountain heights; or if they do, how impossible of access do they seem to their enervated spirits. *Then,* should the moral thunder peal! and the quick lightning of purpose follow, though death lurk in the track. *There be things worse than death.* When men walk with closed mouths, and averted eyes, nor dare look into the mirror of their own souls, and face the marring of God's image there. When with fiendish clutch men strangle in the birth all that is Heaven-given; forgetting the taste of hopes nursed in with a mother's milk, and sacred as her name. When, with iron heel they crush out like so many insects, the soul's breath from thousands, and impiously say, Am I not doing God's service? Is it a time when the smoke of the pit ascends to the very nostrils, for men to coin pretty phrases? When every flower of life lies fainting under the withering Simoom, shall we pray for gentle dews, instead of the quick-coming, purifying, electric shower? Is one to sit down content with a mess of pottage, in place of one's birthright?

Baby-Regiments
August 24, 1861

What has become of those people who objected to seeing little children play with a toy-gun or a sword, lest it should develop war-like proclivities? It strikes us that they must all have gone away on a summer tour, or they would utter their philippics over the juvenile warriors one sees in squads at every street-corner, looking like blood-red flamingoes. To use a phrase more common than classic, "do their mothers know they are out?" We are constrained to admit that they not only *do* know it, but glory in the knowing; else why are so many matronly heads approbatively and admiringly thrust out of the window, as their particular Johnny or Tommy toddles out at the door, staggering under the weight of his miniature knapsack and drinking-cup; not a conscientious scruple visible in their fair happy faces, as they watch the little monkeys strut up the street. How is this? Ah—papa is far away, with just such a uniform as that, and though mamma cried when he went, it was not because she would have kept him from going. That's why Johnny and Tommy are free to wear theirs; *that's* why mamma has forgotten all her old scruples about "children playing soldier." Soldiers don't "play" now-a-days, and Johnny and Tommy at some future time, when they remember the father who is *now* safe and living, may have his and the nation's wrongs to right, with a stouter sword than that they now carry. Mamma thinks of this, and sits down to her work with a heavy sigh, as the little unconscious boy scampers off round the corner to join "the fellows," every one of whom is fed on bread and milk, cries for candy, and sleeps in a crib at night.

Election-Day
December 28, 1861

It is a very cold morning, and this warm room is doubly comfortable by contrast. It is very agreeable too to nurse one's limbs by the fire in this easy chair; but do you suppose were I a man, that the cushion would not be stuffed with pins and needles if I, a voter, sat there inactive, while Rinaldo Brass was being elected, and all because hundreds of just such lazy fellows as I would not put shoulder to shoulder to trip him up? Suppose he *is* "cunning" and "tricky." Is not right a match for wrong when it is as much in earnest? And for shame's sake must right need stipulate for an office, or some equivalent, before it buckles on its working harness? And *need* politics, forever and ever, taint with moral leprosy every man who touches them at the commencement, with clean hands? Again and again I ask these questions of every man of my acquaintance, and get sometimes a shrug of the shoulder, sometimes an uplifted eyebrow, sometimes a jest, sometimes a compliment, but *never* a satisfactory answer. Then, if in vexation, I exclaim I wish to goodness the women could have power to put this matter through; I am told first, that every woman would be sure to vote as her husband did. Now, if half the husbands don't vote at all, I don't exactly see the force of that reply. Then I am told secondly, that if women were allowed to vote, there would be twenty silly women to one intelligent one who would do it. When I answer, that the very fact of the restriction about their voting being taken off, would give them a motive and desire for becoming well informed in these matters, my male opponent, alarmed for his puddings, falls to weeping at thought how the gentle sex will be squeezed and jostled at the polls, and their ears offended by the frequent use of the letter D, &c. How wonderful he never thought of this when pulling some lady through a mob to see the Prince of Wales, or squeezing her into some crowded public assembly, where the levelling rule of first come, first served, had precedence of ears, feet, dresses and decency. The truth is, it is all an immense humbug, and they know it, and whenever I can catch a sensible man long enough to look me straight in the eye, and there is no other man near to witness his laying aside his pontifical shell to talk sense to a woman, he admits it!

Well, there's one thing certain. This war won't leave *women* where it found them, whatever may be said of *men*. The door of the Castle of Folly has been opened by it, and they are gradually coming out into a more bracing atmosphere; and one consequence will be, that the great alleged hindrance to female voting, viz., "a want of intelligence," (and, as I write, there goes a very well dressed man past my window, talking very familiarly with one of the "shoddy" stamp, whose vote he hopes to draw, not from his brain, but through his stomach,) pardon this digression—the great hindrance to female voting—the want of intelligence—will then be done away with. Meanwhile women who are taxed all the same as if they *were* "intelligent," may work worsted dogs and cats in crochet, awaiting that millennium.

Holidays and Holy-People
January 11, 1862

What shall I give you this week? The usual platitudes about Christmas? Such as the meeting of friends and geese;—slaughter of turkeys;—devastation of plum-puddings and pies;—Jack Frost very biting;—hot fires very warming;—Santa Claus;—remember the poor;—and all that? Or, shall I, after the unexceptionable milk-and-water manner of Mr. Never-Sin, tell a story of the immortal conjugal *He*; who was, of course, all wisdom and patience, and virtue and goodness himself, but who was afflicted with a wife who was not at all so,—on the contrary,—over whom he grieved like a forbearing saint? And how, one day, he came in and found this mother of twelve children, who had no right ever to be nervous, or fretful, although she lay awake with them a good part of every night; and "whose sphere being home," consequently ought never to need a breath of fresh air. Shall I tell you how, one day, he came home and found this bad wife in a depressed state of mind, which exhibited itself in moist eyes and other shameful symptoms; and how this perfect He, grieved at the sight, seated himself behind his newspaper until such time as she should, kneeling, ask forgiveness for not being merry when he came in; and how the more he waited the more she didn't do it; *not of course because* she didn't understand his drift, but because she was naturally a fiend in human shape like all other wives; and how, at last, tired of waiting, this majestic He remarked that he was sorry to see her so thankless for the good gifts of a bountiful Providence, (meaning the twelve children whom he himself saw for half an hour every evening, and whom he requested to have put to bed early at that); and how this bad wife only cried the more instead of falling on her knees and asking pardon for being made of flesh and blood, and consequently getting occasionally worn out like her betters; and how, with sublime patience, he did not cleave her head in two on the spot, as he legally might have done, but calmly resolved not to notice her much till she did it; and how that night he found her crying again over her baby's crib; and how he then made up his mind that she was sufficiently miserable to suit even him; and how he took her then and there to his manly waistcoat, and how they lived in peace ever after, owing to this his judicious management; and how the children from that time became sanctified young ones; actually preferring castor-oil to molasses candy, and arithmetic to Mother Goose; and how all husbands and wives who read this story should take warning that when a wife is sick or tired, she should laugh all the merrier, (as men do!) and that the great He does not—never did—never will—and ought not to be expected to have, any patience with any pains or aches, that he does not feel in his own person.[1]

Or—if you don't like this little story, "fit to lie on the family table," suppose I furnish you with some "*War*-Sketches from the Capital," after the manner of Hyppolite Hyacinth.[2] Giving you non-committal descriptions of tea and dinner parties there; and giving you the patterns of the tea and din-ner service; and telling you what the exquisite Mrs. Syllabub immortalized herself by wearing; and at what hour the President changed his clothes, and how long it took him by the watch to do it, and suppose I deplore that the dear lady-traitors who are so condescending as to notice us Yankees, *will* be so killingly charming to a man who is unfortunately under the necessity of considering both his northern and southern subscribers; and suppose I ride through the camps, and give you in these *War*-Sketches a description of the tails of the horses, and the noses of their riders, and linger lovingly like a flunkey over the young French Princes, and all that sort of thing, you know?

Well, I see very plainly there is no use trying to suit you, so you may write your own Christmas article, and a merry Christmas to you!

A Fifth Avenue Scene
July 4, 1863

We are never weary of admiring the ivy-clad churches of New York. One in particular we often pass, half hidden amid trees and flowers and foliage. Often have we lingered on a pleasant Sunday to listen to the soothing strains of the organ through the open doors and windows. It may be heterodox to say it, but devotion has overtaken us in that way that we might not have found in any other. Yesterday the church gate was open, and the fresh green grass was spaded up and tossed on one side; for there was a new-made grave, and on the very brink of it, joyous little birds were singing. Now Pleyel's lovely hymn stole upon the air from a regimental band, and through the street we caught a glimpse of a coffin, draped with the bright flag we all love, and snowy with fragrant white flowers, borne upon the shoulders of pall-bearers; while on either side walked the mourners, with uncovered heads. As the soldiers parted at the gateway, the solemn procession moved slowly on, over the scented grass and under the drooping branches, to the grave. Little children peeped curiously through the iron railing as the flag and the flowers were removed from the coffin lid; the hurried street-driver forgot his busy errand and paused for a brief moment to gaze and think, while from lip to lip, as the coffin was lowered, came the sympathetic inquiry: "Who is it?" Who? Not *your* husband, or son, or brother, or father; but only one of the many whose blood shall never have been shed in vain in this most righteous war. Who? Only Lieutenant———. *You* never saw his face; you scarce catch the name as it trips over the tongue; but for all that, your heart knows a strange pang that he is dead, for well you know that *somewhere*, love sits weeping in that bright sunshine.

And now the slanting sun gilds the painted church windows, and the sexton locks the churchyard gate, and the crowd disperses, and the dead lieutenant is left in the cool dews of evening, and the departing feet of his comrades keep time to the plaintive music of the band, as it grows fainter and fainter in the air.

Our City Camps
September 26, 1863

One could scarcely spend a pleasanter or more suggestive hour than in walking through the different parks in New York where our troops are at present stationed for the safety of the city. One glance shows that these are no holiday fellows, in bandbox trim, playing war. Their bronzed faces, and faded uniforms, tell unmistakably of service, as well as the tattered battle flags fastened to their tents. One sees there, in a very mitigated aspect, it is true, something of what "war" means. The numberless little low tents, just the length of a man's body, and no more, huddled together to make the most of a small space; the impromptu morning toilette, at that universal wash basin, "the fountain," hitherto considered exclusively the ornamental property of the goldfish and the children; the one under-garment, hastily washed out and hung on the trees to dry; the peremptory tattoo summons to bed and "reveille"; the careless, childlike freedom of attitude in sleep, in or out of tent, according as the weather or the humor suits, regardless of curious eyes; the little group gathered round a preacher, who gives out line by line one of Watts' Hymns to be sung, while several of the soldiers, with their arms about each other's shoulders, sing as they used to do in their New England "meeting-houses." All these things were most interesting to me, not to speak of the respectful, intelligent manner of the sons of New England, whom I saw encamped on Washington Parade Ground. Nor was the scene less impressive at night when the tiny tents, dimly illuminated, gleamed out of the grass like fire-flies. Within them one sees now a soldier, stooping over his allotted bit of candle, writing in pencil a letter home. One can "guess" what that letter is, from the honest, frank face bent over it. One feels the salvation it may have been, and will be, to the writer, amid the temptations of camp life, to know, that "at home" hearts will ache, or be glad, as he is true to his country and to himself. Farther on, a contented knot of smokers lounge on the benches; at a little distance a hand-organ is grinding out "Hail Columbia" for their amusement; while scattered at intervals under the trees are weary heads, with knapsacks for pillows, and the stars for a roof.

How I longed to sit down in those little tents, and talk with those heroes of Gettysburg about their New England homes, and the battles they had seen since they bade them farewell. How many questions I would like to have had answered, from *their* point of view, on points vital to all who love their country. Had I been a man, I should have walked straight up to them, and spoken of all these things, with a hearty shake of the hand; but being a woman, I could only use my eyes, and hold up my tormenting skirts from the damp grass and "lean confidingly" on the arm of my companion, and gaze at "the chaste moon" overhead, and *do the pretties*, all the same, as if life were no more earnest to me than to any female butterfly, who hangs enraptured over a fashion plate, or embroiders her apology for a soul, into a crooked worsted dog on a chair cover. Well—one thing I know. If I have to gnaw this file much longer, some Lunatic Asylum will have the pleasure of inscribing my name on its books; for there is not a day that I don't feel it in my feet to jump over some five-barred gate, that custom and "propriety" have set up, to limit female range within the scented clover-fields of lethargic inanity. Now that I have cleared my throat, I tell you—I want a freer range. In plain Saxon, I want to "loaf" about, and see something besides ribbons and laces. I want to be able to go out evenings alone, if the whim suits me, without being spoken to, on any legitimate and proper errand I may see fit. I would like to go to see ship-yards, and wharves, and iron-works, and station-houses, and hospitals, and jails, and penitentiaries; and if there must be riots, I want to see *them*, as well as political meetings, where people are pulled out by the head and shoulders for bad sentiments and bad manners. I know this is neither "refined" nor "lady-like," according to the present perverted sense of these words; and I know you are ready to ask, "Wouldn't I like to be drafted?" Yes, sir; and if I were, I hope I would not buy "a substitute." Wouldn't I like to stand up, and give up my seat in public meetings and conveyances to thankless women? That *would* be a bitter pill; still, sir, I'd swallow it courageously. Wouldn't I like?—oh—pshaw—I would agree to subscribe to almost anything, so that I need not lace, pin and button on so many things every morning, only to take them off every night, and hold them up every time it rained or is damp, and be frightened to death for fear some human hoof will tear them, or some human lips spit upon them. I would agree to anything a self-respecting woman might, could I only have an escape-valve for the superfluous electricity, that refuses the usual conductors of needles and thread, and new bonnets, and flies from my head to my heels, till I long to be a locomotive or a comet. Between you and me, I think the amount of it is, that I want to be taken care of, and petted as a woman, and yet have the independence and freedom of a man. Now any philosopher who will solve this social problem for me shall be entitled to my eternal gratitude. But to return to where we started; those who have not visited the parks, where our troops are now stationed, will have missed a most suggestive and instructive spectacle, and would do well to do so, without loss of time; and those who have done so will scarcely accuse me of over-stating the subject, in point of interest.

The Chief Obstacle to Enlistments
March 5, 1864

Various causes have been assigned by editors, politicians and civilians for tardiness in the enlistment business. None of them having, in our opinion, touched the root of the matter, it may not be inopportune to offer a woman's solution—viz.: *Tobacco!* In our opinion no male creature persistently and slavishly addicted to the use of this drug, dreads any evil which could possibly befall his country or himself like—*exertion! This* "enemy" is his daily and hourly bugbear;—how to dodge and avoid it is his anxious study from rosy dawn till dewy dark. To secure uninterrupted his precious "smoke," he would even allow his wife to be waited upon by some other man, provided he were not *too* fascinating, or she had not an undeniable and irrepressible gift for flirting. To put up his heels and think of nothing but the wreaths of smoke above his nose, is the Paradise of the male creature of 1864. Whoso, or whatsoever, interferes with this, be it family, church or State, has his hearty (though it may be silent) malediction. "The Union must and shall be preserved," of course; but why can't some other fellow go and help do it? Camp beds are horrid things at best; wet clothes worn six weeks without changing are suggestive of scurvy. Powder has been known to hurt; and though the Government finds artificial legs and arms for those it takes off, yet somehow they don't feel exactly like a man's own. And then there's that bitter pill to coat and trousers submission. *Wasn't "man born to rule"?*

Don't the veriest little masculine wasp who ever strutted on the stage of existence feel *that* to his back bone? The whole army can't be Generals and Majors and Lieutenants, and where are the *privates* to come from? Beside, he will have to march when the lazy smoking-mania is on him; and though a wife is often a nuisance in the same way, yet *she* can be scolded and snubbed and fretted till she is sick and quiet; whereas one's commander *may* answer back with a bullet.

Bounties are not to be despised, 'tis true; but then *dead* soldiers, after all, can't "smoke." Shoulder-straps are good in their place; but even officers' cigars have been known to give out and "suttlers" to be "non est."[3]

Beside, one's hearing should be quite perfect to be a soldier; and he has lately had symptoms of deafness; and once when a boy he sprained his little finger, and is now hourly expecting a relapse; then his near-sightedness grows on him, and altogether he has suddenly, for the first time in his life, such a just and overpowering sense of his general good-for-nothingness; that he feels it his duty to find a substitute if drafted; or else do a much more difficult thing, viz., prove himself to be the *comfort and support* of a widowed mother.

Unwritten History of the War
From Folly as It Flies, *1868*

What a four years we had of it! And now that our cheeks no longer grow hot at the name of Bull Run, and peace and victory—terms which no loyal heart ever wished to dissever—are ours; now that we have laid down our muskets and stop to take breath, how strange it all seems! Now that we can snap our fingers at those precious "neutral" friends; now that we can smile complacently upon croakers this side of the water, and enjoy the wry faces which suddenly converted patriots make, swallowing their allegiance; now that we sleep peaceably nights, without tossing up window-sashes and thrusting out night-capped heads, regardless of the modest stars and a shivering bed-fellow, to hail some lightning "Extra"; now that our pockets are no longer picked for standing gaping on the streets spelling out bulletins; now that six-foot cowards have done squabbling about the "draft" that is to tear them from families for which they never half provided, and for which they have suddenly conceived such an intense affection; now that our noble soldiers look back upon their sufferings and privations as some troubled dream, so happy are they in the love of proud wives and glad children and friends; now that Libby—thank God!—holds only its jailer, and kindred spirits, and on the prison ground of Andersonville loyal philanthropy already talks of erecting an institution for the benefit of our brave soldiers;[4] now that Broadway has time to cool, between regiments coming and regiments going; now that the rotten thrones of the old country will have as much as they can do to prop up their shaky foundations, without making mouths at the new cap-stone of our glorious republic, phew! *now* we can untie our bonnets and toss them up in the air, without caring for their descent. For have not dry-goods and groceries gone down? and can't we buy needles, threads and pins without beads of perspiration standing on our faces at the thought? are not pennies plenty? and won't we soon have the dear little clean silver pieces back again, instead of greasy stamps? and isn't there a prospect that when hanging is good for a man he will now be sure to get it? and if I *am* a woman, can't I fold my arms and strut about a little, even though I didn't help fight? Come to think of it, though, I *did*; I can show you a spoiled dress I got, touching off a thirty-two pounder Parrot gun[5] commissioned to throw shells into Petersburg; and I never got a shoulder-strap for it either, like many another fellow, and never grumbled about it, *un*-like many another, but was satisfied with that spot on my dress, and none on my soldierly honor, and when it was told me that "that lady had better leave the field and go somewhere else," I went there.

We've done so much grieving lately, that it is a relief to be silly; so you'll excuse me; but deep down in my heart, I thank God that the dear lost lives, from our President down, have not been in vain; that the blood the monster slavery would have lapped up triumphantly has only gone to strengthen the roots of the tree of Liberty.

Ah! think if tyranny all over the world had flaunted more defiantly for our *uncrowned* struggle! If every despotic chain, the earth over, were fresh riveted! Ah! then indeed we *might* mourn.

But now!—with tender compassion for the bereaved,—for in many a home that bright flag will *always* wear its mourning-border—today! Joy—joy to it! I never see its dear folds waving in and out against the clear blue sky, that my eyes do not fill; I want to fold it round my shoulders, I want to wear it for a dress. I want to sleep under it for a bed quilt—and I want to be wrapped in it when I die.

By and by what a glorious history of our war may be written. Not that the world will not teem with histories of it. But I speak not of great generals and commanders, who, under the inspiration of leadership, and with the magnetic eyes of the world upon them, shall have achieved their several triumphs; but of those who have laid aside the plough, and stepped from behind the anvil, and the printing press, and the counter, and from out the shop, and with leaping pulses, and without hope of reward, laid an honest heart and a strong right arm on the altar of their country; some to languish in prison, with undressed wounds, defying taunts and insults, hunger and thirst, their places of sepulture even unknown, and their names remembered only at some desolate hearthstone, by a weeping widow and orphans, and yet whose last pulse-beat was "for their country." By many a cottage fireside shall old men tell tales to wondering childhood, that shall bring forth their own precious harvest; sometimes of those who, enclosed in meshes too cunningly woven to sunder, wore hated badges over loyal hearts, and with gnashing teeth and listening ear and straining eyeballs, bided their time to strike! Men who planted, that the tyrant might reap; whose wives and children went hungry and shelterless, that he might be housed and fed. Nor shall woman be forgotten, who, with quivering heart but smiling lip bade God-speed to him, than whom only her country was dearer, and turned bravely back to her lonely home, to fight the battle of life, with no other weapon than faith in Him who feedeth the ravens. All these are the true heroes of this war; not alone they who have memorials presented, and if they die, pompous monuments erected, but the thousands of brave fellows who know, if they fall, they will have mention only among the "list of the killed and wounded." Who, untrammelled by precedents, shall write us *such* a history?

~

Let me tell you a story I heard the other day.

He was home at last! It was for three years he had enlisted. When his term was nearly out, and just as his heart leaped at thought of going home, he was taken prisoner. We all know what that word means in connection with "Andersonville" and "Libby." No shelter from rain, or sun, or night dew; stung by vermin; devoured by thirst and hunger. So day after day dragged by, and fewer and fewer came thoughts of home; for the light was fading out from the sufferer's eyes, and one only thought, day and night, pursued him—food, food! At last came the order for exchange, and John was taken with the rest, as he could bear the removal—slowly—*home!* Oh, how joyful they all were as they waited for his coming! How tenderly he should be cared for and nursed. How soon his attenuated form should be clothed with flesh, and the old sparkle of fire come back to his faded eyes. How they would love him ten thousand times better than ever for all the dreadful suffering he had undergone for his country's sake. And when he got better, how they would have the neighbors come and listen to his stories about the war. Oh, yes—they would soon make John well again. Nine—ten—eleven o'clock—it was almost time for him to be there. Susy and Jenny were quite wild with joy; and mother kept saying "Girls, now be quiet"; but all the time she kept smoothing the cushions of the easy-chair by the fire, and fidgeting about more than any of them. Then there was *such* a shout went up from Susy, who was looking down the road from the end window. *He's* coming! father's coming! and fast as her feet could carry her through the door and down the road she flew; and Jenny followed, and mother?—well, *she* stood there, with beating heart and brimming eyes of joy, on the threshold. But what makes the girls so quiet as they reach the wagon where "father" is sitting? Why don't father kiss and hug them, and he three long years away? He is *alive*, thank God, else he couldn't be sitting there—why don't he kiss his girls? He *don't* kiss them: he don't speak to them; he don't even know Susy and Jenny, as they stand there with white lips and young faces frozen with terror. It *is* father—but, look! he is only a crazy skeleton. And when they came to him, he only stretched out his long, bony fingers, and muttered, feebly—"Bread! bread! Oh, give me some bread!" And when they brought him in, crowded round and kissed him, and carried him to the warm fire, and, with streaming eyes of pity, showed him the plentiful table, he only looked vacantly in their faces and muttered, "Bread! bread! Oh, give me some bread!" And to everybody who came into the door till the hour he died, which was very soon, he said still, "Bread! bread!" and this was the last word they ever heard from "father."

And yet they say we must forgive the leader of the rebellion who did such things as these! Spirit of Seventy-six! Can I believe my ears? What sort of mercy is this, that sets the viper of to-day free to raise up a brood of hissing vipers for the future? What is this mercy for one, and this injustice for the million? This mercy which hangs little devils, and erects no gibbet for the arch-fiend himself? This mercy which lets Jeff. Davis glide safely out of the country with his money-bags, and claps the huge paw of the law upon some woman, for giving so much aid and comfort to the enemy as she could carry in her little apron-pocket?[6] What! Forgive Jeff. Davis, with the fresh memory of Forts Pillow and Wagner?[7] What! Because your son, or your husband, are now smiling at you across your table, are you to ignore that poor mother, who night after night paced up and down her chamber floor, powerless to release her husband or boy, who, at Libby or Andersonville, was surely, horribly dying with the slow pangs of starvation! The poor mother, did I say? The thousands of mothers, whose wrung hearts cry out that the land be not poisoned with the breath of their children's assassinator. To whom the sight of the gay flags of victory, and the sound of the sweet chiming bells of peace are torture, while this great wrong goes unredressed. Who can see only by day and night that dreadful dead-cart, with its unshrouded skeleton-freight, and uppermost the dear face, rumbling from that loathsome prison, to be shoveled, like carrion, underground.

Tell me? Is it in nature or grace, either, for these parents to vote that Jeff. Davis and his like be neither expatriated nor deprived of the rights of citizenship? In the name of that "mercy" which would be so burlesqued, let them not suffer this crowning injury. Let them not be pained with this mock magnanimity which so "forgivingly" crosses palms with this wrencher of other people's heartstrings. Let it not be said thoughtlessly, "Oh, we are too happy to think of vengeance." Say rather, "Let us not, in our joy, forget to be just."

And let me, individually, have due notice, if it be in contemplation to present these traitors, either with a costly service of silver plate or an honorable seat in the United States Senate.

Overhead floats the dear old flag, thank God! But countless are the homes where the music of "the holidays" has forever died out; where sorrow will clasp its hands over an aching heart, or sit down by a solitary hearth, with a pictured face it can scarce see for the tears that are falling on it. There seems nothing left now. The country is safe, the war has ended; that rifled heart is glad of that; but oh! What shall make its terrible desolation on these festival days even endurable? *That's* the thought that can't be choked down even by patriotism. It comes up all over the house, at every step. It meets you in parlor, and chamber, and entry. It points where the coat and hat used to hang; it whispers from the leaves of some chance book you listlessly open, where are *his* pencil-marks. Even the dish on the table you loved to prepare for him is turned to poison. The sun seems merciless in its brightness; the music and dancing in unrifled homes is almost heartless. What can you *do* with this spectre grief, that has taken a chair by your fireside, and, change position as you may, insists on keeping you torturing company? You may walk, but it is there when you return. You may read, but you feel its stony eyes on you the while; you may talk, but you keep listening for the answer you will never hear. Oh, what shall you do with it? Face it! Move your chair up as closely to it as you can. Say—I see you; I know you are here, and I know too that you will never, *never* leave me. I am so weary trying to elude you. Let us sit down then together, and recognize each other as inseparable. Between me and happiness *is* that gulf—I know it. I will no longer try to bridge it over with cobwebs. It is there. As you say this, a little voice pipes out—mother, when is Christmas? Ah!—you thought you could do it; but *that* question from that little mouth, of all others! Oh, how can *you* be thankful?

Poor heart, look in that little sunny face, and be thankful for that. Hasn't it a right to its share of life's sunshine, and are you not God-appointed to make it? There's work for you to do—up-hill, weary work, for quivering lips to frame a smile—I grant, but there's no dodging it. That child will have to take up its own burthen by and by, as you are now bearing yours; but for the present don't drop your pall over its golden sunshine. Speak cheerily to it; smile lovingly on it; help it to catch the floating motes that seem to it so bright and shining. Let it have its youth with all its bright dreams, one after the other, as you did. They may not all fade away; and if they should, there's the blessed memory of which even you would not be rid, with all the pain that comes with it. Now would you?

So, little one—Christmas is coming! And coming for you. There's to be turkey and pie, and you shall stuff your apron full. There's to be blind-man's buff, and hunt the slipper, and puss in the corner, and there shall be flowers strewn for *your* feet, you little dear, though we all wince at the thorns.

But for our soldiers' homes where death has literally taken all; where the barrel of meal and cruse of oil too has failed; let a glad country on festival days, of all others, bear its widows and orphans in grateful remembrance.

Speaking of "Unwritten History," reminds me of some curious written chapters of it that I saw the other day.

I begin now to think that an "All-Wise Providence" spent more time finishing off human beings than was at all necessary. I arrived at this sapient conclusion, the other evening, while looking at some hundreds of specimens of the handwriting of our disabled soldiers.[8] Before this I had always supposed that hands and arms were necessary preliminaries to chirography, and *right* hands and above all arms. And there I was, brought up all standing, with the legible, fair proofs to the contrary before my very face. Positively there was one specimen written with the soldier's *mouth*, both hands being useless. It was enough to make an able-bodied man or woman blush to think of cowering for one moment before the darkest cloud of fate. As a moral lesson I would have had every boy and girl in the land, taken there to see the power of the mind over the body. The potency of that one little phrase, "I will try." The impotency of that cowardly plea, "I can't." I wished, as I examined these interesting and characteristic papers, with the signatures and photographs of the writers annexed, that all our schools in order, should be taken there, to learn a lesson that all their books might never teach so impressively. I wished that every man in the nation, whose patriotism needed quickening, (alas that there should be any!) might see that these men who have fought for the peace we are now enjoying, who have languished long months in wretched prisons for us, and through all have but just escaped, maimed and disabled, to reach their homes, are yet self-helpful and courageous, fearing nothing, hoping all things, since they have helped save the nation. *Is* it safe? That is a question I shall not meddle with here. Meantime I, for one, feel proud as an American loyal woman that this collection of manuscripts has been made. I believe it to be purely an *American* idea. I am not aware that in any other country such a novelty exists. I think it as highly creditable to the head and heart of the originator, as to the skill and patience of our soldiers. I felt as though it should have, like a great national picture, its appropriate framing and setting in the most conspicuous spot in the Capitol. How often I think of these "privates," as they are called, when grand "receptions" and "balls" are in progress for some great "General" in our midst. All honor to him; but meantime what of these brave maimed "privates"?

Therefore I was rejoiced when John Smith and Thomas Jones had succeeded in "making their mark" on paper as well as in battle. I was glad that they had placed it on record that an American soldier is still wide awake and hopeful, though he may be so hacked and hewed to pieces that not half his original proportions remain. I wanted to sing "Hail Columbia," and "The Star Spangled Banner," and "John Brown," and "Yankee Doodle," and more than all, I wanted those people who are sticking pins through curious sprawling bugs, and paying fabulous sums for shells, and taking their Bible oaths over some questionable pictures "by the old masters," would just turn their attention to something not only veritable and unique, but honorable and worthy as a legacy to every American child that shall be born to the end of time, or—the end of our Republic, which is one and the same thing.

The History of Our Late War
From Ginger-Snaps, *1870*

Many able works have already appeared on this subject, and many more will doubtless follow. But *my* History of the War is yet to be written; not indeed *by* me, but *for* me. A history which shall record, not the deeds of our Commanders and Generals, noble and great as they were, because these will scarcely fail of historical record and prominence; but *my* history shall preserve for the descendants of those who fought for our flag, the noble deeds of our *privates*, who shared the danger but missed the glory. Scattered far and wide in our remote villages—hidden away amid our mountains—struggling for daily bread in our swarming cities, are these unrecognized heroes. Travelling through our land, one meets them everywhere; but only as accident, or chance, leads to conversation with them, does the plain man by your side become transfigured in your eyes, till you feel like uncovering your head in his presence, as when one stands upon holy ground. Not only because they were brave upon the battle-field, but for their sublime self-abnegation under circumstances when the best of us might be forgiven our selfishness; in the tortures of the ambulance and hospital—quivering through the laggard hours, that might or might not bring peace and rest and health. Oh! What a book might be written upon the noble unselfishness *there* displayed; not only towards those who fought *for* our flag, but *against* it. The coveted drop of water, handed by one dying man to another, whose sufferings seemed the greater. The simple request to the physician to pass *his* wounds by, till those of another, whose existence was unknown to him a moment before, should have been alleviated. Who shall embalm us these?

Last summer, when I was away in the country, I was accustomed to row every evening at sunset on a lovely lake near by. The boatman who went with me was a sunburnt, pleasant-faced young man, whose stroke at the oar it was poetry to see. He made no conversation unless addressed, save occasionally to little Bright-Eyes, who sometimes accompanied me. One evening, as the sun set gloriously and the moon rose, and the aurora borealis was sending up flashes of rose and silver, I said, "Oh, this is too beautiful to leave. I *must* cross the lake again." I made some remark about the brilliance of the North Star, when he remarked simply, "That star was a good friend to me in the war." "Were you in the war?" asked I; "and all these evenings you have rowed a loyal woman like me about this lake, and I knew nothing of it!" Then, at my request, came the story of Andersonville, and its horrors, told simply, and without a revengeful word; then the thrilling attempt at escape, through a country absolutely unknown, and swarming with danger, during which the North Star, of which I had just spoken, was his only guide. Then came a dark night, when the friendly star, alas! Disappeared. But a watch, which he had saved his money to obtain, had a compass on the back of it. Still of what use was that without a light? Our boatman was a Yankee. He caught a glowworm and pinched it. It flashed light sufficient for him to see that he was heading for one of our camps, where, after many hours of travel, he at last found safety, sinking down insensible from fatigue and hunger, as soon as he reached it. So ravenously did he eat, when food was brought, that a raging fever followed; and when he was carried, a mere skeleton, to his home on the borders of the lovely lake where we were rowing, whose peaceful flow had mocked him in dreams in that seething, noisome prison pen, he did not even recognize it. For months his mother watched his sick-bed, till reason and partial health returned—till by degrees he became what he then was.

When he had finished, I said, "Give me your hand—*both of 'em*—and God bless you!"—and—then I *mentioned* his jailers! Not a word of bitterness passed his lips—only this: "I used to gasp in the foul air at Andersonville, and think of this quiet, smooth lake, and our little house with the trees near it, and long so to see them again, and row my little boat here. But," he added, quietly, "*they* thought they were as right as we, and they *did* fight well!"

I swallowed a big lump in my throat—as our boat neared the shore, and he handed me out—and said, penitently, "Well, if *you* can forgive them, I am sure I ought to; but it will be the hardest work I ever did."—"Well, it is strange," said he: "I have often noticed it, since my return, that you who stayed at home feel more bitter about it, than we who came so near dying there of foul air and starvation."

VI

"More than angelic are these soul-responses"

On Grief, Suffering, and Compassion

The counterpoint to her legendary sense of humor and satire, Fern's compassionate voice was equally known and valued by her readers. Drawing upon her own experiences with tragedies and hardships, Fern intimately connected with her readers to explore the universal realities of grief and suffering. While her reflections on loss, memories, and the role of sympathy and compassion in society transcend her own era, Fern's commentary also provides valuable insight into the issues and struggles that mattered to her nineteenth-century readers. Whether commiserating with the personal trauma of grieving parents, an experience all too common at the time, or addressing such societal issues as the inhumane conditions of prisons and asylums, the rise in extreme poverty during an economic crisis, and the unfair treatment of women in workplaces, Fern sympathized with her readers' hardships. She routinely reminded her readers of the healing powers of compassion and promoted an elevated consciousness of the pain and suffering of others.

New York
From Fresh Leaves, *1857*

"There is no night there," though spoken of a place the opposite of New York, is nevertheless true of Gotham; for by the time the ennuied pleasure seekers have yawned out the evening at the theater or opera, and supped at Taylor's, or danced themselves lame at some private ball, a more humble but much more useful portion of the community are rubbing open their eyelids, and creeping by the waning light of the street lamps, and the gray dawn, to another brave day of ill-requited toil; while in many an attic, by the glimmer of a handful of lighted shavings, tear-stained faces resume the coarse garment left unfinished the night before. At this early hour, too, stunted, prematurely-old little boys may be seen, staggering under the weight of heavy shop window shutters, and young girls, with faded eyes and shawls, crawl to their prisoning workshops; while lean, over-tasked omnibus horses, commence anew their never-ceasing, treadmill rounds. God help them all! My heart is with the oppressed, be it man or beast.

The poet says there are "sermons in stones." I endorse it. The most eloquent sermons I ever heard were from "*A. Stone*"; (but that is a theme I am not going to dwell upon now.) I maintain that there are sermons in *horses*.

Crash—crash—crash!

I turned my head. Directly behind me, in Broadway, was a full-freighted omnibus. One of the horses attached had kicked out both his hind legs, snapped the whiffle-tree to the winds, and planting his hoofs into the end window, under the driver's seat, had shivered the glass in countless fragments, into the faces of the astonished passengers, plunging and rearing with the most '76-y spirit. Ladies screamed, and scrambled with what haste they might, out on to the pavement; gentlemen dropped their morning papers, and uttering angry imprecations as they brushed the glass splinters from their broadcloth, followed them; while the driver cursed and lashed in vain at the infuriated hoofs, which abated not a jot of their fury at all his cursing and lashing.

"Vicious beast!" exclaimed one bystander. "Ought to be shot *instanter!*" said a second. "I'd like to lash his hide raw!" exclaimed a third Nero.

Ah! My good friends, thought I, as I went laughing on my way, not so fast with your anathemas. The cause of that apparently malicious and unprovoked attack, *dates a long way back*. Count, if you please, the undeserved lashings, the goadings, and spurings, that noble creature has borne, while doing a horse's best to please! Think of the scanty feed, the miserable stable, the badly-fitting, irritating harness; the slippery pavements, where he has so often been whipped for stumbling; the melting dog-days with their stinging bottle-flies and burning sun-rays, when he has plodded wearily up and down those interminable avenues, sweating and panting under the yoke of cruel task-masters.

'Tis the last ounce which breaks the camel's back; 'tis the last atom which balances the undulating scales. Why should that noble horse bear all this? He of the flashing eye, arching neck, and dilating nostril? He of the horny hoof and sinewy limb? *He!*—good for a *score* of his oppressors, if he would only think so!—*Up go his hoofs!* As a Bunker Hill descendant, I can not call that horse—a jackass.

A Word to Shop-Keepers
June 20, 1857

In one respect—nay, in more, if so please you—I am unfeminine. I detest shopping. I feel anything but affection for Eve every time I am forced to do it. But we must be clean and whole, even in this dirt-begrimed, lawless city; where ash-barrels and ash-boxes, with spikes of protruding nails for the unwary, stand on every sidewalk, waiting the bidding of balmy zephyrs to sift their dusky contents on our luckless clothes. All the better for shop-keepers; indeed, I am not at all sure, that they and the street-cleaning gentry do not, as doctors and druggists are said to do, play into each other's hands!

Apart from my natural and never-to-be-uprooted dislike to the little feminine recreation of shopping, is the pain I experience whenever I am forced to take part in it, at the snubbing system practiced by too many shop-keepers toward those whose necessities demand a frugal outlay. Any frivolous female fool, be she showily dressed, may turn a whole store-full of goods topsy-turvy at her capricious will, although she may end in taking nothing away but her own idiotic presence; while a poor, industrious woman, with the hardly-earned dollar in her calico pocket, may not presume to deliberate, or to differ from the clerk as to its most frugal investment. My blood often boils as I stand side by side with such an one. I, by virtue of better apparel, receiving respectful treatment; she—crimsoning with shame, like some guilty thing, at the rude reply.

Now, gentlemen, imagine yourselves in this woman's place. *I* have no need to do so, because I have stood there. Imagine her, with her fatherless, hungry children by her side, plying the needle late into the night, for the pitiful sum of seventy-five cents a week, as I once did. Imagine her, with this discouraging price of her eye-sight and strength, creeping forth with her little child by the hand, peeping cautiously through the glass windows of stores, to decide unobtrusively upon fabrics and labeled prices, or vainly trying to read human feeling enough in their owners' faces to insure her from contemptuous insult at the smallness and cheapness of her contemplated purchase. At length, with many misgivings, she glides in amid rustling silks and laces, that drape hearts which God made womanly and tender like her own, but which Fashion and Mammon have crushed to ashes in their vice-like clasp; hearts which never knew a sorrow greater than a misfitting dress, or a badly-matched ribbon, and whose owners' lips curl as the new-comer holds thoughtfully between her thin fingers the despised fabric, carelessly tossed at her by the impatient clerk.

Oh, how can you speak harshly to such an one? how can you drive the blood from her lip, and bring the tear to her eye? how can you look sneeringly at the little sum she places in your hand, so hardly, *virtuously*, *bravely* earned?—She has seen you!—See her, as she turns away, clasping so tightly that little hand in hers, that the pained child would tearfully ask the reason, were it not prematurely sorrow-trained.

Oh, *you* have never (reversing the order of nature) leaned with a breaking heart, upon a little child, for the comfort and sympathy that you found nowhere else in the wide world beside. *You* never wound your arms about her in the silent night, drenching brow, cheek and lip with your tears, as you prayed God, in your wild despair, dearly as you loved her, to take her to himself; —for, living, she, too, must drink of the cup that might not pass away from your sorrow-steeped lips.

It is because I have felt all this that I venture to bespeak your more courteous treatment for these my unfortunate sisters who can only weep for themselves.

Mother's Room
August 15, 1857

Mother's room! How we look back to it in after years, when she who sanctified it is herself among the sanctified. How well we remember the ample cushioned chair, with its all-embracing arms, none the worse in our eyes for having rocked to sleep so many little forms now scattered far and wide, divided from us, perhaps, by barriers more impassable than the cold, blue sea. Mother's room—where the sun shone in so cheerily upon the flowering plants in the low, old-fashioned window-seats, which seemed to bud and blossom at the least touch of her caressing fingers; on which no blight or mildew ever came; no more than on the love which outlived all our childish waywardness, all our childish folly. The cozy sofa upon which childish feet were never forbidden to climb; upon which curly heads could dream, unchidden, the fairy dreams of childhood. The closet which garnered tops, and dolls, and kites, and whips, and toys, and upon whose upper shelf was that infallible old-fashioned panacea for infancy's aches and pains—brimstone and molasses! The basket, too, where was always the very string we wanted; the light-stand round which we gathered, and threaded needles (would we had threaded thousands more) for eyes dimmed in our service; and the cheerful face that smiled across it such loving thanks.

Mother's room! Where our matronly feet returned when *we* were mothers; where we lifted our little ones to kiss the wrinkled face, beautiful with its halo of goodness; where we looked on well pleased to see the golden locks we worshiped, mingling lovingly with the silver hairs; where—as the fond grand-mamma produced, in alarming profusion, cakes and candies for the little pets, we laughingly reminded her of *our* baby days, when she wisely told us such things were "unwholesome"; where *our* baby caps, yellow with time, ferreted from some old bag or closet, were tried on our own babies' heads, and we sat wondering where the months and years had flown between then and now;—and looking forward, half sighing, to just such a picture, when we should play what seemed to us now, with our smooth skins, round limbs, and glossy locks, such an impossible part.

Mother's room! where we watched beside her patient sick-bed through the long night, gazing hopelessly at the flickering taper, listening to the pain-extorted groan, which no human skill, no human love, could avert or relieve; waiting with her the dawning of that eternal day, seen through a mist of tears, bounded by no night.

Mother's room! where the mocking light strayed in through the half-opened shutters, upon her who, for the first time, was blind to our tears, and deaf to our cries; where busy memory could bring back to us no look, no word, no tone, no act of hers, not freighted with godlike love. Alas!—alas for us then, if, turning the tablets, they showed us this long debt of love unappreciated—unpaid!

What Shall We Name the Baby?
August 22, 1857

Mary? Not so, my little ones; have you forgotten the head-stone in the church-yard, with that name upon it, and the little sister who lies beneath it? The new babe is welcome, but call her not Mary; there can be but one Mary. *Her* spirit-voice still calls me "Mother." Little feet, all unheard by you, trip softly round me. A little hand, which you see not, gently clasps mine. A little shining head bends low with yours for a mother's good-night blessing. No, no—call not the new babe "Mary." Even a little sister may not wear the robes she wore, or efface the print of the fairy foot in the useless little shoe; the idle needle must rust in the doll's frock, where the busy fingers left it. The half-formed word must not be finished, even by a sister's fingers, in the little blotted copy-book; for between the new-born babe and me stands ever the shadowy form of the first-born. No, no, my little ones, not *"Mary,"*——take not away her birth-right.

"Now there are three of you?" Nay, my little ones, now there are *four*; three here—one with God.

To Young Ladies
December 5, 1857

I was thinking to-day, how many young ladies who read the NEW YORK LEDGER, ever made it their business to relieve the suffering poor. I do not doubt that you have contributed sums of money, when called upon to do so; that is not what I mean; that often requires little or no self-denial. Have you ever left your comfortable homes, and passed through narrow streets and alleys, up rickety stair-ways lined with neglected children, whose cradle-heritage is sorrow, to search out some poor woman, languishing for everything that makes life sweet to you? It is not agreeable, I know, to see and hear nothing from which the sickened soul and senses do not turn shuddering away. But was life intended for a holiday? Is there nothing for the young and happy but to dance, and laugh, and sing? Does it matter nothing to that young heart, that within the very sight of the cheerful firelight from your windows, within sound of your musical laughter, (which God forbid I should find fault with,) sits despair with tearless eye—doubting man, doubting God—to whom the sight of your fresh, cheerful and sympathizing face would be like a flash of sunlight across the captive's dungeon floor; to whom your sweet heart-tones would be like the plank to the ship-wrecked mariner? I am sure you cannot have thought of this, or you would not have contented yourself with sending now and then a coin by the hand of some friend. You can never have suffered, or you would know how beyond all price is—sympathy. You can never have felt that delicious joy which thrills through every nerve, as the bowed head is lifted, the pale cheek flushes, and the ray-less eye overflows with the gratitude which words are so meaningless to express. I am sure you could never have listened to the sad, truthful story, and there are many such, without execrating your own selfishness, that you had eaten, drunk and slept, day after day, as if there were no hungry mouths to feed, no broken hearts to bind. I am sure you can never appreciate your own table, your own fireside, your own bed, till you see them by this contrast.

Oh, there are lessons to be learned up those narrow stairways, in those darkened rooms, which whole libraries were powerless to teach you. Lessons of sublime faith and trust in God under crushing sorrows, which are written in letters of light, read only by angels, and those human angels who see their Father's lineaments in every sorrow-stained face. There is to be seen the fierce, one-handed struggle with temptation, which, whether victorious or not, is *justly* weighed in the balance by Him who made every quivering nerve, and who can make allowance when the sharp cry of childhood nerves the outstretched hand of plunder. Why He permits this, is not for you and me, who believe in, and love Him, to ask. What we know not now, we shall know hereafter—faith can trust and wait—meantime he says to us, "Feed my lambs."

Will you do it, not by proxy, but with your own hands? Will you seek out *one* sufferer at least, to whose necessities you will minister? Some day, though your eyes are so bright, your limbs so round, your locks so glossy; some day, though Heaven forbid it, you may need such ministration yourself. I have seen this very week one as delicately cared for once as you now are, with as little prospect of future want, sitting by her fireless hearth, holding to her breast a little skeleton of a babe, with two other children clamoring for food; and no hope of relief but in Him who feedeth the sparrows. "Oh," said she to me, "when I think of what I *was*, and what I *am*," and she looked about her cold, cheerless room and at her hungry children, "I get *wild* with trouble."

Ah—that thinking!—that contrast of plenty with destitution—of tender care and love, with the cold charity of the world;—that hopeless gaze into the future;—those fettered hands and feet, and yet that weary road to travel;—and the arm—dust—that was once so strong to lean upon, so tender to shield!—Ah—have you no pity for such! Can you not feed those little innocent children, and ask your friends each to contribute something to help to feed them? Can you not, with your own hands, make from your useless dresses something to cover them? Can you not sit down by that sorrowing woman, once so happy, and ask her to try for her own sake, not to look back—not to look forward so repiningly? Can you not ask her to try to *live by the day*, not by the month, or year? Can you not say to her, as you place the loaf of bread on her table; or the coal, or wood on her hearth; *to-day* you have food, warmth and shelter—trust God for the morrow; and will you not be His almoner till the cloud is a *little* lifted, and the sun-light streams through?

I have spoken of lessons to be learned in these abodes of sorrow. Oh, it is beautiful the unselfishness of some of the poor each for the other: the sharing the small loaf, the watching by the sick bed, when the watcher is scarcely less sick; the loan of the ragged shawl, or shoes; the comforting word, when there is nothing else to give. I have seen in those places deeds that would put to blush many, for the reward of which an admiring world clamors so loudly. Are they lost? Neither you nor I believe it. We shall hear of them yet, but not from mortal tongues.

In conclusion I would say, that it would make me very happy if, at this time of distress, when so many, by no fault of their own, are without the means of a livelihood, I should call the attention of only one young lady who reads this article in the LEDGER, to the duty of *personal ministration* to the suffering poor.[1]

What Came of a Violet
May 8, 1858

Before me lies a little violet, the forerunner of spring, with a sweet, faint, delicate perfume like a baby's breath. It should give me joy, and yet my tears are dropping on its purple leaves.

Why? Has life been such a holyday to you, that your heart never grew sick at a perfume or a well-remembered song hummed beneath your window, or a form, or a face, which was, and yet was not, which mockingly touched a chord that for years you had carefully covered over, every vibration of which was torture unutterable? Have you never rushed franticly into a crowd—somewhere, anywhere to be rid of yourself? Did you never laugh and talk so incessantly and so gaily, that your listeners asked wonderingly and reproachfully, "Does she ever *think*?" Did you ever walk till your feet tottered beneath you, and still press on, as if urged by some invisible, irresistible power? Did you never listen to the tick—tick—of your watch, night after night, with dilated eyes that would not close, with limbs so weary that you could not change your posture, and lips so parched you could not even cry, God help me, and your brain one vast workshop, where memory was forging racks, and chains, and screws, and trying their strength on every quivering nerve? Did you never hail the first streak of dawn, as an angel whom you implored to lay a cool hand on your brow, and bring you peace or oblivion? And did you never see that day's sun set in clouds, like its predecessors, and the stars come forth one by one, with searching eyes, staring into the windows of your soul with a free, bold gaze, that irritated and maddened you?

You never did? Well, then, how can you understand why I shed tears over the violet? Ask your Maker that it may be a long day before sorrow brings you such knowledge, and if you have a child, and that child a girl, whose heritage is your intense nature, ask Him to take the cup of life from her lips ere she prays to have it done, ere the fair things of earth shrivel away before her eyes like a scroll.

Poor little violet, live out thy little day. I needs must love thee; I know this was not the story nature told thee to tell me, and yet it will never be an old tale while warm hearts beat, and life's pain is more than life's pleasure.

Blessed is that woman whom a new bonnet or a new dress can satisfy, who can contemplate her diamond rings, and not know a wish ungratified, who leaves reflections to her mirror, and is never reminded of her heart save by her corset-lacings.

Blackwell's Island, Number I[2]
August 14, 1858

Prior to visiting Blackwell's Island last week, my ideas of that place were very forlorn and small-pox-y. It makes very little difference, to be sure, to a man, or a woman, shut up in a cell eight feet by four, how lovely are the out-door surroundings; how blue the river that plashes against the garden wall below, flecked with white sails, and alive with gay pleasure-seekers, whose merry laugh has no monotone of sadness, that the convict wears the badge of degradation; and yet after all, one involuntarily says to oneself, so instinctively do we turn to the cheerful side, I am glad they are located on this lovely island. Do you shrug your shoulders, Sir Cynic, and number over the crimes they have committed? Are *your* crimes against society less, that they are written down only in God's book of remembrance? Are *you* less guilty that you have been politic enough to commit only those that a short-sighted, unequal, human law sanctions? Shall I pity these poor wrecks of humanity less, because they are so recklessly self-wrecked? because they turn away from my pity? Before I come to this, I must know, as their Maker knows, what evil influences have encircled their cradles. How many times when their stomachs have been empty, some full-fed, whining disciple, has presented them with a Bible or a Tract, saying, Be ye warmed and filled. I must know how often when their feet have tried to climb the narrow, up-hill path of right, the eyes that have watched, have watched only for their halting; never noting, as God notes, the steps that did *not* slip—never holding out the strong right hand of help when the devil with a full larder was tugging furiously at their skirts to pull them backward;—but only saying—"I told you so," when he, laughing at your pharisaical stupidity, succeeded.

I must go a great way back of those hard, defiant faces, where hate of their kind seems indelibly burnt in;—back—back—to the soft blue sky of infancy, overclouded before the little one had strength to contend with the flashing lightning and pealing thunder of misfortune and poverty which stunned and blinded his moral perceptions. I cannot see that mournful procession of men, filing off into those dark cells, none too dark, none too narrow, alas! to admit troops of devils, without wishing that some white-winged angel might enter too; and when their shining eye-balls peer at my retreating figure through the gratings, my heart shrieks out in its pain—oh! Believe that there is pity here—only pity;—and I hate the bolts and bars, and I say this is *not* the way to make bad men good; or, at least if it be, these convicts should not, when discharged, be thrust out loose into the world with empty pockets, and a bad name, to earn a speedy "through-ticket" back again. I say, if this *be* the way, let humanity not stop here, but take one noble step forward, and when she knocks off the convict's fetters, and lands him on the opposite shore, let her not turn her back and leave him there as if her duty were done; but let her *there* erect a noble insti-tution where he can find a *kind* welcome and *instant* employment; before temptation joining hands with his necessities, plunge him again headlong into the gulf of sin.

And here seems to me to be the loose screw in all these institutions; admirably managed as many of them are, according to the prevalent ideas on the subject. You may tell me that I am a woman, and know nothing about it; and I tell you that I *want* to know. I tell you, that I don't believe the way to restore a man's lost self-respect, is to degrade him before his fellow-creatures; to brand him, and chain him, and poke him up to show his points, like a hyena in a menagerie. No wonder that he growls at you, and grows vicious; no wonder that he eats the food you thrust between the bars of his cage with gnashing teeth, and a vow to take it out of the world somehow, when he gets out; no wonder that he thinks the Bible you place in his cell a humbug, and God a myth. I would have you startle up his self-respect by placing him in a position to show that you trusted him; I would have you give him something to hold in charge, for which he is in honor responsible; appeal to his *better* feelings, or if they smolder almost to extinction, fan them into a flame for him out of that remnant of God's image which the vilest can never wholly destroy. *Anything but shutting a man up with hell in his heart to make him good.* The devils may well chuckle at it. And above all—tear down that taunting inscription over the prison-hall door at Blackwell's Island—"The way of transgressors is hard"—and place instead of it, "Neither do I condemn thee; go and sin no more."[3]

Blackwell's Island, Number III
August 28, 1858

You can step aside, Mrs. Grundy; what I am about to write is not for your over-fastidious ear. *You*, who take by the hand the polished roue, and welcome him with a sweet smile to the parlor where sit your young, trusting daughters; you, who "have no business with his private life, so long as his manners are gentlemanly"; you who, while saying this, turn away with bitter, unwomanly words from his penitent, writhing victim. I ask no leave of *you* to speak of the wretched girls picked out of the gutters of New York streets, to inhabit those cells at Blackwell's Island. I speak not to *you* of what was tugging at my heartstrings as I saw them, that beautiful summer afternoon, file in, two by two, to their meals, followed by a man carrying a cowhide in his hand, by way of reminder; all this would not interest you; but when you tell me that these women are not to be named to ears polite, that our sons and our daughters should grow up ignorant of their existence, I stop my ears. As if they could, or did! As if they can take a step in the public streets without being jostled or addressed by them, or pained by their passing ribaldry; as if they could return from a party or concert at night, without meeting droves of them; as if they could, even in broad daylight, sit down to an ice-cream without having one for a vis-a-vis. As if they could ride in a car or omnibus, or cross in a ferry-boat, or go to a watering-place, without being unmistakably confronted by them. No, Mrs.

Grundy; you know all this as well as I do. You would push them "anywhere out of the world," as unfit to live, as unfit to die; *they*, the weaker party, while their partners in sin, for whom you claim greater mental superiority, and who, by your own finding, should be much better able to learn and to *teach* the lesson of self-control—to them you extend perfect absolution. Most consistent Mrs. Grundy, get out of my way while I say what I was going to, without fear or favor of yours.

If I believed, as legislators, and others with whom I have talked on this subject, pretend to believe, they best know why, that God ever made one of those girls for the life they lead, for this in plain Saxon is what their talk amounts to, I should curse Him. If I could temporize as they do about it, as "a necessary evil," and "always has been, and always will be," and (then add this beautiful tribute to manhood) "that pure women would not be safe were it not so"—and all the other budget of excuses which this sin makes to cover its deformity—I would forswear my manhood.

You say their intellects are small, they are mere animals, naturally coarse and groveling. Answer me this—are they, or are they not *immortal?* Decide the question whether *this* life is to be *all* to them. Decide before you shoulder the responsibility of such a girl's future. Granted she has only *this* life. God knows how much misery may be crowded into that. But you say, "Bless your soul, why do you talk to *me?* I have nothing to do with it; I am as virtuous as St. Paul." St. Paul was a bachelor, and of course is not my favorite apostle; but waiving that, I answer, you *have* something to do with it when you talk thus, and throw your influence on the wrong side. No matter how outwardly correct your past life may have been, if you *really believe* what you say, I would not give a fig for your virtue if temptation and opportunity favored; and if you talk so for talk's sake, and do not believe it, you had better "tarry at Jericho till your beard be grown."

But you say to me, "Oh, you don't know anything about it; men are differently constituted from women; woman's sphere is home." That don't suspend the laws of her being. That don't make it that she don't need sympathy and appreciation. That don't make it that she is never weary and needs amusement to restore her. Fudge. I believe in no difference that makes this distinction. Women lead, most of them, lives of unbroken monotony, and have much more need of exhilarating influences than men, whose life is out of doors in the breathing, active world. Don't tell me of shoemakers at their lasts, and tailors at their needles. Do either ever have to lay down their customers' coats and shoes fifty times a day, and wonder when the day is over why their work is *not* done, though they have struggled through fire and water to finish it? Do not both tailor and shoemaker have at least the variation of a walk to or from the shop to their meals? Do not their customers talk their beloved politics to them while they stitch, and do not their "confreres" run for a bottle of ale and crack merry jokes with them as their work progresses? Sirs! If monotony is to be avoided in man's life as injurious; if "variety" and exhilaration must always be the spice to his pursuits, how much more must it be necessary to a sensitively organized woman? If home is not sufficient, (and I will persist that any *industrious, virtuous, unambitious* man, may have a home if he chooses); if home is not sufficient for him, why should it suffice for her? whose work is never done—who can have literally *no* such thing as system, (and here's where a mother's discouragement comes in), while her babes are in their infancy; who often says to herself at night, though she would not for worlds part with one of them—"I can't tell what I have accomplished today, and yet I have not been idle a minute"; and day after day passes on in this way, and perhaps for weeks she does not pass the threshold for a breath of air, and yet men talk of "monotony!" and being "differently constituted," and needing amusement and exhilaration; and "business" is the broad mantle which it is not always safe for a wife to lift. I have no faith in putting women in a pound, that men may trample down the clover in a forty-acre lot. But enough for that transparent excuse.

The great Law-giver made no distinction of sex, as far as I can find out, when he promulgated the seventh commandment, nor should we. You tell me "society makes a difference"; more shame to it—more shame to the women who help to perpetuate it. You tell me that infidelity on the wife's part involves an unjust claim upon the husband and provider; and I ask you, on the other hand, if a good and virtuous wife has not a right to expect *healthy* children?[4]

Let both be equally pure; let every man look upon every woman, whatsoever her rank or condition, as a sister whom his manhood is bound to protect, even, if need be, against herself, and let every woman turn the cold shoulder to any man of her acquaintance, how polished soever he may be, who would degrade her sex. Then this vexed question would be settled; there would be no such libels upon womanhood as I saw at Blackwell's Island, driven in droves to their cells. No more human traffic in those gilded palaces, which our children must not hear mentioned, forsooth! Though their very fathers may help to support them, and which our tender-hearted legislators "can't see their way clear about." Then our beautiful rivers would no longer toss upon our island shores the "dead bodies of unfortunate young females."

Sympathy; or, Straws for the Drowning
May 21, 1859

I think the hardest thing for human nature to bear is lack of sympathy. One can endure privation, poverty, disappointment, trial, in almost any form, if there be only *one* loyal human being to whom we can turn our tearful eyes and say, "*Isn't this hard?*"

Nor need there be a verbal reply: the slightest hand-pressure; a quick, responsive moistening of the eye; an arm slid round the waist; an echoing sigh; a touch of the lips to the throbbing forehead. What heaven is in these mute tokens! How they bridge over the yawning gulf of despair! How fair, when the tempest lulls, do they span it with hope's rainbow! True, the clouds may return—the chill mist—the darkness; but the bright, warm tints *have* been there! More than angelic are these soul-responses. Eternity shall show it, when they, over whom the shadows of great trouble fell, till wrong almost seemed right, shall, with these their earth-saviours, serenely untangle the life-web, every fibre of which is spun by the hand of Infinite Love.

A kind word! Don't grudge it. Don't say, "It is a sad pity, but then it is no concern of mine." A kind look, even! Don't withhold it. I remember once, when in great trouble, I was walking the crowded thoroughfare on some errand, in that state of utter hopelessness which must have told its story on my face, suddenly encountering a look from a stranger so full of compassionate tenderness, that I, who had thought never again to shed a tear, so stony seemed my eyes, felt them overflowing. Oh! The hope and courage that look gave me! Some day I shall know more about it—not *here*.

There are those heaven-ordained ones who shed this brightness as they glide past us; and there are others so flinty, yet so polished withal, that we clasp our hands tightly over our heart to still its cries, whispering, Hush!—not *there*—anywhere but *there*! And as they pass us, a chill, like that from a newly opened tomb, creeps slowly over us, and the last flower of hope droops to the earth beneath it.

I suppose such people have their place in the world; but they always seem to me like those artificial plants suspended in pots from drawing-room windows; perennial stiffnesses, mocking our reach, incapable of growth or expansion, without moisture, without fragrance, impervious alike to dew or sunshine—fit only to accumulate the grime and dust of years.

Night and Sleep
December 24, 1859

Blessed be sleep! How many thousands, heart-weary and body-weary, say this to the stars every night, as they close their eyes upon their brightness. Blessed be sleep! We often say so, as we look upon the care-worn faces threading their way through the streets at twilight, jostling each other at corners,—each perhaps with their own heavy burthen to bear, with which no stranger can intermeddle. Another day may come indeed to each, (God knows); but meanwhile there is a blessed season of forgetfulness when nothing has power to pain. *Then angels minister!* Soft, unseen fingers are laid gently on aching brows and drooping lids. Long years ago they crumbled to dust,—we folded them over the still breast ourselves—and oh, how yearningly in our waking hours have we longed for their kindly pressure, but—only in sleep—to feel it. Blessed be sleep! For then *they* "have charge to keep us." Else why do we sometimes wake, if not happy, yet calm and patient, like those unavoidably detained and crossed by the way, who will *yet* see the bright lights of "home." But for these blessed reprieves, how many tired feet would halt utterly on life's journey.

Alas for those from whom sleep flies, though they woo it ever so earnestly! They who count each lagging hour, as it solemnly announces itself to the silent night. Upon whom every wave of trouble that ever beat upon their life-shore, comes surging and rolling, till they lie breathless under the dreadful spell, and yet so vitally conscious! Praying for the tardy morning light to exorcise the spirits,—listening to the gradual stir and hum of the waking streets, and yet turning—oh, so wearily away from the first bright sun-ray. *You* have felt it—and you—and you—if you were not born an oyster. Pity you hadn't been!

Vivid Life
August 3, 1861

" 'Tis not the whole of life to live,
    Nor all of death to die."[5]

I have been reading a live book by one of those persons to whom the simple gift of existence were alone blessing enough. One who walked the earth with bounding step, and to whom every blossom and cloud-tint was a special gift of love. A happy, joyous, rich, exuberant nature, that it seemed death and decay could never touch. Ah! How sad to turn away, as we close a book like this, knowing that even for such there can be no exemption. We never saw the author; we never met the beam of the eyes which so revelled in this beautiful world, and yet we finger as tenderly the closed volume, as if we were smoothing the hair over the brow of the departed author. With a sigh we go out into the bright sunshine, and mutter querulously—Why was he born for this? You must have felt this—and you—and you—at the live words of some one, who being dead yet speaketh.

And who of us has not had personal friends who could never—never—die to us? Whose waving locks *always* touch us; whose garments still flutter past us; whose fragrant breath we inhale, till our souls grow faint; and for whose footstep we never cease listening. True—the moss may have gathered round their tombstone long since; and we go there, and read their name, and age, and the day they died, with as stupid a bewilderment, years after, as if we saw it for the first time. It seems like some sad mistake. It cannot be—that some day, at the threshold, or round the street-corner shall not beam upon you that face, bright-eyed, cherry-lipped and radiant. Perhaps we turn upon our finger restlessly, a ring that dust once wore; perhaps in a locket, sleeping on our breast, nestles a bright tress, whose fellows, thread by thread, have decayed long ago; but still, our yearning hearts turn away from all these convincing proofs of bereavement, and cry out piteously—come—oh, come!

And sometimes we meet a strange face so mockingly like the dead one; or a form sways past us, that makes our breath come quick, and our heart throb, and our fingers move nervously to touch it, as we chokingly murmur the dear name it evokes. And when we see anything beautiful, we so long that *they* should see it; and who knows they do *not*? and by the great deep sea, and on the mountain-top, and in the valley, we listen for that sympathetic echo, and will not *be* denied. Can love like this, die when *we* die? Blessed be God for immortality!

Whose Business Is It?
September 28, 1861

We suppose it is useless to draw attention, for the thousandth time, to the way in which the poor cattle are abused, who are brought through the city to be slaughtered. But the sight is so harrowing and revolting that we cannot hold our peace. On one of the hottest days this summer, we saw a crowded cart full of poor calves, bound by the legs, that were being jolted mercilessly over the stones, their heads hanging over the sides of the cart, and one head certainly being grazed till it bled, with every revolution of the wheel; while the protruding eyes and tongues but too plainly told the agony of the poor animals! Such sights as these are a disgrace to a civilized city. Is it not time that our children and young people ceased being taught these heathenish lessons of cruelty?

Poisoned Arrows
May 10, 1862

It is wonderful how slight a thing may waken an endless train of association. A lady may take out her handkerchief in passing, and the subtle perfume in its folds brings the tears to our eyes; for lo! A vision is evoked from "the long ago." Eyes that were long since closed on all things earthly; flowing hair, and dimpled cheek, and swaying limbs, and breezy motion; the old bright smile, and the glad, welcoming tones; and with a sigh of pain we pass on. There are flowers, too, lovely as they may be, that are more deadly to our peace than the most venomous "night shade." The heart needs a long torpidity before these things shall pass away. With some natures, indeed, they may never.

How They Look at It
May 30, 1863

With what different feelings different persons will look upon the coming of this bright spring. To some it will speak only hope, and joy, and blessedness. To others the tender blade of grass, upon which the eye falls—the budding trees, the serene blue skies, the fragrant, many-hued flowers—will all be so many elements of pain and distress; for that soft breeze stirs the grass over a new-made grave, and all that brightness and beauty seems but a wretched mockery. *"Why? Why? Why?"* the impatient soul constantly reiterates, as it vainly seeks to reconcile itself to the change between the hope of the last spring-time and the sadness of this. There are moments when one is satisfied submissively to leave this question, unsolved; but nature, strong and self-asserting, soon moans again in her pain; and so all over the land are they who will turn away, sick at heart, from the brightness and beauty of this coming spring.

"New York, with all thy faults, I love thee still"

On Life in the City

Fanny Fern's perspective as a transplant from Boston, and as the most famous newspaper writer in New York, gave her a fresh perspective about life in the city. In her articles about New York scenes, she builds a kinship with her fellow city-dwelling readers, while providing *Ledger* subscribers outside of the city with a glimpse into the unknown pleasures and horrors; conveniences and annoyances; magnificence and squalor that the city had to offer. As a former Bostonian, she frequently compares the two cities in everything from public parks and cemeteries to personalities, manners, and fashion. And while her preference for the grittier and more bohemian vibe of New York is clear, she nevertheless gave vent to her occasional frustration or dismay over the disorder, crime, and injustices she witnessed in her beloved city. Following the selection of Fern's writing about life in New York, the chapter includes several columns about her vacations away from the city.

Greenwood and Mount Auburn[1]
September 6, 1856

I have seen Greenwood. With Mount Auburn for my ideal of what a cemetery *should* be, I was prepared for disappointment. But the two are not comparable. Greenwood is the larger, and more indebted to the hand of art; the gigantic trees of Mount Auburn are the growth of half a century; but then Greenwood has its ocean view, which, paradoxical as it may seem, is not to be overlooked. The entrance to Mount Auburn I think the finer. Its tall army of stately pines stand guard over its silent sleepers, and strew their fragrant leaves on the pathway, as if to deaden the sound of the carriage wheels, which, at each revolution, crush out their aromatic incense, sweet as the box of spikenard which kneeling Mary broke at Jesus' feet.

Greenwood has the greater monumental variety, attributable, perhaps (more than to design), to the motley population of New York; the proprietors of each tomb, or grave, carrying out their national ideas of sepulture. This is an advantage. Mount Auburn sometimes wearies the eye with its monumental monotony. Mount Auburn, too, *had* (for he long since laid down in its lovely shade) a grey-haired old gate-keeper, courteous and dignified: "a man of sorrows," whose bald, uncovered head, many will remember, who have stood waiting at the portal to bear in their dead. Many a bouquet, simple but sweet, of my favorite flowers have I taken from his palsied hand; and many a sympathizing look, treasured up in my heart from him whom Death had also bereft of all. Greenwood has, at least if my afternoon visit was a fair exponent, its jocund grave-diggers, who, with careless poise, and indecent foot of haste, stumble on with the unvarnished coffin of the poor, and exchange over the fresh and narrow mound, the comrade's time-worn jest. Money has its value, for it purchases gentler handling and better manners.

Let those who will, linger before the marble statue, or chiseled urn of the rich; dearer to me is the grave of the poor man's child, where the tiny, half-worn shoe, is sad and fitting monument. Dearer to me, the moldy toys, the whip, the cap, the doll, the faded locks of hair, on which countless suns have risen and set, and countless showers have shed their kindly tears. And yet for the infant army who slumber there, I cannot weep; for I bethink me of the weary toil and strife; the wrecks that strew the life-coast; the plaint of the weary-hearted, unheard in life's fierce clamor; the remorseless, iron heel of strength, on the quivering heart of weakness; the swift-winged, poisoned arrow of cruel slander; the hearts that are near of kin as void of love; and I thank God that the little shoes were laid aside, and the dreary path untrod.

And yet, not all drear, for, as I pass along, I read, in graven lines, of those who periled life to save life; who parted raging billows and forked flames, at woman's wild, despairing shriek, and childhood's helpless wail. Honor to such dauntless spirits, while there are eyes to moisten and hearts to feel!

Beautiful Greenwood! with thy feathery swaying willows, thy silver-voiced fountains and glassy lakes: with thy grassy knolls and shady dells; with thy "Battle Hill," whose sod, of yore, was nourished by brave men's blood. The sailor here rests him well, in sound of old Ocean's roar;

the fireman heeds nor booming bell, nor earthly trump, nor hurried tramp of anxious feet; the pilot's bark is moored and voyage o'er; the school-boy's lesson conned; beauty's lid uncloses not, though rarest flowers bloom above her; no husband's hand is outstretched to her who stoops with jealous care to pluck the obtrusive weed which hides the name she, lonely, bears; no piping, bird-like voice, answers the anguished cry, "My child, my child!" but, still the mourners come, and sods fall dull and heavy on loved and loving hearts, and the busy spade heeds never the dropping tears; and for her who writes, and for them who read—ere long—tears in their turn shall fall. God help us all.

Knickerbocker and Tri-Mountain
October 11, 1856

The New York woman doateth on rainbow hats and dresses, confectionery, the theater, the opera, and flirtation. She stareth gentlemen in the street out of countenance, in a way that puzzleth a stranger to decide the question of her respectability. The New York woman thinketh it well-bred to criticize *in an audible tone* the dress and appearance of every chance lady near her, in the street, shop, ferry-boat, car, or omnibus. If doubtful of the material of which her dress is composed, she draweth near, examineth it microscopically, and pronounceth it—"after all—silk." The New York woman never appeareth without a dress-hat and flounces, though the time be nine o'clock in the morning, and her destination the grocer's, to order some superfine tea. She delighteth in embroidered petticoats, which she liberally displayeth to curious bipeds of the opposite sex. She turneth up her nose at a delaine, wipeth up the pavement with a thousand-dollar silk, and believeth point-lace collars and handkerchiefs essential to salvation. She scorneth to ride in an omnibus, and if driven by an impertinent shower therein, sniffeth up her aristocratic nose at the plebeian occupants, pulleth out her costly gold watch to—ascertain the time! and draweth off her gloves to show her diamonds. Arrived at Snob-Avenue, she shaketh off the dust of her silken flounces against her fellow-travelers, trippeth up her aristocratic steps, and holding up her dress sufficiently high to display to the retreating passengers her silken hose, and dainty boot, resigneth her parasolette to black John, and maketh her triumphant exit.

At the opera, the New York woman taketh the most conspicuous box, spreadeth out her flounces to their fullest circumference, and betrayeth a constant and vulgar consciousness that she is in her go-to-meetin-fixins, by arranging her bracelets and shawl, settling her rings, and fiddling at her coiffure, and the lace kerchief on her neck. She also talketh incessantly during the opera, to show that she is not a novice to be amused by it; and leaveth with much bustle, just before the last act, for the same reason, and also to display her toilette.

On Sunday morning, the New York woman taketh all the jewelry she can collect, and in her flashiest silk and bonnet, taketh her velvet-bound, gilt-clasped prayer-book out for an airing. Arrived at Dives church, she straightway kneeleth and boweth her head; not, as the uninitiated may suppose, to pray, but privately to arrange her curls; this done, and raising her head, she sayeth, "we beseech thee to hear us, good Lord!" while she taketh a minute inventory of the Hon. Mrs. Peters's Parisian toilette. After church, she taketh a turn or two in Fifth Avenue, to display her elaborate dress, and to wonder "why vulgar people don't confine themselves to the Bowery."

The *Boston* woman draweth down her mouth, rolleth up her eyes, foldeth her hands, and walketh on a crack. She rejoiceth in anatomical and chemical lectures. She prateth of Macaulay and Carlyle; belongeth to many and diverse reading-classes, and smileth in a chaste, moonlight kind of way on literary men. She dresseth (to her praise be it spoken) plainly in the street, and considereth india-rubbers, a straw bonnet, and a thick shawl, the fittest costume for damp and cloudy weather. She dresseth her children more for comfort than show, and bringeth them up also to walk on a crack. She maketh the tour of the Common twice or three times a day, without regard to the barometer. She goeth to church twice or three times on Sunday, sandwiched with Bible-classes and Sabbath-schools. She thinketh London, Vienna, or Paris—fools to Boston; and the "Boulevards" and "Tuileries" not to be mentioned with the Frog Pond and the Common. She is well posted up as to politics—thinketh, "as Pa does," and sticketh to it through thunder and lightning. When asked to take a gentleman's arm, she hooketh the tip of her little finger circumspectly on to his male coat-sleeve. She is as prim as a bolster, as stiff as a ram-rod, as frigid as an icicle, and not even matrimony with a New Yorker could thaw her.

Knickerbocker and Tri-Mountain, Number 2
October 18, 1856

The New York male exulteth in fast horses—stylish women—long-legged hounds—a coat-of-arms, and liveried servants. Beside, or behind him, may be seen his servant, with folded arms and white gloves, driven out daily by his master, to inhale the gutter breezes of Broadway, to excite the wonder of the curious, and to curl the lips of republicanism. The New York male hath many and diverse garments; some of which he weareth bob-tailed; some shanghai, some with velvet collars, some with silk; anon turned up; anon turned down; and some carelessly a-la-flap. The New York male breakfasteth late, owing to pressing engagements which keep him abroad after midnight. About twelve the next morning he lighteth a cigar to assist his blear-eyes to find the way down-town; and with his hands in his pockets, and arms akimbo, he navigateth tortuously around locomotive "hoops";—indefatigably pursueth a bonnet for several blocks, to get a peep it its owner; nor getteth discouraged at intervening parasols, or impromptu shopping errands; nor thinketh his time or shoe leather wasted. The New York male belongeth to the most ruinous club and military company; is a connoisseur in gold sleeve-buttons, and seal-rings, and diamond studs. He cometh into the world with an eye-glass and black ribbon winked into his left eye, and prideth himself upon having broken all the commandments before he arrived at the dignity of coat-tails.

The *Boston* male is respectable all over; from the crown of his glossy hat to the soles of his shiny shoes; and huggeth his mantle of self-esteem inseparably about him, that he may avoid contaminating contact with the non-elect of his "set." The Boston male is for the most part good-looking; and a staunch devotee of starch and buckram; he patronizeth jewelry but sparingly, and *never discerneth a diamond in the rough*. If, as Goethe sayeth, "the unconscious is the alone complete," then is the male Bostonian yet in embryo. He taketh, and readeth all the newspapers and magazines, foreign and domestic; and yet, strange to say, sweareth by the little tea-table "Transcript." When the Boston male traveleth he weareth his best clothes; arrived at his destination he putteth up at the most showy hotel, ordereth the most expensive rooms and edibles, and maketh an unwonted "splurge" generally. He then droppeth the proprieties—pro tem.—being seized with an anatomical desire to dissect the great sores of the city; fancying, like the ostrich, that if his head only be hidden, he is undiscernible.

The Boston male is conservative as a citizen, prosaic as a lover; humdrum as a husband, and hath no sins—*to speak of!*

Living in Brooklyn
January 2, 1858

It is a very common remark of the New York city press, that "the monotony of Brooklyn was broken in upon, last week, by this or that novel incident."

As if Brooklyn were some provincial place, where loungers gathered around the village pump, or blacksmith's shop, or tavern, to take a drink, and discuss the price of chicken-feed or grain, and where the drawing out of *the* fire engine on the village green to be washed, was an object of stunning importance to every biped who swung his heels over his barnyard fence. I wonder do not the New York press know that there may be intolerable monotony in hubbub, gas, gilding, glitter and confusion, as anybody who has sojourned for a year or two in the Broadway hotels, and listened to the ceaseless Niagara roar of equestrian and pedestrian life past its windows, can testify. The great human tide ever surging on, bearing on its mighty bosom the straws and feathers of the hour; the eloquent voices of the midnight stars, never heard for the clamors of human need and human passions, till the very soul grows sick with the changeful, yet changeless, purposeless, yet fore-ordained, eternal drifting, yet never passing away.

Brooklyn is a heaven after it. The chest expands, the breath comes freer, the step grows lighter, the moment the crowded boat strikes the pier, and we spring ashore. Clean streets await us; smokers, thank goodness, are few and far between; pretty gardens greet us; healthy children jump, and run and shout; mothers dare indulge in the luxury of taking out their own little rosebud babies, instead of mounting guard over a hireling nurse; papas can walk about in old hats and comfortable boots; ladies can run out after dark, without danger of being taken for what they are not, or ramble bonnetless in couples round whole blocks, without fear of molestation, or comb their hair leisurely before the window, without anxiety on account of an opposite eye-glass.

Our shop-keepers are civil, respectful and obliging, our "cakes and ale" as good as yours, our carriages—ah, there you have us—I never get into one but I see small pox and yellow fever, *perdu* in its dirty cushions, floor mat, and soiled window "fixin's," or without wondering what makes all the servant girls whom we pass grin at the graceless driver.

And as to dogs, we knock under to nobody. Every cur, of high degree and low degree, agrees with me when I say that Brooklyn is a heaven; the bob-tailed, ugly, yellow terrier, the kingly Newfoundland, the waggly little podge of incipient bulldog-ism, the lithe, fleet, graceful greyhound, and the dog whose tail might be pulled out a little farther to advantage, or driven clear in out of sight, "ary one"—every one of them knows that muzzles are a dead letter, and Brooklyn safe barking ground.

And as to schools, male and female, they are as good and as plentiful as yours, and like yours, keep their pupils, I am sorry to say, doubled up over their grammars about five times as long as common sense and good health give them any right to do. And as to preachers, have we not the magnetic Beecher, who is yet guilty, every Sunday, of turning his friends out doors; and the scholarly Storrs, who, by right of inheritance, should be a man of talent and mark, and who, when he reads a hymn, makes you fancy you hear an angel singing it; and Bethune, and many others of whom New York is not worthy.[2]

And have we not our horticultural shows and our library, though the least said about that last, the better—and our undertakers' shops, with ghastly coffins, piled, like your own, on the sidewalks and in the windows, in tempting rows, and butchers and bakers, and candlestick makers—why not?

Then, where will you show me a finer view of its kind than may be seen from Washington Park, once the old battle ground? And have we not a famous "Navy-yard," and "Marine Hospital," and close by, "An Asylum for Aged and Indigent Females," the lettering of which I would jog the Directors' elbows about, as better readers than myself might peruse it as I did, viz., an Asylum for Aged and *Indecent* females.

And when "hard up" for fun, can we not go to the New York Opera? Take tea, for instance, at goodly country hours in the middle of the afternoon, then ride in the cars from the extreme end of Brooklyn to the Fulton Ferry, which cross, to gain the "right up Broad'ay" omnibus, tightly packed in with other pleasure-seekers, bound to the different theatres and concerts, each of whom is desirous to stow his party of six or eight into the *very first* omnibus going. Driver swearing—horses prancing—wheels hitching—gentlemen stepping on ladies' toes, and crushing their bonnets, as they hand up the fare. Driver at last gives the signal to start, with an accompaniment of jolts and jerks, more edifying to himself than his impatient freight, whom (by a strange perversity, reversing his usual break-neck speed) he drags at a snail-pace up interminable Broadway, to that interminable Fourteenth street. Arrived there, we are pushed, without any volition of our own, into the vestibule, trod on, spit on, punched in the back, punched in the ribs, punched in the stomach, if I may be allowed the expression, and shoved into a crowd, while our respective gallants show or buy tickets, and finally are ushered into the perfumed atmosphere of song, to dispute our seats, or yield them up to avoid doing so, or to find our party separated by a huge pillar, which was not down in the plan of the house when seats were selected, and which, how architecturally beautiful soever, can neither be seen through nor whispered across, nor, alas! got out of the way.

Opera over, we go through the same operation getting out, which we did getting in, and reach the vestibule at 12 o'clock to find a pouring rain, Broadway omnibuses done running for the night, no conveyance for love or money; street cars—one, two, three—crowded double and treble; stand in the rain till No. four passes—*that* full, too, but gentlemen cry, "Get in!"—so we do, and ride in a vapor bath of steam to the City Hall; no buss to the ferry; walk down Fulton street in the rain; wait in the ferry house for a boat, all of a perspiration for fear the last car will have ceased running for the night on the other side; catch it, after crossing, just as it starts; pile in—wet feet, wet skirts, and yawning fearfully; reach home between one and two; rub ourselves down with bay water and arnica; eat some supper, get into bed, and feel like stewed fools in the morning;—there, if you call that "monotony," I should like to know what dictionary is your standard.

For all that, Brooklyn is a little heaven; a heaven for writers who, within sound of New York, can yet compass the necessary hours for work, there so difficult or impossible. And listen, ye parents who sepulcher your offspring by scores in the stifled city—*a heaven for children, who have here plenty of fresh air, and plenty of safe playgrounds.*

Why I Like New York
June 5, 1858

New York, with all thy faults, I love thee still; and yet thy long-suffering pavements know thou never art still! Yes, I love thy rush, and hurry, and clatter, and din; it sounds as if the world was really "going round," as the geographers tell us, which a sojourn in Boston might tempt one to doubt. It suits my restless moods, though I must say I prefer my bed to be located in Brooklyn. I don't always find myself frowning when the impudent omnibusses coolly take off the hind wheel from the smaller fry, never turning a head to hear the ripping anathemas launched after them. I like the distant whiz of the breathless cars. I like the booming of cannon, announcing a steamer's arrival, which comes to us on every breeze. I like the slap-dash, pell-mell rush of the fire-engines, round corners, and through thoroughfares, regardless of every description of puppy and nondescript young kittens. The impudent persistence of thy beggars amuseth me, with their stock of blessings and curses ready to order, according to the generosity, penuriousness, or indifference of the listener; also the horse-leech cry of the venders of small wares; also the street "ballads," festooning park gates and railings, or held down by stones to counteract their exceeding *lightness.* Thy sprinkling of priests and dandies is funny. Thy Babylonish women also, bloated with high living, nothing to do, and no place to do it in. Thy vivacious little school-girls—the nature, not yet "moral science"-d out of all of them—more bewitching with their shining hair, plain collars, and satchels, than all the after-trickeries of fashion can make them. Thy jaded editors and merchants, to whom one must give a wide berth as they pass home up-town to dinner—the very incarnation of jack-knives, cast-wind, and vinegar; but how radiant in the evening at opera or concert, like all their sex after that male quietus—a good feed! (N. B.)—No wife, who knows anything, will ask a favor of her husband at any less auspicious moment.—Thy stylish equipages, with their liveried coachmen, and anything but patrician-looking occupants. Thy opera's, and theater's, and minstrel's, and mammoth women—the latter shown at twenty-five cents a head; likewise skeleton men; likewise learned pigs. Thy long-tailed, humbugging Chinamen, bent double on the sidewalk, with intense scrutiny of their toes, meantime drawing sympathy and coppers from unsophisticated "green-horns." Thy bewitching shop-windows, which wise husbands never pass in company with their wives. Thy surfeit of church-steeples and dentists. (N. B.)—How is it that dentists are generally handsome?—Thy heterogeneous, panoramic mixing-up of races and costumes. Thy better than Babel-confusion of tongues. Good gracious! How refreshing to rush plump into the maelstrom, and sink one's self; to shut one's mental eyes, and be borne carelessly off on the current of the hour, ignoring the mosquito-stinging cares, annoyances, disgusts, perplexities, aye, even responsibilities, from which our overcharged hearts need an escape valve.

Heaven help the excitable wretch, doomed to vegetate like a turnip in the sleepy humdrumness of a country village, with its one town-pump, its one blacksmith's shop, its one fire-engine, and its one desolate "meeting-house"—and that always perched on an arid sand-bank, forty miles at least from any green thing, save the sexton.

The Rival Cities
December 18, 1858

It is amusing to see the pop-gun war of words between New York and Philadelphia, as to the respective merits and demerits of each as a city; the respective bigness of its big men and big churches, big theaters, big hotels, and big opera-houses. Let Philadelphia enjoy its clean streets, and New York its dirty ones; who cares how large or how little a place may be, if there one is at home and happy? A diversity of taste is the most blessed thing in existence; imagine everybody fancying the same thing! What countless nose-pullings would be the result. What is the use of pelting the Quakers for their broad brims, or Broadway for its narrow brims? Isn't the latter at least *brim-full?* If New York has her "Morrissey and Heenan,"[3] has not Philadelphia her pugilistic fire companies? If New York has her mammoth oysters, has not Philadelphia her golden butter and fresh cream? If the New York woman beats Babylon with her stunning raiment, does not the female Philadelphian sway past you like a white lily on its stem? If Philadelphia is "always bragging," does not New York brag *that it don't brag?*

Never mind your noisy, bold-eyed, showy sister, you little vestal; there are plenty like me to whom the remembrance of your spotless thresholds, and elm-shaded streets, and clear-browed men and dove-eyed women, is as refreshing as a clover field in June to a Five Points child, to whom the senses only seem to have been avenues of pain.[4]

A Phase of City Life
October 22, 1859

A hearse stands before your door, and a long line of carriages is creeping slowly up, one after another, behind it. Within the carriages heads are bowed, and tears are falling beneath sable vails. "One of the neighbors," quietly remarks a bystander, in answer to your query, and passes on. "One of the neighbors." You never noticed the face and form now lying in that plumed and tasselled hearse, behind those tall black horses; and yet for months, perhaps years, he has passed and re-passed your house every day, and two or three times a day, on his way to and from his business. His joys and sorrows, hopes and fears, whatever they might have been, were nothing to you when he was living; they are less so now that he is dead. And yet you watch that hearse, as it creeps away with him, and the carriages that follow with their grief-freighted burthen, with a strange fascination; and you say to yourself—it will be just so when *I* die. Somebody will say, carelessly, "One of the neighbors"; and the ranks will close up again, and the world jog on as usual, and I shall never be missed. And this is life in the jostling city! Only a brick wall between us and the breaking hearts through whose sobbing and moaning we slumber on so peacefully, and yet the ocean itself could not wider divide us. Sorrowful as true!

A Housekeeper's Views on Street-Cleaning
December 3, 1859

Where I came from, street-sweeping was one of the fine arts. First came a gang of men with watering-pots, to lay the dust. Followed as many more, with vigorous-looking brooms to sweep it into piles. Close upon their heels came executive drivers, with carts—to shovel it up. In fifteen minutes—without an extra particle of dust—your street was clean as a floor. Did you ever see street-cleaning done in New York? Three or four rickety, sleepy specimens of humanity come crawling round the corner, as if they were going to execution, each bearing a broom worn to the hub. Part go on one side the street, and part on the other, and toss the dirt back and forth, like a shuttlecock, for about half-an-hour, without one drop of preliminary sprinkling; now and then stopping to hitch up their waistbands, or tinker the insane-looking old brooms with which they are doing such choking execution. This done, they produce several rakes with one tooth apiece in them, and scrape the dirt up, and down, and across, till they lose it; then they crawl off down street, to repeat the thriftless operation elsewhere, and are succeeded by a small, lout-ish looking boy, with a crazy old cart, the hindboard knocked out, drawn by a "Praise-God-Barebones"-looking-horse, who has evidently made up his mind to die in the service of his country. Small boy begins to search for the dirt, and finally discovers a pile which the wind has blown together. Slapping the sharp rump of "Praise-God-Barebones" with the flat of the shovel, he entices him to the spot. Small boy then, with many grunts and contortions, inserts his shovel, *full of holes*, under the pile of dirt; and what don't sift through the holes, or isn't lodged on the horse's tail, (which having only three hairs on it, can't retain much,) is tossed—*over*—the cart, and back into the street again—smack up against your bright window-panes, which Betty has nearly broken her back that very morning trying to polish. Well—there's no help for it, as I see, till women are allowed to vote; and I won't have another pane of glass washed till they do.

Dear Crazy Gotham
June 22, 1861

"De'il take the hindmost" should be written on every man, woman, child, door-post, street, corner, dray-cart, cab, cat and dog in Gotham. It is the first trait that presents itself to the bewildered stranger. The daily nuisances in the shape of encumbered sidewalks, which a busy public scramble over, tear their clothes and stub their toes against, day after day, for the temporary convenience of some private individual—owner of a store or house, without ever taking breath to inquire by what right they thus incommode a long-suffering public. The way the milkmen, sitting in their carts, shriek out their unearthly yells, disturbing sick people and babies, every morning in the year, instead of getting off their perch, and going quietly to the back-gate with their milky treasures, as in scandal-loving Boston. The horribly thriftless way in which strawberries are brought to market, in petty little three or six cent baskets, exposed to dust and sun, instead of being nicely hulled and packed in a covered box, after being spread over with dewy green leaves, all ready for instant use. The wretched cow-bells attached to the crazy carts of itinerant rag-men, that ding-dong into your very brain day after day; the prolonged howls and horns of fishmen and rag-men, which everybody execrates, and yet nobody has time to drive away; the horrible smoking nuisance, without the slightest regard to the female portion of pedestrianism, in our public thoroughfares. The shocking expectoration across narrow omnibuses and *over shrinking female shoulders, out of omnibus windows,* and over shrinking female faces from the roof; the foul plastered straw in which your foot plunges in its floor—ugh!—be these *"gentlemen"* prithee? The utter impossibility of getting any job done in New York, short of building a meeting-house, under a three years' dunning-process of workmen so much in demand, that they can well afford to let your blind or door swing on its hinge till it drops off, or your roof leak till you are drowned. In short, the general pell-mell scramble, jostle, hurry, rush and row, from one day to another—well I've got used to it now, and I dare say I should stagnate without it, but I nearly died in the process of becoming Gotham-ized.

New York Parks
September 21, 1861

Blessed be the parks of New York. Fifty times a week we say it, as we see the children of the poor creeping from noisome dwellings and narrow alleys to look at the green grass and blue sky, and sit upon the benches and let soul and body breathe in an atmosphere free from natural and moral filth. Ah, of what is that pale weary mother, with veiled eyes, thinking, as she sits with her chin on her palms, while her little stunted, half-grown baby toddles upon the gravel walk, reaching out its hands at the gay trimmings of the little one whose every step must be guarded and watched, lest harm come to its dainty feet? We cannot read her thoughts; but more than likely *her* babyhood was just as carefully tended. More than likely they who tended it never dreamed of such an ending as this. And how carelessly we pass along through these life-tragedies, nor heed the wan looks, or deep-drawn sighs about us. And so we are glad of the New York parks, where poverty may escape, even for a brief hour, the sickening sights and odors which daily surround it.

Central Park and Boston Common
November 16, 1867

I don't know what would become of New York had it not its Paradise in the Central New Park. I never go there without blessing its originator, and wishing it might be re-baptized with a more suggestive and prettier name. But never mind names. In its lovely October dress, with its sparkling lake, and drooping willows, its white swans, its lovely velvet greensward; the myriads of sweet children alighting here and there, in their bits of gay dresses, like little humming-birds or orioles, with happy mothers and fathers who have left their cares and frets in the city, and come there to be young again for too brief an hour, with the little ones; all this is a picture to feast the eye and gladden the heart. In one respect Central Park might borrow a hint from Boston Common. *There* the *little children* are allowed to run upon the grass at *all* times; not on certain days of the month or week as in the Central Park. Said a bright little child of six the other day, when asked if it would like to go to the Central Park: "No! (emphatically) *no!* I don't want *to waste my time going* where they won't let me step on the grass."

I sometimes wish that the policemen on duty there—so Argus-eyed to arrest the tiny shoe when temptation is too strong for childhood cooped within city limits—would bestow some of their notice upon the *men loafers* who stretch themselves at *full length* upon benches, occupying them to the exclusion of the children; puffing vile tobacco, and making a spittoon of the path through which ladies pass. It strikes me there might be an improvement on the straining-at-a-gnat and swallowing-a-camel system now in vogue there.

To return to Boston, which I always like to do occasionally: that city *needs* not our Central Park drives, with its lovely and easily accessible

188 | A Fanny Fern Reader

environs. Here in New York one does not *get* to the environs until it is time to come home; what with clogged streets, and ferry-boats, and Babel-hindrances too numerous to mention, such as scratched sides of the pet carriage, and often-recurring "locked wheels," the fright of prostrate horses, and the music of profanity from the lips of hurried and irate drivers of teams, and drays in every direction. All this is death to the repose one seeks in "a drive." *Therefore* we New Yorkers love our quiet, accessible Central Park. May its boundaries be limitless as our tax bills! I couldn't say more. But my first love—that dear old gem of a Boston Common! How happy were the Saturday and Wednesday afternoons, when, under the blessed old school system, before children were forced on grammar and geography, like hothouse plants, and we had short forenoon and *afternoon* sessions, with the exception of the above-mentioned holidays; how happy were the afternoons I spent there, picking buttercups, and blowing off thistle-down "to see if our mothers wanted us at home"; which, by the way, was sure to be answered in the negative. And as to the Frog-Pond—what was the Atlantic Ocean to that? On the Atlantic Ocean, they had dreadful shipwrecks; on the Boston Frog-Pond, we sent out our tiny ventures, sure to find safe arrivals when we ran 'round the other side of the Pond. And the big Tree—hooped all 'round like a modern belle—with what big eyes of wonder we looked up into its branches, as our elders told us wonderful stories of what it had seen in its long, eventful life. And *now* there are many big trees where *little* ones used to stand. Bless me! It shows how old I must be; just as it does to go back there and meet in the street some radiant, fresh young girl, "the very image of her mother," with whom I used to play buttercups, on Saturday afternoons. There are the same bright eyes, and lovely hair, and smiling lips—bless me, how old I *really* must be! And why don't I walk with a stick?

And then I laugh as I look up to Boston State-House and its awe-inspiring dome of our childhood; and recall the "members of the Legislature," crawling up and down stairs and galleries, like great black ants; and think of the terrific "*Inquisition*" doings which we used to be sure *must* be going on inside those wonderful halls, and to which Blue-Beard's locked apartment was nothing. Oh, it is all very funny now, when I go there; and, though I sit on a seat in the Common and try to conjure all the myriad hours, and days, and years, between then and now, and try to feel like the second Methuselah[5] I am, I declare to you I never can do it,—but, instead, catch myself trotting off home, under the trees, as briskly as a squirrel. I suppose, some day, I shall be dead though, for all that.

About Some Things in New York Which Have Interested Me
From Folly as It Flies, *1868*

The Battery was my first New York love.[6] I shall never forget how completely it took possession of me, or how magnetically it drew me under the shade of its fine trees, to breathe the fresh sea-breeze, and watch the graceful ships come and go, or lie calmly at anchor, with every line so clearly defined against the bright sky. It was not "the fashion," even then, to go there; so much the better. It is still less the fashion now; but there I found myself, one bright Sunday not long since, as I left the leafy loveliness of Trinity church, with its sweet choral music still sounding in my ears.

Alas! For my dear old Battery. The sea is still there, to be sure—no "corporation" can meddle with that; and still the picturesque ships come and go; but the blades of grass grow fewer and thinner, and the dirty, dusty paths call aloud for a "vigilance committee." What a sin and shame! I exclaimed, that this loveliest spot in New York should present so forlorn an appearance. Is there not room enough in the purses and affections of New Yorkers for the Central Park and the Battery too? In good truth, when I reflect upon it, I am jealous of this new aspirant for the public favor. What is a *horse* to a ship? Sacrilege though it be to say so. What is the gaudy, over-dressed equestrian "swell" of fine ladies and fine "Afghans" to the majestic *swell of the sea*? What are the stylish equipages and liveries, to the picturesque crowd of newly-arrived emigrants, with their funny little, odd-looking babies, their square, sturdy forms and bronze faces, chattering happy greetings in an unknown tongue, and gazing about them bewildered, at the strange sights and sounds of a great new city; or sauntering up to Trinity church, and in happy ignorance of novel steeples and creeds, dropping on their catholic knees in its aisles, in thankful, devout recognition of their safe arrival in a new country. What is the pretty toy-lake, and the hearse-like "gondola," and "the swans," and the posies, and the "bronze-eagle," and the blue-coated policemen, who stand ready to handle rogues *with* gloves, and *white ones* at that, to my dear old Battery, battered as it is.

I call capricious, fickle New York to order, for thus forsaking the old love for the new. I demand an instant settlement of any protracted dispute there may be on hand, as to "whose business it is" to renovate the Battery, before it quite runs to seed, like the City Hall Park. Not that *I* won't keep on going to the Battery, though they should build a small-pox hospital on it; for it is not my way to forsake an old friend because he is shabby; but

I *should* like to be a female General Butler,[7] for one month, and put this business through in his chain-lightning executive fashion.

It is a great plague to be a woman. I think I've said that before, but it will bear repeating. Now the wharves are a great passion of mine; I like to sit on a pile of boards there, with my boots dangling over the water, and listen to the far-off "heave-ho" of the sailors in their bright specks of red shirts, and see the vessels unload, with their foreign fruits, and dream away a delicious hour, imagining the places they came from; and I like to climb up the sides of ships, and poke round generally, just where Mrs. Grundy would lay her irritating hand on my arm and exclaim—"What *will* people think of you?"

I am getting sick of people. I am falling in love with things. They hold their tongues and don't bother.

I like also to stroll forth in New York, just at dusk, and see the crowds hurrying homeward. The merchant, glad to turn his back at last on both profit and loss. The laboring man with his tools and his empty dinner pail. The weary working-girl, upon whose pallid face the fresh wind comes, like the soft caressing touch of her mother's fingers. The matron, with her little boy by the hand, talking lovingly, as he skips by her side. The young man, full of hope for the future, looking, with his eagle eye, and fresh-tinted cheek, as if he could defy fate. The young girl, rejoicing in her prettiness, for the power it gives her to win love and friends. The little beggar children, counting their pennies on some doorstep, to see how much supper they will buy. The small boot-blacks, who stoop less, after all, than many men whose feet they polish, singing as merrily as if they were sure of a fortune on the morrow. The bright glancing lights in the shop windows, touching up bits of scarlet, and yellow, and blue, and making common beads and buttons gleam like treasures untold. The lumbering omnibuses, crawling up and down, heavy with their human freight. The rapid whirl of gay carriages, with their owners. The little bits of conversation one catches in passing, showing the depth or shallowness of the speakers. The tones of their voices, musical or otherwise. The step, awkward or graceful, and the sway of the figure. The fading tints of the sky, and the coming out of the stars, that find it hard to get noticed among so many garish lights. The interior glimpses of homes, before caution draws the curtains. Now—some picture on the wall. Now—a maiden sitting at the piano. Now—a child, with its cunning little face pressed close against the window. Now—a loving couple, too absorbed in the old—old—but ever *new* romance, to think that their clasped hands may be noted by the passer by. Now—a woman for whom your heart aches; walking slowly; glancing boldly; going anywhere, poor thing! But—*home*. Now—oh! The contrast—a husband and wife, with locked arms, talking cheerily of their little home matters. Now—a policeman with folded arms, standing on the corner, past being astonished at anything. Now—a florist's tempting window, whence comes a delicious odor of tube-roses, and heliotrope, and geranium. There is a huge, fragrant pyramid for some gay feast. There is a snowy wreath and cross, white as the still, dead, face, above which they are soon to be laid. There is a snowy coronal for a bride. There is a gay, bright-tinted bouquet for an actress. Lingering, you look, and muse, and spell out life's alphabet, by help of these sweet flowers; and now you are jostled away by a policeman, dragging a wretched, drunken woman to the station-house.

People talk of Niagara, and tell how impressive is its roar. What is the roar of a dumb thing like that to the roar of a mighty city? There, *souls* go down, and alas! The shuttle of life flies so swiftly that few stop to heed.

There are persons who can regard oppression and injustice without any acceleration of the pulse. There are others who never witness it, how frequent soever, without a desperate struggle against non-interference, though prudence and policy may both whisper "it's none of your business." I believe, as a general thing, that the shopkeepers of New York who employ girls and women to tend in their stores, treat them courteously; but now and then I have been witness to such brutal language to them, in the presence of customers, for that which seemed to me no offence, or at least a very trifling one, that I have longed for a man's strong right arm, summarily to settle matters with the oppressor. And when one has been the innocent cause of it, merely by entering the store to make a purchase, the obligation to see the victim safe through, seems almost imperative. The bad policy of such an exhibition of unmanliness on the part of a shopkeeper would be, one would think, sufficient to stifle the "damn you" to the blushing, tearful girl, who is powerless to escape, or to clear herself from the charge of misbehavior. When ladies "go shopping," in New York, they generally expect to enjoy themselves; though Heaven knows, they must be hard up for resources to fancy this mode of spending their time, when it can be avoided. But, be that as it may, the most vapid can scarcely fancy this sort of scene.

The most disgusting part of such an exhibition is, when the gentlemanly employer, having got through "damning" his embarrassed victim, turns, with a sweet smile and dulcet voice, to yourself, and inquires, "what else he can have the pleasure of showing you?" You are tempted to reply, "Sir, I would like you to show me that you can respect womanhood, although it may not be hedged about with fine raiment, or be able to buy civil words with a full purse." But you bite your tongue to keep it quiet, and you linger till this Nero has strolled off, and then you say to the girl, "I am so sorry to have been the innocent cause of this!" and you ask, "Does he often speak this way to you?" and she says, quietly, as she rolls up the ribbons or replaces the boxes on the shelves, "Never in any other!" It is useless to ask her why she stays, because you know something about women's wages and women's work in the crowded city; and you know that, till she is sure of another place, it is folly for her to think of leaving this. And you think many other things as you say Good-morning to her as kindly as you know how; and you turn over this whole "woman-question" as you run the risk of being knocked down and run over in the crowded thoroughfare through which you pass; and the jostle, and hurry, and rush about you, seem to make it more hopeless as each eager face passes you, intent on its own plans, busy with its own hopes and fears—staggering perhaps under a load either of the soul or body, or both, as heavy as the poor shop-girl's, and you gasp as if the air about had suddenly become too thick to breathe. And then you reach your own door-step, and like a guilty creature, face your dressmaker, having forgotten to "match that trimming"; and you wonder if you were to sit down and write about this evil, if it would deter even one employer from such brutality to the shop-girls in his employ; not because of the brutality, perhaps, but because by such a short-sighted policy, he might often drive away from his store, ladies who would otherwise be profitable and steady customers.

There is an animal peculiar to New-York, who infests every nook and corner of it, to everybody's disgust but his own. He is a boy in years, but a man in vicious knowledge. Every woman who is unfortunate enough to be in his presence is simply a *she*—nothing more. He may be seen making a charmed circle of expectoration, about the seat he occupies in a ferry-boat, ferry-house, or car, while she stands half fainting with exhaustion, in hearing distance of his coarse, prurient remarks to some other little beast like himself. Pea-nuts are the staple food of this creature, the shells of which he snaps dexterously at those about him, when other means of amusement give out. When a public conveyance has reached its point of destination, this animal is the first to make an insane rush for egress, treading down young children, and tearing ladies' clothing in his triumphal march. Sometimes he stops on the way to "bung out the eye" of an offending youngster, in so tight a place for a combat that somebody's corpse seems inevitable. Terrified ladies, who would fain give him elbow room if they had it, faintly ejaculate "Oh!" as they squeeze themselves into the smallest breathable space; nor does he desist, till h's adversary is punished for the crime of existing, without this brute's permission; he then emerges into the open street, settling his greasy jacket and indescribable hat, muttering oaths, and squaring off occasionally, as he looks behind him, as though he wished somebody else was "spiling for a licking."

Often this animal may be found in the city parks; where the city corporation generously furnishes about one seat to every hundred children, and selecting the shadiest and most eligible, stretches himself on it upon his stomach, while tired little children and their female attendants, wander round in vain for a resting-place. Sometimes sitting upon it, he will stretch out his leg so as to trip some unwary, happy little child in passing; or perhaps he will suddenly give a deafening shout in its ear, for the pleasure of hearing it cry; or from a pocket well stuffed with pebbles will skillfully pelt its clean clothes from a safe distance; and sometimes this animal, who smokes at ten years like a man of forty, will address a passing lady with such questions as these:

"Oh, aint *you* bully? Oh, give *her* room enough to walk!—oh, yes!" Or, "Who's *your* beau, Sally?" which last cognomen seems with them to constitute a safe guess.

When not otherwise occupied, this young gentleman writes offensive words on door-steps and fences with bits of chalk, which he keeps on hand for this purpose. Or, if a servant has just nicely cleaned a window, he chews gum into little balls wherewith to plaster it; or he kicks over an ash-barrel in passing upon a nicely swept side-walk; or he rings the door-bell violently, and makes a flying exit, having ascertained previously the policeman's "beat" on that district; or he climbs the box round a favorite tree, which has just begun by its grateful shade to refresh your eye and reward your care, and, stripping off the most promising bough for a switch, goes up street picking off the leaves and scattering them as he goes; or he will stand at the bottom of a high flight of steps, upon the top step of which is a lady waiting for admittance, and scream, "Oh, my—aint *you* got bully boots on?" He also is expert at stealing newspapers from door-steps, and vociferating bogus extras about shocking murders and fires, and "lass of life"; and flowers out in full glory in a red shirt, in a pit of a Bowery theatre of an evening.

Sometimes he diverts himself throwing stones at the windows of passing cars, and splintering the glass into the eyes of frightened ladies and children, and suddenly disappearing as if the earth had opened and swallowed him, as you wish some day it would.

What this boy will be as a man, it is not difficult to tell. He counts one at the ballot-box, remember that, when you deny cultivated, intelligent, loyal *women* a vote there.

~

. . . Let me speak of a pleasanter topic: my visit to the newsboys. One Sunday evening I went to "The Newsboys' Lodging House, 128 Fulton Street, New York."[8] Few people who stop these little fellows in the street to purchase a paper, ever glance at their faces, much less give a thought to their belongings, associations or condition. Oh! had you only been down there with me that evening, and looked into those hundred and fifty intelligent, eager faces, numbered their respective ages, inquired into their friendless past, given a thought to the million temptations with which their *present* is surrounded, spite of all the well directed efforts of Christian philanthropy, and looked forward into their possible future, your eyes would have filled, and your heart beat quicker, as you have said to yourself, Oh, yes; something *must* be done to save these children.

Children! for many of them are no more. Children! already battling with life, though scarce past the nursery age. Imagine your own dear boy, with the bright eyes and the broad, white forehead, whom you tuck so comfortably in his little soft bed at night, with a prayer and a kiss; whom you look at the last thing on retiring; for whom you gladly toil; whom you hedge around with virtuous, wholesome influences from the cradle; who does not yet know even the meaning of the word "evil"; who jumps into your arms as soon as he wakes in the morning, with the sweet certainty of a warm love-clasp; who has the nicest bit, at breakfast, laid on his little plate; whose little stories and questions always find eager and sympathizing ears; imagine this little fellow of seven or eight, or ten years, getting out of his bed at one or two o'clock in the morning, going out into the dark, chill, lonesome street, half-clad, hungry, alone to some newspaper office, to wait for the damp morning papers, as they are worked from the press, and seizing his bundle, hurrying, barefoot and shivering, to some newspaper stand or depot, at the farther part of the city. Imagine *your* little Charley doing that! Then, if that were all! If this drain on the physical immaturity of childhood were the worst of it. The devil laughs as he knows it is not. Big boys—*men*, even—*cheat*; why not he? If he can pass off bad change—surely, who has more need to make a sixpence, though it be not an honest one? What care customers if he grow up a good or a bad man, so that the newspaper comes in time to season their warm breakfast? Who will ever care for him living, or mourn for him dead? What does it matter, anyhow?

That's the way this poor friendless child reasons. I understood it all last night. All too that this noble philanthropy called "The Newsboys' Lodging House" meant. And as I looked round on those boys, I felt afraid when they were addressed, that the right thing might not be said to so peculiar an audience. For children though they were, they had seen life as men see it. Untutored, uneducated, in one sense, in others they knew as much as any adult who should address them. Sharpened by actual hard-fisted grappling with the world, let him be careful who should speak to these grown-up children of seven, and ten, and fourteen years. Thinking thus, I said, as their friend, Mr. C. L. Brace, rose to speak—pray God, he may take all this into consideration.[9] Pray God, he may give them neither creeds nor theology; but, instead, the wide open arms of the good, pitiful, loving Saviour, whose home on earth was with the lowly and the friendless. And he did! It was a human address. The God he told them of was not out of their reach. It was every word pure gold. Bless him for it! He had them all by the hand, and the heart too. I saw that. Promptly, frankly, and with the confidence of children in the family, they answered his questions as to their views on the chapter in the Bible he read them. And if you smiled at some of their queer notions, the tear was in your eye the next minute at the blessed thought that they had friends who cared whether the immortal part of them slumbered or woke; who recognized and fanned into a flame even the smallest particle of mentality. Now and then among the crowd a head or face would attract your eye, and you would be lost in wonder to see it *there*! The head and face of what I call "*a mother's boy*." God knows if its owner had one, or, if it had, if she cared for him! And as they sang together of "The Friend that never grew weary," my heart responded, aye—aye—why should I forget that?

I hope you will go—and you and you—on some Sabbath evening, if you come to New York. They love to feel that people take an interest in them. It brightens and cheers their lives. It gives them self-respect and motive for trying to do right; and don't forget to ask the Superintendent, Mr. O Conner, to show you the nice little beds where they sleep. *Do* go; and if you can say a few words to them, or tell them a bright short story, so much the better. They will know you next time they sell you a newspaper; don't forget to shake hands with them *then*. And take your little pet boy Charley down there. Show him the little fellows who go into business in New York at seven and ten years old, and have no father or mother at night to kiss them to sleep. It will be a lesson better than any he will ever learn at school. He will find out that all boys are not born to plum-cake and sugar candy, and some of the best and smartest boys too. He will open his eyes when you tell him that without plum-cake, or candy, or a grandpa, or an aunt, or father or mother to care for them, some of the newsboys who came from that very house, to-day own farms in the West, that they earned selling newspapers, and have since come back for other newsboys to go out there and help them work on it. Tell Charley that. I think he will be ashamed to cry again because there was "not sugar enough in his milk."

~

People who visit a great city, and explore it with a curious eye, generally overlook the most remarkable things in it. They "do it up" in Guide-Book fashion, going the stereotyped rounds of custom-ridden predecessors. If *my* chain were a little longer, I would write you a book of travels that would at least have the merit of ignoring the usual finger-posts that challenge travellers. I promise you I would cross conservative lots, and climb over conservative fences, and leave the rags and tatters of custom fluttering on them, behind me, as I strode on to some unfrequented hunting-ground.

That's the way I'd do. Never a "lord" or "lady," or a "palace," or a "picture gallery," should figure in my note-book. "Old masters" and young masters would be all the same to me. When my book was finished, if nobody else wanted to read it, I'd sit down and read it myself. Of course you know such a method pre-supposes a little capital to start with, at the present price of paper; but really, I put it to you, wouldn't that be the only honest and racy way to write a book?

Don't be alarmed—there's no chance of my doing it. I dream of it, though, sometimes—this deliciousness of "speaking right out in meetin'" without fear of the bugbear of excommunication. And speaking of "meetin,'" that's what I have been coming at. The "Fulton-street daily prayer-meeting."

It is one of the most wonderful sights in New York. In the busiest hour of the day, in its busiest business street, noisy with machinery of all kinds, even the earth under your feet sending out puffs of steam at every other step, to remind you of its underground labor, is a little plain room, with a reading-desk and a few benches, with hymn-books scattered about. Take a seat, and watch the worshippers as they collect. *Men*, with only a sprinkling of bonnets here and there. Business men, evidently; some with good coats, some with bad; porters, hand-cartmen, policemen, ministers; the young man of eighteen or twenty, the portly man of forty, and the bent form, whitening head, and faltering step of age. For *one* hour they want to ignore, and get out of, that maelstrom-whirl, into a spiritual atmosphere. They feel that they have souls as well as bodies to care for, and they don't want to forget it. How lonely soever yonder man, in that great rough coat, may be, in this great, strange city, to which he has just come, here is sympathy, here is companionship, here are, in the best sense, "brethren." Never mind creeds; that is not what they assemble to discuss. *But has that man a burden, a grief or a sorrow, which is intensified tenfold by want of sympathy?* Nobody knows his name; nobody is curious to know. He has sent a little slip of paper up to the desk, and he wants them all to pity and pray for him. It may be the man on this seat, or that yonder—nobody knows. Yes—*"pray"* for him. Perhaps you are smiling. You "don't believe in prayer." Oh, wait till some strand of earthly hope is parting, before you are quite sure of that. Was there ever an hour of peril or human agony through which he or she who "did not believe in prayer," was passing, that the lips did not involuntarily frame the short prayer, "Oh, God?"

Well, they "pray" for him. He feels stronger and better as he listens. He has found friends, even here in this great whirling city, who are sorry for him; of whose circle he can make one, whenever he chooses; and to whom he can more fully introduce himself, if he cares to be better known.

I say it is a good and a noble thing. It warmed and gladdened my heart to see it. And all the more, that at every step, on leaving, I saw the "traps" of the Evil One, sprung for that man's return footsteps.

One of the pleasantest features of this "one-hour meeting" to me was the hymns. I don't know or care whether they were "sung in tune." It wasn't *hired* singing, thank God! It came straight from orthodox lungs, with a will and a spirit. Those old "come-to-Jesus" hymns! I tell you I long for them sometimes with a homesick longing, like that of the exiled Swiss for his favorite mountain song. You may pick up the hymn-books containing them, and with your critical forefinger point to "hell" and "an angry God," and all that. It makes no difference to me. Don't I take pleasure in looking at your face, though your nose isn't quite straight, and your eyes are not perfect, and your shoulders are not shaped to my mind. I don't mind *that*, so that there's a heart-tone in your voice, a love-look in your eye, when I'm heart-sore—don't you see?

Oh! I liked that meeting. I'm going again. It was so homely, and hearty, and Christian. One man said, "*them* souls." Do you think I flounced out of the meeting for that? I liked it. One poor foreigner couldn't pronounce straight, for the life of him. So much the better. His stammering tongue will be all right some day. I haven't the least idea who all those people were, singing and praying there; but I never can tell you how I liked it. That "Come to Jesus" was sung with a *heart-ring* that I haven't stopped hearing, yet, though I have slept on it once or twice. You may say "priestcraft!" "early education!" and all that. There are husks with the wheat, I know; but for all that—I tell you there is *wheat!*

A Morning at Stewart's[10]
From Folly as It Flies, *1868*

It is not often that I treat myself to a stroll into Stewart's great shop. Mortal woman cannot behold such perfection *too* often and live. It is like a view of the vast ocean, so humiliating and depressing by its immensity and sublimity that little atoms of humanity are glad to creep away from it, to some locally-big elevation of their own. Once in a while, when I feel strong enough to bear it, when the day is very bright, and the atmosphere propitious, I put on a bold face and plunge in with the throng. When I say "throng" I don't wish to be understood as meaning anything like a mob. It is a very curious circumstance that how objectionably soever "throngs" may behave elsewhere, even that most disorderly of all throngs, a *woman*-throng—yet at Stewart's so suggestive of order and system is the place, that immediately on entering, they involuntarily "fall into line," like proper little Sunday scholars in a procession, and never shuffle or elbow the least bit. Perhaps they are astonished into good behavior by the sight of those well-behaved statuesque clerks—I don't know. Perhaps with the artistic manner in which yonder silky-inky bearded Italian-looking, red-neck-tied gentleman, has arranged the different shades of silk on yonder counter; so that, as the light falls on it from the window, it looks like a splendid display of folded tulips and roses. Perhaps it is the imposing well-to-do portly individual who walks up and down between the rows of counters, snapping his eyes about, as if to say—"Ladies, if this don't suit you, what in heaven's name *will?*" Perhaps it is the eel-like manner in which little "Cash" winds in and out, with his neatly-tied parcels, and bank-bills and change. Perhaps it is the astounding sight of yonder fur-cape, as displayed to advantage on one of those revolving lay-figures. Perhaps it is the cloak room up-stairs, where the ladies sigh as they tumble over heaps of beautiful garments, unable to choose from such a superfluity. "How happy could I be with either, were the other dear charmer away!" Perhaps 'tis the thought of the money that must have been expended in this wonderful Juniper store, inside and out, first and last, and "if *they* only had it," how many diamonds, and laces, and silks it would buy, *all at once*; instead of taking it in disgraceful little installments from their stingy husbands, so that they positively blush when Stewart's factotum inquires, "Any thing more this morning, ma'am?" to be obliged to answer "No." I don't pretend to comprehend the talismanic spell; but I know that at other than Stewart's I see those very women, snub and brow-beat clerks, and put on astounding airs generally, as women will when let out on a shopping spree.—I see none of it there. Indeed, I sometimes think that if the great Stewart himself were bodily to order them out, they would neither mutter, nor peep mutinously; but turn about, like a flock of sheep, and obediently leap over the threshold. The amount of it is, Stewart is a sort of dry-goods "Rarey." Perhaps husbands wink at the thing and give the little dears coppers to spend there on purpose—I don't know.

The Working-Girls of New York
From Folly as It Flies, *1868*

Nowhere than in New York does the contest between squalor and splendor so sharply present itself. This is the first reflection of the observing stranger who walks its streets. Particularly is this noticeable with regard to its women. Jostling on the same pavement with the dainty fashionist is the care-worn working-girl. Looking at both these women, the question arises, which lives the more miserable life—she whom the world styles "fortunate," whose husband belongs to three clubs, and whose only meal with his family is an occasional breakfast, from year's end to year's end; who is as much a stranger to his own children as to the reader; whose young son of seventeen has already a detective on his track employed by his father to ascertain where and how he spends his nights and his father's money; swift retribution for that father who finds food, raiment, shelter, equipages for his household; but love, sympathy, companionship—never? Or she—this other woman—with a heart quite as hungry and unappeased, who also faces day by day the same appalling question: *Is this all life has for me?*

A great book is yet unwritten about women. Michelet has aired his wax-doll theories regarding them.[11] The defender of "woman's rights" has given us her views. Authors and authoresses of little, and big repute, have expressed themselves on this subject, and none of them as yet have begun to grasp it: men—because they lack spirituality, rightly and justly to interpret women; women—because they dare not, or will not, tell us that which most interests us to know. Who shall write this bold, frank, truthful book remains to be seen. Meanwhile woman's millennium is yet a great way off; and while it slowly progresses, conservatism and indifference gaze through their spectacles at the seething elements of to-day, and wonder "what ails all our women?"

Let me tell you what ails the working-girls. While yet your breakfast is progressing, and your toilet unmade, comes forth through Chatham Street and the Bowery, a long procession of them by twos and threes to their daily labor. Their breakfast, so called, has been hastily swallowed in a tenement house, where two of them share, in a small room, the same miserable bed. Of its quality you may better judge, when you know that each of these girls pays but three dollars a week for board, to the working man and his wife where they lodge.

The room they occupy is close and unventilated, with no accommodations for personal cleanliness, and so near to the little Flinegans that their Celtic night-cries are distinctly heard. They have risen unrefreshed, as a matter of course, and their ill-cooked breakfast does not mend the matter. They emerge from the doorway where their passage is obstructed by "nanny goats" and ragged children rooting together in the dirt, and pass out into the street. They shiver as the sharp wind of early morning strikes their temples. There is no look of youth on their faces; hard lines appear there. Their brows are knit; their eyes are sunken; their dress is flimsy, and foolish, and tawdry; always a hat, and feather or soiled artificial flower upon it; the hair dressed with an abortive attempt at style; a soiled petticoat; a greasy dress, a well-worn sacque or shawl, and a gilt breast-pin and earrings.

Now follow them to the large, black-looking building, where several hundred of them are manufacturing hoop-skirts. If you are a woman you have worn plenty; but you little thought what passed in the heads of these girls as their busy fingers glazed the wire, or prepared the spools for covering them, or secured the tapes which held them in their places. *You* could not stay five minutes in that room, where the noise of the machinery used is so deafening, that only by the motion of the lips could you comprehend a person speaking.

Five minutes! Why, these young creatures bear it, from seven in the morning till six in the evening; week after week, month after month, with only half an hour at midday to eat their dinner of a slice of bread and butter or an apple, which they usually eat in the building, some of them having come a long distance. As I said, the roar of machinery in that room is like the roar of Niagara. Observe them as you enter. Not one lifts her head. They might as well be machines, for any interest or curiosity they show, save always to know *what o'clock it is*. Pitiful! pitiful, you almost sob to yourself, as you look at these young girls. *Young?* Alas! it is only in years that they are young.

"Only three dollars a week do they earn," said I to a brawny woman in a tenement house near where some of them boarded. "Only three dollars a week, and all of that goes for their board. How, then, do they clothe themselves?" Hell has nothing more horrible than the cold, sneering indifference of her reply: "*Ask the dry-goods men.*"

Perhaps you ask, why do not these girls go out to service? Surely it were better to live in a clean, nice house, in a healthy atmosphere, with respectable people, who might take other interest in them than to wring out the last particle of their available bodily strength. It were better surely to live in a house cheerful and bright, where merry voices were sometimes heard, and clean, wholesome food was given them. Why do they not? First, because, unhappily, they look down upon the position of a servant, even from *their* miserable stand-point. But chiefly, and mainly, because when six o'clock in the evening comes they are their own mistresses, without hindrance or questioning, till another day of labor begins. They do not sit in an under-ground kitchen, watching the bell-wire, and longing to see what is going on out of doors. More's the pity, that the street is their only refuge from the squalor and quarrelling and confusion of their tenement-house home. More's the pity, that as yet there are no sufficiently decent, cleanly boarding-houses, within their means, where their self-respect would not inevitably wither and die.

As it is, they stroll the streets; and who can blame them? *There* are gay lights, and fine shop-windows. It costs nothing to *wish* they could have all those fine things. They look longingly into the theatres, through whose doors happier girls of their own age pass, radiant and smiling, with their lovers. Glimpses of Paradise come through those doors as they gaze. Back comes the old torturing question: Must my young life *always* be toil? *nothing* but toil? They stroll on. Music and bright lights from the underground "Concert Saloons," where girls like themselves get fine dresses and good wages, and flattering words and smiles beside. Alas! the future is far away; the present only is tangible. Is it a wonder if they never go back to the dark, cheerless tenement-house, or to the "manufactory" which sets their poor, weary bodies aching, till they feel forsaken of God and man? Talk of virtue! Live this life of toil, and starvation, and friendlessness, and "unwomanly rags," and learn charity. Sometimes they rush for escape into ill-sorted marriages, with coarse rough fellows, and go back to the old tenement-house life again, with this difference, that their toil does *not* end at six o'clock, and that from *this* bargain there is no release but death.

But there are other establishments than those factories where working-girls are employed. There is "Madame———, Modiste."[12] Surely the girls working there must fare better. Madame pays six thousand dollars rent for the elegant mansion in that fashionable street, in the basement or attic of which they work. Madame cuts and makes dresses, but she takes in none of the materials for that purpose. Not she. She coolly tells you that she will make you a very nice *plain* black silk dress, and find everything, for two hundred dollars. This is modest, at a clear profit to herself of one hundred dollars on every such dress, particularly as she buys all her material by the wholesale, and pays her girls, at the highest rate of compensation, not more than six dollars a week. At this rate of small wages and big profits, you can well understand how she can afford not only to keep up this splendid establishment, but another still more magnificent for her own *private* residence in quite as fashionable a neighborhood. Another "modiste" who *did* "take in material for dresses," and—ladies also! was in the habit of telling the latter that thirty-two yards of any material was required where sixteen would have answered. The remaining yards were then in all cases thrown into a rag-pen; from which, through contract with a man in her employ, she furnished herself with all the crockery, china, glass, tin and iron ware needed in her household. This same modiste employed twenty-five girls at the starvation price of three dollars and a half a week. The room in which they worked was about nine feet square, with only one window in it, and whoso came early enough to secure a seat by that window saved her eyesight by the process. Three sewing-machines whirred constantly by day in this little room, which at night was used as a sleeping apartment. As the twenty-five working-girls were ushered in to their day's labor in the morning before that room was ventilated, you would not wonder that by four in the afternoon dark circles appeared under their eyes, and they stopped occasionally to press their hands upon their aching temples. Not often, but *sometimes*, when the pain and exhaustion became intolerable.

One of the twenty-five was an orphan girl named Lizzy, only fifteen years of age. Not even this daily martyrdom had quenched her abounding spirits, in that room where never a smile was seen on another face—where never a jest was ventured on, not even when Madame's back was turned. Always Lizzie's hair was nicely smoothed, and though the clean little creature went without her breakfast—for a deduction of wages was the penalty of being late—yet had she always on a clean dark calico dress, smoothed by her own deft little fingers. In that dismal, smileless room she was the only sunbeam. But one day the twenty-five were startled; their needles dropped from their fingers. Lizzie was worn out at last! Her pretty face blanched, and with a low baby cry she threw her arms over her face and sobbed: "Oh, I *cannot* bear this life—I cannot bear it any longer. George *must* come and take me away from this." That night she was privately married to "George," who was an employee on the railroad. The next day while on the train attending to his duties, he broke his arm, and neither of the bridal pair having any money, George was taken to the hospital. The little bride, with starvation before her, went back that day to Madame, and concealing the fact of her marriage, begged humbly to be taken back, apologizing for her conduct on the day before, on the plea that she had such a violent pain in her temples that she knew not what she said. As she was a handy little workwoman, her request was granted, and she worked there for several weeks, during her honeymoon, at the old rate of pay. The day George was pronounced well, she threw down her work, clapped her little palms together, and announced to the astonished twenty-five that they had a married woman among them, and that she should not return the next morning. Being the middle of the week, and not the end, she had to go without her wages for that week. Romance was not part or parcel of Madame's establishment. Her law was as the Medes and Persians, which changed not. Little Lizzie's future was no more to her than her past had been—no more than that of another young thing in that work-room, who begged a friend, each day, to bring her ever so little ardent spirits, at the half hour allotted to their miserable dinner, lest she should fail in strength to finish the day's work, upon which so much depended.

Oh! if the ladies who wore the gay robes manufactured in that room knew the tragedy of those young lives, would they not be to them like the penance robes of which we read, piercing, burning, torturing?

There is still another class of girls, who tend in the large shops in New York. Are they not better remunerated and lodged? We shall see. The additional dollar or two added to their wages is offset by the necessity of their being always nicely apparelled, and the necessity of a better lodging-house, and consequently a higher price for board, so that unless they are fortunate enough to have a parent's roof over their heads, they will not, except in rare cases, where there is a special gift as an accountant, or an artist-touch in the fingers, to twist a ribbon or frill a lace, be able to save any more than the class of which I have been speaking. They are allowed, however, by their employers, to purchase any article in the store at first cost, which is something in their favor.

But, you say, is there no bright side to this dark picture? Are there no cases in which these girls battle bravely with penury? I have one in my mind now; a girl, I should say a lady; one of nature's ladies, with a face as refined and delicate as that of any lady who bends over these pages; who has been through this harrowing experience of the working-girl, and after years of patience, virtuous toil, has no more at this day than when she began, *i.e.*, her wages day by day. Of the wretched places she has called "home," I will not pain you by speaking. Of the rough words she has borne, that she was powerless, through her poverty, to resent. Of the long walks she has taken to obtain wages due, and failed to secure them at last. Of the weary, wakeful nights, and heart-breaking days, borne with a heroism and trust in God, that was truly sublime. Of the little remittances from time to time forwarded to old age and penury, in "the old country," when she herself was in want of comfortable clothing; when she herself had no shelter in case of sickness, save the hospital or the almshouse. Surely, such virtue and integrity, will have more enduring record than in these pages.

Humanity has not slept on this subject, though it has as yet accomplished little. A boarding-house has been established in New York for working-girls, excellent in its way, but intended mainly for those who "have seen better days," and not for the most needy class of which I have spoken. A noble institution, however, called "The Working Woman's Protective Union,"¹³ has sprung up, for the benefit of this latter class, their object being to find places *in the country*, for such of these girls as will leave the overcrowded city, not as servants, but as operatives on sewing-machines, and to other similar revenues of employment. Their places are secured before they are sent. The person who engages them pays their expenses on leaving, and the consent of parents, or guardians, or friends, is always obtained before they leave. A room is to be connected with this institution, containing several sewing-machines, where gratuitous instruction will be furnished to those who desire it. A lawyer of New York has generously volunteered his services also, to collect the too tardy wages of these girls, due from flinty-hearted employers. Many of the girls who have applied here are under fifteen. At first, they utterly refused to go into the country, which to them was only another name for dullness; even preferring to wander up and down the streets of the city, half-fed and half-clothed, in search of employment, than to leave its dear kaleidoscope delights. But after a little, when letters came from some who had gone, describing in glowing terms, their pleasant homes; the wages that one could live and save money on; their kind treatment; the good, wholesome food and fresh air; their hearty, jolly country fun; and more than all, when it was announced that one of their number had actually married an ex-governor, the matter took another aspect. And, though all may not marry governors, and some may not marry at all; it still remains, that *inducing them to go to the country is striking a brave blow at the root of the evil*; for we all know, that human strength and human virtue have their limits; and the dreadful pressure of temptations and present ease, upon the discouragement, poverty and friendlessness of the working-girls of New York, must be gratifying to the devil. I do not hesitate to say, that there is no institution of the present day, more worthy to be sustained, or that more imperatively challenges the good works and good wishes of the benevolent, than "The New York Working Woman's Protective Union." May God speed it!

GETTING AWAY FROM THE CITY

Trip to the Caatskills, Number One
September 12, 1857

Well—I've "done" the Caatskills! I've tugged up that steep mountain, one of the hottest days in which a quadruped or a biped ever perspired, packed to suffocation, with other gasping sufferers, in that crucifying institution called a stage-coach, until I became resignedly indifferent, whether it reached its destination, or rolled head over heels—or rather head over wheels—over the precipice. Landing at last, at the hotel I was conscious of only one want, a bed-room; which, when obtained, was close enough, and which I shared with three other jaded mortals. The next morning, thanks to a good Providence and the landlord, I emigrated into unexceptionable quarters.

Ah—now I breathe! now I remember no more that purgatorial reeling stage-coach, and its protracted jigglings—wrigglings—joltings and bumpings. Now I am repaid—now I gaze—oh, how *can* I gaze with only one pair of eyes, on all this beauty and magnificence? This vast plain spread out so far below our feet like an immense garden, with its luxuriant foliage—its little cottages, smaller than a child's toy;—its noble river, specked with white sails, lessened by distance to a silver thread, winding through the meadows; and beyond—still other plains, other streams, other mountains—on—on—stretching far beyond the dizzy ken, till the eye fills, and the heart swells, and leaning in an ecstasy of happiness on the bosom of "Our Father" we cry—"Oh—what is man that Thou art mindful of him?"

Now—as if the scene were too gorgeous for mortal sight, nature gently, compassionately drops a silvery veil of mist before it, veiling, yet not hiding—withdrawing, yet not removing—giving us now sunshine, now shadow; bringing out now the vivid green of a meadow, now the silver sheen of the river; now the bold outline of a pine-girdled mountain. And now—the scene changes, and fleets of clouds sail slowly—glide ghostly, round the mountain's base; winding-sheets wrapped round the shapely trees, from which they burst with a glorious resurrection; while over and above all arches the blue heavens, smiling that it canopies a scene so fair. See—village after village, like specks in the distance—where human hearts throb to human joys and sorrows; where restless ambition flutters against the barred cage of necessity, pining for the mountain-top of freedom; when, gained, oh, weary traveler, to lose its distant golden splendor, and wrap thee in the chill vapors of discontent. What matter—if thou but accept this proof of thy immortality? Yes—village after village;—farmers plodding on, as farmers too often will, turning up the soil for dollars and cents, seeing only in the clouds the filter for their crops; in the lakes the refrigerator for their fish; in the glorious trees their fuel; in the waving grass and sloping meadows, feed for their cattle; in the sweet sunrise an alarm bell to labor, in the little bird's vespers but a call to feed and sleep.

Now—twilight steals upon the mountains, calm as Heaven. The bright valleys sleep in their deepening shadows, while on the mountain-tops lingers the glory, as if loth to fade into the perfumed night. With a graceful sweep the little bird mounts to the clouds, takes his last circling flight, and sings his evening hymn, sweet and soft as the rapt soul's whispered farewell to earth. And yet—oh, God!—this is but the porch to the temple, before whose dazzling splendors even thy seraphs veil their sinless eyes.

Trip to the Caatskills, Number Four
October 3, 1857

A lack of competition is said to affect progress. That the traveler to the Caatskills has no choice but "The Mountain House," should not, it seems to me, act as an extinguisher to enterprise upon its well patronized landlord.[14] I might make many suggestions as to improvements, by which I am sure he would, in the end, be no loser. It needs no great stretch of the imagination to fancy the carriage which conveys victims to "The Falls," a relic of the Inquisition. I did not know till I had tried it, how many evolutions a comfortably-fleshed woman could perform in a minute, between the roof and floor of such a ve-higgle! (Result—a villainous headache—and the black and blues.) I noticed a small book-shelf in the very pleasant ladies' parlor. "Praise God Barebones," I think, must have made the selection of the volumes. But it is pleasanter to commend than to find fault. I could forgive many short-comings for the privilege of feasting on the wholesome light bread, which to a saleratus-consuming,—saleratus-consumed New Yorker, was glory enough to nibble at.[15] Blessings, too, on the skillful fingers which stirred up those appetizing omelettes, and sublime orange-puddings. What an amusement it is, to be sure, to watch a man when he gets hold of the dish he fancies! What fun to bother him with innumerable questions while he is trying to eat it in undisturbed rapture—meanwhile wishing you at the North Pole. How cynical the creatures are, the last interminable half hour *before* meals, and how sweetly amiable, and lazy, *after*. Then is your time to try men's soles; to insist upon their taking a walk with you, when they can scarce waddle,—when visions of curling Havana smoke invite them to two-legged piazza-chairs, digestion, and meditation. *Then* is your time to be suddenly seized with an unpostponable longing for a brisk game of ten-pins, to test the sincerity of all their disinterested speeches. My dears,—the man who continues amiable while you thus stoke his inclinations the wrong way, may safely be trusted in any matrimonial crisis. I endorse him.

With regard to the Falls it may be a delusion, but I think it is rather a damper to sentiment to fee a man to turn on the water for them! and I know it is a damper to the slippers to go down into the ravine beneath—which, joking aside, is very beautiful, and a great place for a bear to hug you in. Instead of which, I met a young parson whom I knew by token of his very black coat, and very white neck-tie; and who actually pulled from his sacerdotal pocket a profane handkerchief which I had carelessly dropped, presenting it with as much gravity as if he had been giving me "the right hand of fellowship." Heaven help him—so young—so well made—and so solemn!—I felt immensely like a frolic. And speaking of frolics—oh, the mountains I had to leave unclimbed—the "campings out" foregone—and all because I was foreordained to petticoats—hampering, bush-catching petticoats!—all because I hadn't courage to put on trousers, (in which, by the way, I have made several unsatisfactory private rehearsal attempts to unsex myself but nature was too much for me,) and wade knee-deep in moss to see what man alone, by privilege of his untrammeled apparel, may feast his eyes upon. It is a *crying* shame. Ten-pins, too—who can get a "ten-strike" in petticoats? See what I would do at it in a jacket and unmentionables—though I really think nature had no eye to this game when she modeled a woman's hand and wrist. Now I dare say there are strait-laced people who will be shocked at the idea of a woman playing ten-pins. Well—let them be shocked. I vote for it for two reasons: first, for the exercise, when dripping grass and lowering skies deny it to us elsewhere; secondly, because it is always a pleasant sight to see husbands sharing this, or any other innocent recreation, with their wives and daughters, instead of herding selfishly in male flocks. I like this feature of domesticity in pleasure-seeking in our friends, the Germans. I like the Germans. Their joy is infectious. A sprinkling of such spirits would do much towards infusing a little life into the solemn business way in which Americans too often pursue, but seldom overtake, pleasure. Yes—it is a lovely sight to see them with their families! and oh, how much more honorable and just, to a pains-taking economical wife and mother, than the expensive meal, shared at a restaurant with some male companion, while she sits solitary—to whom a proposal even for a simple walk would be happiness, as an evidence of that watchful care which is so endearing to a wife's heart.

Not the least among our enjoyments were our evenings at the Caatskills. When warm enough, promenading on the ample piazza with pleasant friends; when the out-door temperature forbade this, seated in the parlors, listening to merry voices, looking on young and happy faces,—or what is never less beautiful, upon those who, having reached life's summit, did not, for that reason, churlishly refuse to cast back approving, sympathizing glances upon the young loiterers, who were still gleefully gathering flowers by the way.

Then, too, we had music—*heart* music,—from our German friend, Ferdinand Ulrich; whose artistic fingers often, also, gave harmonious expressions upon the piano to our *sunrise* thoughts, before we had left our rooms. Happy they, whose full souls can lighten their secret burdens by the low musical plaint, understood only by those who have themselves loved and suffered! Of how many tried and aching hearts has music been the eloquent voice? The ruffled brow grows smooth beneath its influence; the angry feeling,—calm as a wayward child, at a mother's loving kiss. Joy, like a white robed angel, glides softly in, and on the billows of earthly sorrow she lays her gentle finger, whispering—"Peace—be still!"

Notes of a Summer Tour, Number VI
October 9, 1858

Slow old Boston is waking up at last. Washington street is nearly as dirty as New York streets. Old landmarks are fast disappearing, new stores are springing up on the sites of old dwelling houses, and the wheel of progression is going round in that latitude, in a way to make an old resident stare. What a pity it could not extend to the Boston *newspapers*!

Tortured with a slow fever and racking cough during my stay there, I could only ride round to make my investigations, with the exception of one short walk, during which I had the felicity of meeting the greatest scoundrel that Boston can boast—a sight hardly worth rising from a sick bed to see. For months I had so longed to see "The Common"; (how I like that good, homely name.) How I feasted my eyes upon its fountain and trees, its green banks and its nicely-kept gravel walks, over which time has so closely woven its network of leaves, that you can scarce believe them to be the same your feet used to tread, up and down, and across, in all weather and moods, but chiefly when nature seemed to you the only safe and soothing confidant of anguish of spirit else intolerable. Old associations, how thick and fast they came. Tripping feet flew over the greensward, that no eyes but mine could see; golden locks floated on the wind, whose rare beauty had only a parallel in a severed tress, precious as the little head lying low in Mount Auburn.

"Mother! mother!" not from around this tree, nor yet that, did the little, merry face peep, nor from this grassy bank, nor that shaded pathway, nor yet by the cool plash of the fountain, where childish feet loved best to stray, did that most musical call come. Other little forms there were there—God grant them long to bless the homes they brighten—but not *hers*—not *hers*.

Beacon street, Boston's Fifth Avenue, is looking its loveliest now, since its inhabitants have had the good taste to drape their balconies and doorways with the luxuriant woodbine, tossing out its long, green tendrils, as the wind comes sweeping over Charles River, laden with sweets rifled from the hay-fields beyond. I should marvel, did I not know how powerless are outside belongings to secure happiness, or even content, that such residences should be abandoned by their inmates when most attractive; putting aristocracy out of the question of neighborhood, no lovelier spot could be found for a city home all the year round. What lunatic was permitted to daub the "State House" its present sulphureous hue I did not inquire; astonishment struck me dumb; I drove quickly past it to feast my eyes on the rural beauty of Cambridge, of which one never tires, no more than of sweet Mt. Auburn, which I will persist in preferring to Greenwood, though I have been talked out of breath so many times by the admirers of the latter, among whom I number myself, with the above amendment. Ah, here we are, now the old gateway is the same, under which so many bereaved ones have passed tearfully, saying, "Thou hast taken away my idol, and what have I left?"

Stay—what is this? Where are the tall sentinel pines, whose aromatic leaves, dropping upon the pathway, muffled the sound of our carriage wheels as we slowly passed into their dim shades, softening so tenderly the garish, mocking sunlight for weeping eyes, as the wind whispered through them, "Peace—be still!" Where are they? Like the face of a dear, long absent friend, upon whose breast I had often leaned, I yearned to see them. *Hewn down!* by the hand of "modern improvement!" Heaven grant us patience to look upon such sacrilege by the stupidity of somebody—it is little matter who—since a century could scarce make good the cruel devastation. I should like to take down a tall monument I saw in Mt. Auburn to a bogus philanthropist, and, effacing the lying inscription, write one to the memory of those giant pines, and erect it on the spot where they fell.[16] May the tongue be palsied that spoke their death-knell, before it does any more mischief. Well, it is of no use fretting—everybody says that when they are through doing it, and Mt. Auburn is not the place for anger; and yet, if there ever was an exceptionable case, this is it. I call upon every one whose dead are garnered there—to whom the place is holy—to join issue with me against this unpardonable desecration. One word more while on this subject. It seems hard that the owners of "lots" in Mt. Auburn, *living at a distance,* should see them, on their annual visits, overgrown with weeds and nettles for that reason. As I stood over *my* dead I felt grieved that the flowers planted by love, and watered by tears, should be so neglected by those who should perform the duty for which they are hired, without regard to eye-service.[17] Some day I shall lie there myself; till I do, this will not cease to pain me.

Apart from these things of which I have spoken, the general appearance of Mt. Auburn is much improved. The chapel especially, which has been renovated and adorned with two fine statues. The one to Chief Justice Story is a just tribute to the worth of the original, and a glory to the filial heart and hand of the sculptor.[18] The Tower is a great accession, and though I was too ill to get out of the carriage to see the view from the top, those of our party who did so, used up the dictionary in its praise. We returned by way of Brighton, which announced itself to our olfactories in the usual manner; from thence over the Western Avenue, home to our hotel. For the one hundred and fiftieth time I smiled at the wooden look of those Boston women, and the wooden way they locomote the streets. Boston and New York should be shook up in a bag together. It would be the salvation of both.

A Broad Hint to New Haven
August 3, 1867

MY DEAR LEDGER: I have had about as much pleasure crowded into my life since I left New York, as a mortal could well bear. Without abating one jot of my *mountain*-worship, I am magnetized over again by my old love—Lake Champlain. I can never tell you what a trance of delight was our lovely sail upon it to St. Albans. They who are in a hurry are welcome to take to the dusty, deafening, whizzing railroad cars; but for me, a seat on the nice, cleanly deck of a Lake Champlain boat, gliding past lovely wooded shores on either side, listening to the cool plash of the waves as they dash against them, and the sweet song of the birds as they come faintly to our ears; after weeks of hurry and fret, to pass from city entanglements and cares to this, was like the soothing caress of a dear hand on fevered temples. Ah! I am all right when I get with Nature—*she* has only words of peace for me. They who like may sit beside me reading the regulation-novel, or any other book, indeed, while the boat glides along; or they may retire stolidly to their state-room and doze the charmed hours away. Every moment to me is precious; every ripple on the lake, every shadow on the mountain side, every cloud on the sky. So I rather owed St. Albans a grudge, when that city abruptly put a stop to my nice dreams. Since, I have spent four days there, and I take it all back. I shake hands with her as though I had known her four years instead of four days. To breathe her air is like tasting rare wine. To gaze upon her glory of lake and mountain at sunrise and sunset, and mid-day, is to pray. How anybody manages in such a pure atmosphere to be sick or die, astonishes me. I pity the doctor who settles in that region, expecting to thrive by tombstones.

All hail to the St. Albanians for the example they have set New Haven in erecting a monster depot, airy, cleanly, substantial and handsome, for the benefit of the thousands of travellers whom it so comfortably shelters and welcomes. After perspiring in the close, dirty *sheds*, miscalled "depots," up and down in the land, one may be permitted a passing tribute to the model depot of St. Albans. It is a letter of introduction. Stepping from the cars into such a depot, one is sure of a hotel in the place, where can be found Christian beds, a sumptuous bill of fare, and civil treatment, all of which promises made by that imposing depot were fulfilled to the letter in our case. But I want St. Albans, before I come again, to plant shade trees on either side of *all* its principal streets. I want to see some flowers, too, around its houses, although if ever the absence of flowers might be forgotten, it is in a country possessing such grand lake and mountain scenery.

New York is to be well represented at St. Albans this summer. Where can you go where this is *not* the case? I found it so years ago, even at the head of Lake Superior, where I thought to see only wolves and Indians. It is not my intention to go abroad till I have seen something of my own dear land, though perish the thought that in *any* case I should ever admit that another was lovelier or better! Come up here and join us, dear *Ledger*, and see what a big parish you have, *out*side as well as *in*side of New York.

VIII

"Coats and trowsers have the best of it *everywhere*"

On Gendered Fashion

While the fashions may have changed since Fanny Fern's time, her commentary about gendered clothing norms will feel uncannily familiar to many readers today. In her writing about the fashion trends and rules for women and men, Fern raised awareness about the ways in which women's health was directly impacted by the restrictive clothing they were expected to wear. She also pointed out the hypocrisy of men who criticized women's fashion in a patriarchal society that demanded women's strict adherence to unrealistic standards of beauty and dress. Fern does not go as far as more radical clothing reformers of her time, such as Amelia Bloomer (and she admits that she is not a fan of the loose trousers popularized by the famous feminist lecturer), but she often pointed out the consequences of the arbitrary rules for women's attire and expressed envy of the bodily freedom men enjoyed in pants.

A Law More Nice than Just
July 10, 1858

Here I have been sitting twiddling the morning paper between my fingers this half hour, reflecting upon the following paragraph in it: "Emma Wilson was arrested yesterday for wearing man's apparel." Now, why this should be an actionable offense is past my finding out, or where's the harm in it, I

213

am as much at a loss to see. Think of the old maids (and weep) who have to stay at home evening after evening, when, if they provided themselves with a coat, pants and hat, they might go abroad, instead of sitting there with their noses flattened against the window-pane, looking vainly for "the Coming Man." Think of the married women who stay at home after their day's toil is done, waiting wearily for their thoughtless, truant husbands, when they might be taking the much needed independent walk in trowsers, which custom forbids to petticoats. And this, I fancy, may be the secret of this famous law—who knows? It *wouldn't* be pleasant for some of them to be surprised by a touch on the shoulder from some dapper young fellow, whose familiar treble voice belied his corduroys. That's it, now. What a fool I was not to think of it—not to remember that men who make the laws, make them to meet all these little emergencies.

Everybody knows what an everlasting drizzle of rain we have had lately, but nobody but a woman, and a woman who lives on fresh air and out-door exercise, knows the thraldom of taking her daily walk through a three weeks' rain, with skirts to hold up, and umbrella to hold down, and puddles to skip over, and gutters to walk round, and all the time in a fright lest, in an unguarded moment, her calves should become visible to some one of those rainy-day philanthropists who are interested in the public study of female anatomy.

One evening, after a long rainy day of scribbling, when my nerves were in double-twisted knots, and I felt as if myriads of little ants were leisurely traveling over me, and all for want of the walk which is my daily salvation, I stood at the window, looking at the slanting, persistent rain, and took my resolve. *"I'll do it,"* said I, audibly, planting my slipper upon the carpet. "Do what?" asked Mr. Fern, looking up from a big book. "Put on a suit of your clothes and take a tramp with you," was the answer. "You dare not," was the rejoinder; "you are a little coward, only saucy on paper." It was the work of a moment, with such a challenge, to fly up stairs and overhaul my philosopher's wardrobe. Of course we had fun. Tailors must be a stingy set, I remarked, to be so sparing of their cloth, as I struggled into a pair of their handiwork, undeterred by the vociferous laughter of the wretch who had solemnly vowed to "cherish me" through all my tribulations. "Upon my word, everything seems to be narrow where it ought to be broad, and the waist of this coat might be made for a hogshead; and, ugh! this shirt collar is cutting my ears off, and you have not a decent cravat in the whole lot, and your vests are frights, and what am I to do with my hair?" Still no reply from Mr. Fern, who lay on the floor, faintly ejaculating, between his fits of laughter, "Oh, my! by Jove!—oh! by Jupiter!"

Was that to hinder me? Of course not. Strings and pins, woman's never-failing resort, soon brought broadcloth and kerseymere to terms. I parted my hair on one side, rolled it under, and then secured it with hair-pins; chose the best fitting coat, and cap-ping the climax with one of those soft, cosy hats, looked in the glass, where I beheld the very fac-simile of a certain musical gentleman, whose photograph hangs this minute in Brady's entry.[1]

Well, Mr. Fern seized his hat, and out we went together. "Fanny," said he, "you must not take my arm; you are a fellow." "True," said I, "I forgot"; "and you must not help me over the puddles, as you did just now, and do, for mercy's sake, stop laughing. There, there goes your hat—I mean *my* hat; confound the wind! and down comes my hair; lucky 'tis dark, isn't it?" But oh, the delicious freedom of that walk, after we were well started! No skirts to hold up, or to draggle their wet folds against my ankles; no stifling vail flapping in my face, and blinding my eyes; no umbrella to turn inside out, but instead, the cool rain driving slap into my face, and the resurrectionized blood coursing through my veins, and tingling in my cheeks. To be sure, Mr. Fern occasionally loitered behind, and leaned up against the side of a house to enjoy a little private "guffaw," and I could now and then hear a gasping "Oh, Fanny!" "oh, my!" but none of these things moved me, and if I don't have a nicely-fitting suit of my own to wear rainy evenings, it is because—well, there *are* difficulties in the way. Who's the best tailor?

Now, if any male or female Miss Nancy who reads this feels shocked, let 'em! Any woman who likes, may stay at home during a three weeks' rain, till her skin looks like parchment, and her eyes like those of a dead fish, or she may go out and get a consumption dragging round wet petticoats; I won't—I positively declare I won't. I shall begin *evenings* when *that* suit is made, and take private walking lessons with Mr. Fern, and they who choose may crook their backs at home for fashion, and then send for the doctor to straighten them; I prefer to patronize my shoe-maker and tailor. I've as good a right to preserve the healthy body God gave me, as if I were not a woman.

A Law More Nice than Just, Number II
July 17, 1858

After all, having tried it I affirm, that nothing reconciles a woman quicker to her feminity, than an experiment in male apparel, although I still maintain that she should not be forbidden by law to adopt it when necessity requires; at least, not till the practice is amended by which a female clerk, who performs her duty equally well with a male clerk, receives less salary, simply because she is a woman.

To have to jump on to the cars when in motion, and scramble yourself on to the platform as best you may without a helping hand; to be nudged roughly in the ribs by the conductor with, "your fare, sir?" to have your pretty little toes trod on, and no healing "beg your pardon," applied to the smart; to have all the nice-looking men who used to make you such crushing bows, and give you such insinuating smiles, pass you without the slightest interest in your coat-tails, and perhaps push you against the wall, or into the gutter, with a word tabooed by the clergy. In fine, to dispense with all those delicious little politenesses, (for men are great bears to each other,) to which one has been accustomed, and yet feel no inclination to take advantage of one's corduroys and secure an equivalent by making interest with the "fair sex," stale to you as a thrice-told tale. Isn't *that* a situation?

To be subject to the promptings of that unstifleable feminine desire for adornment, which is right and lovely within proper limits, and yet have no field for your operations. To have to conceal your silken hair, and yet be forbidden a becoming moustache, or whiskers, or beard—(all hail beards, I say!). To choke up your nice throat with a disguising cravat; to hide your bust (I trust no Miss Nancy is blushing) under a baggy vest. To have nobody ask you to ice cream, and yet be forbidden, by your horrible disgust of tobacco, to smoke. To have a gentleman ask you "the time, sir?" when you are new to the geography of your watch-pocket. To accede to an invitation to test your "heft," by sitting down in one of those street-weighing chairs, and have one of the male bystanders, taking hold of your foot, remark, "Halloo, sir, you must not rest these upon the ground while you are being weighed," and go grinning away in your coat-sleeve at your truly feminine faux pas.

And yet—and yet—to be able to step over the ferry-boat chain when you are in a distracted hurry, like any other fellow, without waiting for that tedious unhooking process, and quietly to enjoy your triumph over scores of impatient-waiting crushed petticoats behind you; to taste that nice lager beer "on draught"; to pick up contraband bits of science in Medical Museums, forbidden to crinoline, and hold conversation with intelligent men, who supposing you to be a man, consequently talk sense to you. That is worth while.

Take it all in all, though, I thank the gods I am a woman. I had rather be loved than make love; though I could beat the makers of it, out and out, if I did not think it my duty to refrain out of regard to their feelings, and the final disappointment of the deluded women! But—oh dear, I want to do such a quantity of "improper" things, that there is not the slightest real harm in doing. I want to see and know a thousand things which are forbidden to flounces—custom only can tell why—I can't. I want the free use of my ankles, for this summer at least, to take a journey; I want to climb and wade, and tramp about, without giving a thought to my clothes; without carrying about with me a long procession of trunks and boxes, which are the inevitable penalty of femininity as at present appareled. I hate a Bloomer,[2] such as we have seen—words are weak to say how much; I hate myself as much in a man's dress; and yet I want to run my fingers through my cropped hair some fine morning without the bore of dressing it; put on some sort of a loose blouse affair—it must be pretty, though—and a pair of Turkish trousers—*not* Bloomers—and a cap, or hat—and start; "nary" a trunk—"nary" a band-box. Wouldn't that be fine? But propriety scowls and says, "aint you ashamed of yourself, Fanny Fern?" *Yes, I am*, Miss Nancy. I *am* ashamed of myself, that I haven't the courage to carry out what would be so eminently convenient, and right, and proper under the circumstances. I am ashamed of myself that I sit like a fool on the piazza of some hotel every season, gazing at some distant mountain, which every pulse and muscle of my body, and every faculty of my soul, are urging me to climb, that I may "see the kingdoms of the earth and the glory of them." I *am* ashamed of myself that you, Miss Nancy, with your uplifted forefinger and your pursed-up mouth, should keep me out of a dress in which only I can hope to do such things. Can't I make a compromise with you, Miss Nancy? for I'm getting restless, as these lovely summer days pass on. I'd write you such long accounts of beautiful things, Miss Nancy—things which God made for female as well as male eyes to see; and I should come home so strong and healthy, Miss Nancy—a freckle or two, perhaps—but who cares? O-h—n-o-w, Miss Nancy, d-o.—Pshaw! you cross old termagant. May Lucifer fly away wid ye.

Give It Up
January 7, 1860

Those women who are wasting their precious time trying to satisfy the male portion of our population as to the matter of dress, may as well draw a long breath, and rest from their labors. For a long time past, paragraph after paragraph, has been hurled at "hoops" by anxious fathers, husbands, brothers, lovers, and an army of men besides, whose pipe and cigar being wife, mother and child to them, had of course no call to say a word about it. Well—now hoops are gone out: or at least the use of them is mostly confined to Dinah and Biddy. Are the men well pleased? Not they. *Now* a new horror. They "suppose the women now will slink down Broadway looking like churns, or thread-papers."

Anon, the papers were lamenting that women would persist in wearing thin soled boots in sloppy and cold weather, in defiance of consumption and fever. The alarmed women, fearing that their coffins were bespoke, adopted the sensible india-rubber knee boot. Did the men encourage that? Not they. A general howl went up from all Corduroy-dum, of "disenchanting," "horrid," "frightful"; and suppressed grins greeted every female who ventured out in these dry-ankle-covers. Caricaturists were busy turning them into ridicule, and they were frowned down instanter.

Anon—male pocket-handkerchiefs were in request for the hecatombs of lovely creatures who were about to fall victims to neuralgia from the use of little bonnets. All coat-tail-dom wrung its manly hands and—*told the belle!* The frightened belle rushed into big bonnets. What is this day her reward? These very philanthropists are bewailing "that they cannot turn a street corner without a horrid vision of a coal-scuttle bonnet."

Now, don't all the world know that if women were actually to follow men's advice, and "dress sensibly," not a man would be seen in public with them? If any unbeliever doubts, let her try it. They'd dodge round corners, rush into shop-doors, and grow near-sighted to a degree that would be annihilating. I repeat it: if woman should *really* set about disregarding fashion whenever it interfered with her comfort or health, or both,—though she compromised neither her delicacy nor modesty by doing it—not one of these men who are eternally making such a pother about "dressing sensibly," would stand by her, much less walk with her. *They haven't the moral courage.*

As to "dressing sensibly"—let *them* set the example. Nothing more senseless than a shirt was ever invented. Washerwomen frightened into fits lest the bosom shouldn't be as rigid as a pine table. Collars stiffened up till the wearer is red—if not black in the face.—Wearing a thing on their heads that they are obliged to chase through the street-gutters every windy day.—Victims to tight boots, and tight gloves.—Experimenting on their beard and whiskers at the risk of being poisoned, on the appearance of every new hair-dye. Oh, pshaw—a fig for their advice or opinion.

A Voice from the Skating Pond
February 1, 1862

Coats and trowsers have the best of it *everywhere*, I exclaimed, for the thousandth time, as I looked at the delightful spectacle of the male and female skaters at the Central Park. Away went coat and trowsers, like a feather before the wind; free and untrammelled by dry-goods, and independent of any chance somerset; while the poor skirt-hampered women glided circumspectly after their much-needed health and robustness, with that awful omnipresent sense of *the proprieties*, (and—horror of horrors—a tumble!) which sends more of the dress-fettered sex to their graves every year than any disease *I* wot of. That a few women whom I saw there had had the perseverance to become tolerable skaters, with all that mass of dry-goods strung round their waists, is infinitely to their credit. How much *longer* and better they could have skated, disembarrassed, as men are, of these swaddling robes, common sense will tell anybody. I should like to see how long a *man's* patience would hold out, floundering round in them, while *he* learned to skate! And yet were a lady to adopt any other costume, how decent soever, or how eminently soever befitting the occasion, what a rolling of eyes and pursing of mouths should we see from the strainers at gnats and swallowers of camels. All these thoughts passed through my mind as I mixed in with the merry crowd on that bracing winter day, whose keen breath was like rare old wine. So did it stir and warm the blood; and I wondered, as I gazed at those dress-fettered women, whether those heathen nations who strangled their female babies at birth were as naughty as we had been told they were!

"Why don't *you* get up a skating costume, Fanny, and set them an example?" whispers a voice at my elbow. *Me?* why don't *I?* Because, sir, custom has made me a poor, miserable coward in these matters, like the rest of my sex, and because, moreover, sir, you would have no more courage to walk by my side in such a costume, than I should have to wear it. No, no; a crowd of curious men in my wake would be no more agreeable in reality than it is in perspective. It is brave *talking*, I know, but the time has not yet come when men, by refraining from rude remarks on a female pioneer, in such a cause, would remove one of the chief obstacles to its advancement. They "like healthy women"—oh, of course they do! but then, unfortunately, they like dainty prettiness of attire much better. Else, why don't they encourage women when they try to do a sensible thing? Why do they grin, and stroke their beards, and shrug their shoulders, and raise their eyebrows, and go home to Jane Maria, and say, "Let me catch *you* out in such a costume!" Till all that is done away with, we must be content to see puny, waxy-looking children, and read in "Notes on America" the usual number of stereotyped pages on "the fragility of our women." Now, let me say in closing that I don't wish to be misunderstood on this matter. I approve of no costume which a delicate-minded, self-respecting, dignified woman might not wear in public. But I will insist that nothing *can* be done in the way of reform, while husbands and fathers and brothers *sniff* the whole subject "under the table," as soon as it is mentioned. May every one of them have a yearly doctor's bill to pay as long as the moral law!

Sense and Shoes
February 8, 1862

Ladies have made a great advance lately in the matter of being properly *shod* for walking. We can remember when paper soles and silk stockings were quite as often seen on a winter pavement as anything more sensible. Now, even gentlemen themselves, scarce wear a thicker sole or warmer stocking. As a consequence, red cheeks have taken the place of blue noses; and though the family physician may have a fee or two less, we know of nobody else who can grumble. Ah! we forgot—the shoe-maker. *He* tells us, that since ladies took to thick soles he sells only one pair of boots where he used to sell a dozen. So that, as a matter of economy, it seems the ladies have reason to congratulate themselves on this blessed reform. Well, *"there's always something happening most times,"* as the old lady remarked. What next?

Fashion Edicts
April 26, 1862

With what oracular solemnity and deep sense of responsibility fashion-mongers promulgate their high and mighty decrees, which consign to oblivion a check or a stripe, or raise into favor a flounce or a tuck. Imagine a mother anxiously gazing over a newspaper for the list of killed or wounded, among which, perchance, might be her son, lighting upon the following paragraph:[3] "A shadowy hint reaches us that dresses are to be *gored* this summer, instead of being worn full, as usual." Or this: "As to the question of flowers in the hair, we hasten to inform our readers that this important question has not yet been definitely settled; in the mean time, let them rest assured that knots of ribbon will be perfectly safe to venture upon, though no lady, of course, who has a fair complexion, would peril her reputation by selecting yellow." Imagine a woman to whom life is earnest, who has a heart and soul, as well as a body, pondering absorbedly for hours over the unsolved mystery of a sleeve plaited or gathered, round, square or pointed, or searching precedents with a keen, lawyer-like gaze for six ruffles or ten. Heavens! what butterflies must those women needs be, who think and talk and live solely for these things, like the peacock, retiring into dark corners when they cannot strut in the sunshine in gorgeously spread plumage. One can imagine that a sensible, soulful woman may yet apparel herself, when there is a necessity for getting a change of clothing, in a tasteful manner, but to make it the *chief* object in life, to which everything else must bend; to dream of it, rising and sitting, going out and coming in, lying down and rising up, at any time, but more especially now, when such great issues are pending and such great questions are being solved before our eyes, and the eyes of the whole civilized world, the puerility of this is past all belief. There is indeed one aspect of this subject which may be viewed with complacency, and that is the amount of employment these chameleon edicts afford to thousands of operatives, mostly women. Every turn of fashion's revolving wheel, if it throw one portion of them in shadow, shedding pecuniary sunshine on the other. Of course dependent woman must earn her support, whenever, wherever, and howsoever she honestly can; all honor to her for bravely doing it, according to her several opportunities and capacities; but if she *could* set types in a printing office, though her fingers might not be so clean, yet her mind would stand less chance of *belittlement* than when employed in the various stages of dress-ornamentation. As to the unfitness of this or that employment, not usual for females, it is my opinion that a self-respecting, dignified woman need not always employ her whole existence in tossing peace-offerings to Mrs. Grundy.

What May Be Done in the Country
September 14, 1867

I have done marvelling that city-women walk so little. Gradually they will cease altogether, unless the dress-mania "lets up." Directly after breakfast, a healthy person desires out-of-door air; but at that time, in the city, a lady has on her "breakfast-robe," so-called; and, in order to go presentably out, she imagines it necessary to go to her room and remodel herself entirely. The robe must be exchanged for a walking-dress; the slippers must be discarded for boots; these boots have about six dozen buttons,—the button-fastener must be found, to secure them to the ankle. The white underskirt must be exchanged for a Balmoral, to match the outer-skirt.[4] The gloves, belt, and collar which accompany the suit must be hunted up. The hair must be re-arranged for the particular sort of hat worn. The parasol must be found, and the veil; and, by that time, if my lady's vitality and temper are not entirely exhausted, she *may* be able to walk 'round one block, without creeping into an omnibus or ordering a carriage.

Now, here in the country, all this ceremony is dispensed with. If a woman has common sense, she will strike for her freedom *here*, what vassalage soever she may feel constrained to undergo on city pavements. With a sun-umbrella and thick shoes, she may go bonnet-less, in her morning-calico, all day; and never change her apparel from sunrise to sunset, unless she meets with some accident. The blessed, dewy, fresh hours of early morning may be devoted to something else than the looking-glass; and, if she is anything but a stick, she will be better, and happier, and healthier for this untrammelled enjoyment of them. Compared to the stiff, artificial, slow promenading of a city pavement, it is woman's heaven.

Here she may go over fences, if she have a gift for gymnastics, without instruction; and the clumsier she is, the more fun is to be got out of it. As to clothes,—haven't I said that they were of no account? Then there are hills to be climbed, and hills to be chased down, and ditches and brooks to cross, and snakes and cows with vicious facial expression to extemporize a shrill concert at very short notice.

And oh, my dear girls, with what a railroad-velocity does *love* travel in the country! the city, for a hunting-ground, is a fool to it. When a man has nothing else to do, he makes love as naturally as a duck goes into water; and you might *lasso* here in the country with half the pains you usually take when there. Now, in the *city,* you—Maria—stand no chance at all; there are too many other Marias engaged in the same business. And then, if you succeed in securing his attention there, your mamma, or papa, or your brother, or some prying "poke" of an aunt, or uncle is always in the parlor, if he calls; but, here, you may "spear" your fish at any moment. There is the piazza, where the hint is dropped—not to him, of course, (you are not so green as that,) but *at* him—about the grove, or the hill, or the wood, or the lake where *you*, Maria, always go at such a time. You are perfectly and properly "astonished," when, afterwards, you find him there,—by accident! Then, the little coquetry of lingering on the fences, because *he* is helping you over, and because your boots fit so nicely. Then the flower or the leaves, which you "can't really put in your hair without a looking-glass"; and which he kindly volunteers to secure for you. Then the terrors you undergo at frogs and things, which necessitate his manly protection!

Then, if he chance to sleep late in the morning, after such a day of arduous devotion, what is to hinder your borrowing somebody's baby from its nurse, and strolling directly under the window where "you hadn't the slightest idea he slept," and singing the dear little "titsy-witsy" the whole of Mother-Goose, from beginning to end, till you accomplish the desired result? Now, you *know* that's the way you do; and, if you had sixty more freckles than you have, and your shoulder-blades were much more prominent, and your nose sharper, and your waist square-er, he would still think you an angel, because you can keep at him all the time and follow him cunningly up, without any competition worth speaking of; and, moreover, because every thing in nature as well as you—birds, beasts, fish, and fowl—are also in the wooing line. Oh, mark my words, girls: the *city*, as a hunting-ground, is a fool to the country!

IX

"What a pity all editors are not *gentlemen*"

On Newspapers and Editors

Immersed in the world of newspapers throughout her entire life, perhaps no nineteenth-century woman was more qualified than Fanny Fern to offer criticism and advice to editors. In her comments about newspaper trends of the time, she held editors accountable for the power they wielded with the presentation of current events, information, and entertainment for their readers. As a humorist herself, she nevertheless believed that some topics were off limits; she objected to satirical reporting of police blotters, for example, because of the undue pain and embarrassment it would cause the innocent loved ones of those who were arrested. She also took aim at misogynistic editorial commentary and exposed the double standards that newspaper editors perpetuated.

Editors
From Fern Leaves from Fanny's Port-Folio, *1853*

"We know of no state of slavery on earth like that attendant upon the newspaper life, whether it be as director or subordinate. Your task never ended, your responsibility never secured, the last day's work is forgotten at the close of the day on which it appeared, and the dragon of tomorrow waits open-mouthed to devour your thoughts, and snap up one morsel more of your vexed existence. Be as successful as is the nature of things to be;—write with the least possible degree of exertion;—be indifferent to praise, and lion-hearted against blame;—still will the human heart wear out before its time, and your body, if not your mind, exhibit every symptom of dry rot."—*Newspaper.*

"Dry" fiddlestick! That man's dinner did not digest; or the wind was "dead east"; or his wife had astonished him with a pair of twins; or his boots pinched him.

I will wager you a new neck-tie that he is one of the cross-grained sort, who would go to fisticuffs with Gabriel and raise a rebellion in Paradise. There is not a word of truth in what he says. I have been behind the curtain, and I will speak this time! I tell you that editors are just the fattest, sleekest, happiest, most rolicksome, the cleverest, brightest, most intelligent and lovable set of humans in existence; and the only reason they don't "own up," is because they are afraid to let the world in general know how many little favors and perquisites fall to their lot!

They go down to the office in the morning,—after a careful toilette and a comforting breakfast,—make up a fire in the stove hot enough to roast an Icelander, "hermetically seal" every door and window, put on a pair of old slippers, light a cigar, draw up a huge easy-chair, stick their feet up twice as high as their heads, and—proceed to business (?); that is to say, between the whiffs of that cigar they tell excruciatingly funny stories, poke each other in the ribs, agree to join the mutual admiration society, retail all the "wire-pulling" behind the scenes, calculate which way the political cat is going to jump, and shape the paragraphs accordingly;—tell who threw that huge bouquet, at last night's concert, to Madam Fitz Humbug;—shake hands, and make room for all the "hale-fellows-well-met" that drop in to see them;—keep their intellects sharpened up by collision with the bright and gifted,—in short, live in one perpetual clover-field, and when they die, all the newspapers write nice little obituary notices, and give them a free pass to Paradise. I would like to know if that looks like a "vexed existence?"

Time would fail me to tell of the wedding-cake, and flowers, and fruits, and annuals, embroidered purses and tasselled smoking-caps, pretty little notes, braided watchchains, the handkerchiefs they get perfumed, and gloves mended,—for nothing!

How everybody nudges his neighbor, when they appear at lecture, or concert, or opera, and says, "There's that clever fellow, the editor of The Comet!" How he has a season-ticket to a free seat by a Frog Pond;

how he has,—but there is no use in telling all a body knows! Christopher Columbus! Editor's life a "vexed existence!"

"Let those laugh now who never laughed before, And those who always laughed now laugh the more."

A Breakfast Reverie on Ledger Day
November 6, 1858

What *did* Adam and Eve do without newspapers? That's what I want to know. Nobody killed or married, no steamboat explosions, no railroad accidents. The beasts and beastesses all tame and well behaved; breakfast cooked to their taste, hanging ready on vine and bush; no clothes to mend; nothing to do but to make love all day long—not even the consolation of a cigar for Adam, or a bit of scandal for his rib. The serpent must have been a blessing; no wonder Eve dallied with him. "Satan finds some mischief still for idle hands to do," and heads, too. A newspaper would have saved her. In the first place, there would have been the excitement arising from her aggravating husband having the first reading of it, smoking all the while, so that she was obliged to pass it through quarantine before she could read all about "the frightful *lass* of life," as the pathetic newsboys have it. I wonder would she have considered it swerving from her conjugal allegiance not to agree with Adam in politics, or on the great stirring questions of the day, and if she would have waxed warm in the discussion of them, and pulled his whiskers. I wonder if he *had* whiskers. I thought of it the other Sunday "in meetin'" when the minister was reading about him. Of course I ought not, but I did; and I thought, too, how nice it must have been to be loved by the *first* man, before his heart was riddled through and through like a target, as men's hearts are now-a-days, before they are twenty. I am afraid, though, Adam grew tame and stupid, else Eve never would have flirted with the serpent; not that I consider that an excuse—I wouldn't have you think so. Oh, no. In fact, I don't know why I made that remark. I suppose it must have been a natural one, though, else it would not have suggested itself; not that I approve of everything natural, either—not at all—and I wish you would not keep catching me up so on everything I say, as if I need weigh every word before I put it down. If there is anything I hate, it is writing that way; I won't do it for anybody except Mr. Bonner, who has too much good sense to ask it—who gives me a wide pasture to prance in, because he is sure that I will not jump the fence, though the conservatives sometimes needlessly hold their breath for fear I will.

Well, it is a long jump from Adam and Eve to Mr. Bonner, and yet I can't help wishing they had been acquainted. I can't help thinking that if Adam had subscribed, like other good husbands, for the NEW YORK LEDGER, Eve never would have got into trouble. I'm convinced of it, and have long since ceased upbraiding her for that very reason. It was not her fault that Sylvanus Cobb, Jr., and Emerson Bennett were not born.[1] The panthers and lions about her were all well enough, but they didn't show fight; there were no perilous adventures, no hair-breadth escapes, no storms, no "row" any how; she tired of dew and humming birds, just as I should. Now think what a blessing Bennett and Cobb would have been; think of the agonizing delight of leaving a heroine hanging by the eyelids, not to be extricated from her perilous position till the following Thursday, when the next LEDGER should be "out," for they know too much to leave their readers easy in their minds a whole week. Ah, you may sniff at them, you superfine fellows, who find it difficult to keep yourselves in cigars; but if they were not wanted they would not be run after, I can tell you that.

I should like to compute the lips which say every Thursday, "Ah, 'tis LEDGER day, is it not?" I never see that printing press flying round like mad in Fulton street, throwing the sheets to the four winds, that I don't feel like giving three cheers for Robert Bonner, whose heart is as big as his subscription list, and that's saying considerable, and who deserves, a hundred times told, every mill that his industry and energy have earned; and now, when he reads this, he may blush if he likes—I shan't.[2]

For Whom the Cap Fits
November 20, 1858

The other day I took up my morning paper, one third of which was filled with an elaborate account of the beastly, disgraceful fight between two human battering rams, called—par courtesy—pugilists.[3] Turning to the other side of the paper I saw an editorial article denouncing in no measured terms the brutality of the thing, denouncing the laws which wink at such nuisances, but still—deeming it their duty as journalists "catering to the desire of the public," minutely to chronicle the alpha and omega of the whole affair *to lay upon our family table.* Beautiful consistency. It won't do, gentlemen; if, instead of hiding yourselves behind the flimsy screen of "duty as public journalists," and all that transparent trash, you had said—honestly—"confound the morality of the thing, we must make hay while the sun shines—*it will sell so many hundreds more of our paper,* and if we don't do it the other papers will pocket the coppers"; you should have said it, and I would have respected you. What humbugs you must be when *"a woman"* can see through you!

Comic Tragedies
October 29, 1859

We are about to say a word on a practice quite too common in some newspapers. We refer to the flippant manner in which the misfortunes and misdemeanors of certain classes,—brought to the notice of our courts,—are reported for the amusement of the community at large. Surely, it is melancholy enough that a drunken mother should be picked up in the gutter with her unconscious babe, or a young girl, scarcely in her teens, be found guilty of theft; or, that a husband and father should beat or murder her whom he had sworn to cherish, without narrating it after this heartless fashion.

For instance:

> John Flaherty, after beautifully painting a black-and-blue rim round his wife's eyes, was brought into court this morning to answer the question why he preferred that particular color; and not being able to give a satisfactory reason for the same, he was treated to a pleasant little ride to a stone building, where he was accommodated with a private room, board and lodging included.

Or thus:

> Mary Honoria, scarlet-lipped, plump, and sweet sixteen, being fond of jewelry on her pretty person, and having stolen her mistress's watch, was waited upon by a gallant policeman, who escorted her little ladyship into court, in the presence of an admiring crowd, before whom her black eyes sparkled with a rage that but added new beauty to their lustre.

Now, we protest against this disgusting, demoralizing and heartless mention of the sins and follies of poor wretches, the temptations of whose lot are as the sands of the sea-shore for multitude; who—ill-paid, ill-fed, worse-lodged, disheartened, discouraged—fall victims to the snares, in the shape of low groggeries, set for them by the very men who laugh over *their* well-spread breakfast tables, at this pitiful and revolting recital of their success. *Oh, write over against the poor wretch's name—as God does—why he or she fell!* or at least cease making it the subject for a jeer. Make it *your* son, *your* daughter, and then pen that flippant, heartless paragraph if you can. And yet, it was somebody's son, or daughter, or sister, or husband, unworthy it may be, (who is not?) but alas! often forgiven, and still dearly loved, to whose home that paragraph may come like a poisoned arrow, wounding the innocent, paralyzing the hand which was powerless enough before, to struggle with its hapless fate; for not on the guilty does such blight fall heaviest. The young boy—the toiling, unprotected daughter—the aged mother—ah!—what if they were *yours?*

A Word to Editors
January 21, 1860

I wonder are Editors aware of how much importance is their Poet's corner! I wonder if they know that the most inveterate pursuer of brooms and gridirons that ever kept a good man's house tidy, likes a bit of sentiment, in that shape, in the family paper. I wonder do Editors know, how, when the day's work is done, she likes to pull that paper out from some old tea-caddy, or broken flower-pot—that long ago fell into disuse, and seating herself with a long-drawn breath of relief in the old fashioned chair, where all her Tommys and Marys have been rocked, give herself up to the quiet enjoyment of its pages. Presently—as she reads—a tear gathers in her eye; she dashes it quickly away with an "ah—me," and laying her head back upon the chair, and closing eyes that were once much bluer than now, she is soon far—far away from the quiet home where her treadmill round of every-day duties has been for many years so faithfully performed, and—perhaps—alas! so thanklessly accepted. The cat comes purring round her feet, and Tray comes scratching at the door, but she does not move, till the sound of a heavy and familiar footstep is heard, in the entry or hall; then—starting up, and taking her scissors from the long pocket at her side, she clips the precious verses from the paper and hides them in her bosom. Perhaps *you* might turn up your critical nose at those verses; never mind—they have touched *her* heart; and many times when she is alone, she will read them over; and so long as they hold together, she will keep them in a little needle case in her work-box, to read when "things go wrong," and a good, safe cry will ease the heart.

Her good man picks up the mutilated paper and she says, "it was only a bit of poetry, John." Now, there are more Johns than one in the world, but he don't think of *that*, as turning to some political article he says, "oh, you are quite welcome to all that sort of stuff"; nor does he know how much that other John, had to do with her crying over those verses, which somebody certainly must have written, who—like herself—had married the wrong John.

And now, gentlemen Editors, crowd what else you may out of your papers, but *don't crowd out the poetry, or think it of small consequence.* Take the affidavit of one who has seen the clipped verses from your papers, hid away in pocket-books, tucked away in needle-cases, speared upon pin-cushions, pinned up on toilet glasses, and murmured over in the mystic hour of twilight, just before *"John comes home to tea,"*—and always have a bit of poetry in your columns for her who has so potent a voice in the choice of a family paper. I publicly promulgate this bit of wisdom, though I am very well aware, that you will pass it off for your own, and neither credit *me* nor yet the LEDGER for it!

Gentle Shepherd Tell Me Why?
February 16, 1861

I rise, Mr. Public, with some hesitation (being born to a bonnet, through no fault of mine), to ask a question: *Why is it necessary to sexualize newspapers?* Why cannot an intelligent woman appreciate a paper which commends itself to the perusal of an intelligent man? I don't fancy this Shaker way of seating the sisters on one side of the house, and the brethren on the other. It is my present intention to cross over and take a seat, on this question, with the brethren. Perhaps you will answer that the majority of women are *not* "intelligent." Granting this for the sake of the argument,—though I will say I've found as many male as female fools in my travels,—are these "ladies'" papers and periodicals particularly adapted to the purpose of rendering the dear creatures more intelligent? I trust there's no harm in asking the question. Now, a "Family paper" does not excite my ire; although it is my private opinion that what generally comes recommended as "fit to lay on the family table," had better be *under* it. A family paper, I say, don't irritate me; because it puts my understanding on a level with those of the hats in the house; but when you hand me a regular out and out "ladies' paper," so called, I am very apt to throw up the window for a little fresh air.

The Fly in the Ointment
From Ginger-Snaps, *1870*

I do not know who writes the editorials on the "Woman Question" in its various aspects, in our more prominent New York papers. I read them from day to day, with real disappointment at their immaturity, their flippancy, their total lack of manliness, and respect for, or appreciation of, true womanhood. I say this in no spirit of bitterness, but of real sorrow, that men stepping into the responsible position they hold on those papers, have not better considered the subjects of which they treat. That the writers are not known outside the office, seems to me a very unmanly reason for their misrepresentations. Every morning I ask, over my coffee, Have these men mothers, sisters, wives, who so persistently misrepresent the doings of self-respecting, self-supporting, intelligent women? Does *Congress* make no mistakes, that women should be expected, in their pioneering, to have arrived at absolute perfection? Is there no heat, in debate, on *its* floor; no uncourteousness of language? Did not one member, a short time since, call out there to have another member "spanked"? Does the speaker's mallet never call to order, men selected by their constituents, because supposed most intelligently to represent the various local and other interests of the country? Does the cut of a man's hair or coat injuriously or approbatively affect his speech upon the floors? Does anybody care what color it is, or how worn? I ask myself these questions when I read reports of "strong-minded women's meetings," as they are sneeringly termed, which consist mainly on the absence of a "long train" to their dresses, or the presence of it; on the straightness of their hair, or the frizzing of it; on the lack of ornamentation, or the redundance of it. This mocking, Mephistopheles-dodging of the real questions at issue, behind flimsy screens, seems to me not only most unworthy of these writers, but most unworthy of, and prejudicial to, the prominent journals in which they appear.

If they think that women make such grave mistakes,—mistakes prejudicial to the great interests they seek publicly to promote, the great wrongs they seek to right,—would it not be kinder and more manly, courteously to point them out, if so be that they themselves know "a more excellent way"?

Among all these women, are there *none* who are intelligent, intellectual, earnest, *and modest withal?* Have the editors of these very papers in which these attacks appear, never gladly employed just such, to lend grace, wit, and spirit to their own columns, that they have only sneers and taunts for the cause they espouse, and never a brave, kind, sympathetic recognition of their philanthropic efforts? Is the cause so utterly Quixotic, espoused by such women, who make their own homes bright with good cheer, neatness, taste, and wholesome food, that they cannot gallantly extend a manly hand after it and help them *over* those bright thresholds, and out into a world full of pain and misery, to lift the burden from their less favored sisters?

If they have the misfortune not to know such women among "the strong-minded," would it not be well to seek them out, and better inform themselves on the subjects upon which they daily write?

The pioneer women who have bravely gone forward, and still keep "marching on," undaunted in the face of this unmanly and ungenerous dealing, have, doubtless, counted the cost, and will not be hindered by it. I do not fear that; but I *do* regret that any editor of a prominent paper in New York should belittle it and himself, by allowing any of his employés to keep up this boyish pop-gun firing into the air.

The other night, I attended a lecture, the proceeds of which were to be devoted to a charitable institution for women.

Now here was a man willing to do this for the particular women's charity to be benefited by it, but he couldn't do it without stepping out of his way to sneer at female suffrage and kindred movements which are advocated and engineered by pure, intelligent, cultivated, earnest women, or fixing his seal of approbation on this particular branch of philanthropy, as the only remedy for all the ills that come of an empty purse and a grieved heart.

And just here is the fly in all these philanthropic ointments. Mix your medicines in *my* shop, or they will turn out poisons. That is the spirit. Now I don't believe that one society, or one man or woman, is the pivot on which this universe turns; and wishing well, as I do every progressive, humanitarian movement, I deplore that its leaders will not keep this fact in mind. I don't say that I wish *women* would keep it in mind, for I am a diligent reader of newspapers, and I see men every day ignoring this broad foundation of civilization. I see them making mouths at each other over a political bone or religious fence; or I hear naughty names called, because one man grabbed a bit of news for his paper, and scampered off with it to the dear public, before his editorial neighbor got scent of it. Oh, women don't do all the gossip and slander and back-biting in the world. They don't make all the silly or stupid speeches either. Nor do they "rush into print," any oftener than certain unquiet male spirits, "thirsting for notoriety," as the phrase goes, who think they know when a colt is a horse, and *vice versa*, better than any other man, because they studied Greek at Oxford. Humbug is not always a female, but when humbug *is* a female, she generally hails from the top round of the ladder! I am happy to say that, though I may be putting a stone into the hands of mine adversary by the admission!

Human nature might be improved, even in the year 1869. How glad the pop-gun clergyman of a small parish is, when some clerical big-gun is supposed to make a false move on the sacerdotal chequer-board! How he rushes publicly to "deplore" that his "dear brother in Christ should lay himself open to the world's censure in this manner"! His "dear brother's" popularity and big salary were not the animus of *that* criticism—oh, no! Now I'm not one of those who believe that "a minister" is certainly a saint, above his fellows; or that Christianity is benefited by refusing to admit the shortcomings of church-members. I once heard Rev. Dr. Hall preach a sermon on this subject, every word of which was pure gold and ought to be printed in pamphlet form and placed in the pews of all our churches.

"Mix your medicines in my shop, or they will be poisons!" How sick I am of it! There is so much elbow room in the world, why fight only for one corner? But men, set us "weak women" such a terrible example, fighting and squabbling about straws, and whining when they are defeated. Now, if instead of wasting their time this way, or idling it away as fashionable loungers,—I speak after the manner of the New York————to women,—if instead of belonging to useless up-town clubs, where with the heads of their canes in their mouths, they sit in the day-time, measuring passing female ankles, or drinking and talking male scandal, or betting;—if instead they would—each butterfly son of them—take some good, interesting book, and finding some tenement house, sit down of an evening and amuse some laboring man, who would else flee from the discomforts of such a place to the nearest grog-shop, how noble would this male butterfly of Fifth Avenue then appear! In fact, this particular form of benevolence commends itself to me as the only one that could rescue him from the butterfly existence of up-town clubs.

A thought strikes me! As the "New York————" remarks, when advising women to teach sewing to poor girls, "but perhaps these female butterflies of Fifth Avenue don't know themselves how to sew." Alas! Should these male butterflies of the Fifth Avenue club-houses not know how to read, when they get to the tenement house of their poor brother!

Now, to conclude, I see nothing antagonistic to a sewing-machine in a woman's vote, but the Editor of the New York——is always throwing a blanket over a woman's head, for fear she will see a ballot-box. You may make soup, my dear, graciously says he, for poor women; or flannel shirts for very little paupers, if you'll promise not to burn your fingers in politics. That never'll do, my dear! It is *not* coarse for you to scramble at a matinee for seats, and elbow and jostle, and push men's hats awry—oh, no! that's legitimate—but to subject yourself to this kind of thing at the ballot-box, would be to forfeit man's love, and soil both your skirts and reputation.

Some Hints to Editors
From Ginger-Snaps, *1870*

What a pity when editors review a woman's book, that they so often fall into the error of reviewing the *woman* instead. For instance, "she is young and attractive, and will probably before long find her legitimate sphere in matrimony; or she is an old maid—what can she know of life except through a distorted medium? Let her wait, if so she be able, till some man is deluded into inviting her to change her name. That appears to be her present need. Or she has the affectation of writing over a *nom de plume*—and must, perforce, be a fool. Or she *did* write a preface to her book; or she *omitted* writing a preface to her book, as one might expect of a woman. Or we hear she is a widow; and notoriety is probably her object in writing."

I introduced this article by saying what a pity that editors in reviewing a woman's book should so often only review the woman. Perhaps I should have said, what a pity all editors are not *gentlemen*. It is very easy to determine this question, if one keeps the general run of editorial articles. Not that it does not sometimes happen that, in the editor's necessary absence, some substitute may get him into "hot water"; or, as a foreigner who once tried to use this expression, called it "*dirty water*,"—but taking the general tone of editorial articles, from one day or one week to another, the want of courtesy and self-respect, or the lack of it, are patent to the intelligent reader.

It is a pity that an editor should not be a gentleman, *for his own sake*, and because no position can be more honorable than his, if he choose to make it so, nor more influential for good or evil. Think of the multitude he addresses—the thinking men and women who pass his columns under critical review. Surely, this is a career not to be lightly esteemed, not to be slurred over bunglingly. Surely, this messenger crossing the sacred threshold of home, might well step carefully, reverentially, discreetly, and discuss fairly, justly, all topics especially connected with home duties and home responsibilities. Surely, his advertising list, if he have one, should be a *clean* one, such as any frank-browed, hitherto innocent young boy, might read. Surely, the maiden, whose horizon is not bounded by a strip of ribbon or silk, or even the marriage altar; should have the great questions of the day, relating to the future of her sex, not brushed aside with a contemptuous sniff, or treated with flippant ridicule, because this is the shortest and easiest way of disposing of that which requires thought and fair deliberation.

It seems so strange to me, who hold in such exalted estimation an editor's calling, that one should ever be found willing to belittle it; it is also a great comfort to know that there are those who hold this their position, for honor and interest second to none, and in this light conscientiously conduct their paper, so far as their strength and means allow.

This would be a very stupid world, I grant, if individuality were not allowed in the editorial chair as well as elsewhere; but leaving a wide margin for this, is there not still room in many newspapers for more justice, manliness, courtesy, and, above all, respectful mention of woman, even though the exigencies of her life may compel her to address the public.

There is a practice of certain penny-a-liners which cannot be too severely reprehended. We do not refer to their personal descriptions of public persons, male and female, which are often wholly false—they having mistaken some one else for the individual they wished to describe; and if certain of the identity, generally "doing" the description in the worst possible taste. All this is bad enough; but we refer now to cases where a forgery or a murder is committed. Not contented with working up these cases in all their harrowing and often disgusting details, your barren penny-a-liner, catching at the least straw of an idea to secure another penny for another line, states that the criminal in question is son of the Hon. Samuel So-and-so, nephew of Mr. So-and-so, a gentlemen well known in the fashionable world, and brother of the beautiful Miss Smith who was so much admired in society last winter. Now, to say that a man who would recklessly carry distress to innocent persons, already sufficiently crushed by their calamity, should be horse-whipped, is a mild way of putting it. No dictionary could do such cold-blooded atrocity justice. Of course such items help sell a paper; but, alas, how low must be that editor's standard of journalism who permits his employés to pander to so corrupt and ghoul-like a taste! I think, could he sometimes look in upon the sorrowing family circle, which he has assisted to drag into this kennel publicity, or if he could suffer in his own family that which he so remorselessly deals out to another, he might realize the deadly nature of these poisoned arrows which he aims at his neighbor's heart.

Again, because the victims so assailed have not the prefix of "Hon." to their names, and have no "fashionable and beautiful sister," or "prominent and wealthy uncle," shall we therefore excuse this cowardly attack upon their poor hearths and homes? Let any one run over certain police reports of the day, if he would see how misery and misfortune are treated as a jest, by these small, brainless wits hard up for a subject. One's blood boils, that the human being exists who could regard such things from the standpoint of a circus clown. In fact, a circus clown is respectable in comparison, since his jests are legitimate and harmless.

These gentry never did me any personal harm.

True, black hair has often been awarded me, instead of light, by these scribblers, "who were on very intimate terms with me," and I have measured six feet in height, instead of four and a half; and I have "a stylish carriage and footmen," which I fervently wish the international copyright law would drive up to my door, bating the usual vulgar livery; also, half the things which they have asserted I "waste my earnings upon" would be agreeable to possess, and of course I grieve to take them down a single peg on all these statements; but lying did not die with the serpent in Eden, for his slimy trail is all through newspaperdom, save and except the——now don't you wish you knew?

No humane or decent person, can read the police reports in some of the papers in New York, without feeling unutterable loathing and contempt for the writers. Is it not enough that these poor wretches, in their down-ward course, have lost almost the faintest impress of immortality, that one who at least bears the semblance of manhood, can stand over them and manufacture coarse jibes by the yard, to be perused by young people at the family hearth-stone? It is a disgrace to our civilization, and to the paper in whose columns they appear.

How would these writers like it, if the sister who once shared their cradle—having, in some mad moment, thrown away all in life that is pure and sweet to women—should she be brought up among that wretched crowd for sentence, how would he like it, to have her spoken of in this manner?—

"Miss Josephine Jones, a frail sister, with a bruised nose that once had been prettier, and a bonnet that did *not* originate in Paris, was charged with getting drunk, and tearing the hair from Miss Alice Carr's red head. The hair was produced in court, but for some inexplicable reason the clerk of the court seemed disinclined to touch it. Miss Josephine was found guilty, and gathering up the remnant of a greasy silk gown in her fair hand, she walked gracefully forth, to be provided with lodgings and grub, free of expense, on Blackwell's Island, where so many of her sex rusticate for the pleasant winter months."

Or, suppose he had a young brother, who had recklessly thrown off home influences, and, before reaching maturity, was brought into court as a common drunkard, how would he relish, having him spoken of in this manner?—

> "An infant of twenty-one, named Harry Dexter, with blear eyes, and torn hat slouched over his swollen mug, was next called up. His boots and the blacking-brush seemed not to have had a very intimate acquaintance of late, and the laundress had evidently, for some cause or other, neglected his linen. His youthful hands also would have been improved by a dexterous use of soap and water. Young Harry had no occasion to inquire the way to his future boarding house, having often ridden down on previous occasions in that accommodating omnibus called the Black Maria, to take a sail at the city's expense to Pauper's Island."

We might multiply instances of this heartless and disgusting way of speaking of the faults and vices of our fellow-creatures, but this specimen will suffice to show the spirit in which they are penned. Nor is it any excuse, that many of the friends of these wretched beings can neither read or write, nor by any possibility ever be wounded by these so-called *jocular* allusions. I insist that the effect on the young people of our community is demoralizing. God knows that in the crowded city, with its whirling life, we have hard work enough to avoid jostling aside the urgent claims of the erring and unfortunate around us, without such help as this from the devil. It is bad enough "to pass by on the other side" when Christian charity challenges pity and help; but what must that man be made of, who would stand over a crushed fellow-being, and, for a few dollars, make merry with his misery? Surely, it seems to me, that the editors of the papers where these disgraceful items appear, cannot be aware how disgusting they have become, to those who would else gladly welcome their daily issues in the family.

X

"I am sick of flummery and nonsense and humbug and pretension of every kind"

On Pet Peeves, Nuisances, and Miscellaneous Grievances

Snoops, show-offs, snobs, and smokers: they were all regularly skewered in Fanny Fern's weekly column. Fern also had little patience for hypocrites, headaches, or annoying smells, and some of her edgiest humor and most relatable observations are found in these articles about everyday aggravations. In her savaging of annoying personality types, Fern targeted men and women in equal measure, perhaps appeasing the readers who accused her of a bias against men. Fern's readers undoubtedly speculated about the real-life models for her pointed caricatures of irritating people, but they could also easily picture the insufferable "Aunt Peckey" or "*blasé* man" in their own lives. A selection of Fern's more cheerful and uplifting commentary is featured in the next chapter.

A Headache
March 21, 1857

Now I am in for it, with one of my unappeasable headaches. Don't talk to me of doctors; it is incurable as a love-fit; nothing on earth will stop it; you may put that down in your memorandum-book. Now, I suppose everybody in the house to-day will put on their creakingest shoes; and everybody will go up and down stairs humming all the tunes they ever heard, especially those I most dislike; and I suppose everything that is cooked in the kitchen will boil and stew over, and the odor will come up to me; and I have *such* a nose! And I suppose all the little boys in the neighborhood, bless their little restless souls, will play duets on tin-pans and tin-kettles; and I suppose everybody who comes into my room to ask me how I do, will squeak that horrid door, and *keep* squeaking it; and I suppose that unhappy dog confined over in that four-square-feet yard, will howl more deliriously than ever; and Mr. Jones's obnoxious blind will flap and bang till I am as crazy as an omnibus-driver who has a baulky horse, and whose passengers are hopping out behind without paying their fare; and I suppose some poor little child will be running under the window every now and then, screaming "Mother," and whenever I hear that, I think somebody wants *me*; and I've no doubt there will be "proof" to read to-day, and that that pertinacious and stentorian rag-man will lumber past on his crazy old cart, and insist on having some of my dry goods; and I feel it in my bones that oysters and oranges, and tape, and blacking, and brooms, and mats, and tin-ware, will settle and congregate on this side-walk, and assert their respective claims to my notice, till the sight of an undertaker would be a positive blessing.

Whack! how my head snaps! Don't tell me any living woman ever had such a headache before—because it will fill me with disgust. What o'clock is it? "Twelve." Merciful man! only twelve o'clock! I thought it was five. How am I to get through the day, I would like to know, for this headache won't let up till sundown; it never does. "Read to me?" What'll you read? "Tom Moore!"[1]—as if I were not sick enough already! Moore! with his nightingales, and bulbuls, and jessamines; and loves and doves, and roses and poesies—till the introduction of an uneducated wildcat, or the tearingest kind of a hyena in his everlasting gardens, would be an untold relief. No—I hate Moore. Beside—he is the fellow who said, "When away from the lips that we love, we'll make love to the lips that are near."[2] No wonder he was baptized *more*—carnivorous old profligate.

"Will I have a cup of tea?" No, of course I won't. I'm not an old maid. Tea! I'd like a dose of strychnine. There goes my head again—I should think a string of fire-crackers was fastened to each hair. Now the pain is in my left temple; now it is in my eyeballs; now—oh dear—it is everywhere. Sit down beside me, on the bed—don't jar it; now put your cold hand on my forehead—so—good gracious! there's a hand-organ! I knew it—the very one I moved here to get rid of. Playing the same old tune, too, composed of three notes: "tweedle—dum—tweedle—dee!"

Now if that organ-man would pull each of my finger and toe-nails out by the roots, one by one, I wouldn't object, but that everlasting "tweedle—" oh dear!—Or if a cat's tail were to be irretrievably shut into yonder door—or a shirt-sleeve should be suddenly and unexpectedly thrown around an old maid's neck in this room, anything—everything but that eternal, die-away "tweedle." What's the use of a city government? What is the use of anything? What is the use of *me*?

In the Dumps
July 4, 1857

What does ail me? I'm as blue as indigo. Last night I was as gay as a bob-o'-link—perhaps that is the reason. Good gracious, hear that wind howl! Now low—now high—till it fairly shrieks; it excites me like the pained cry of a human. There's my pretty California flower—blue as a baby's eyes; all shut up—no wonder—I wish my eyes were shut up, too. What *does* ail me? I think it is that dose of a Boston paper I have just been reading (for want of something better to do), whose book critic calls "Jane Eyre" an "*immoral* book."[3] Donkey! It is vain to hope that *his* life has been as pure and self-sacrificing as that of "Charlotte Brontë." There's the breakfast-bell—and there's Tom with that autumn-leaf colored vest on, that I so hate. Why don't men wear pretty vests? why can't they leave off those detestable stiff collars, stocks, and things, that make them all look like choked chickens, and which hide so many handsomely-turned throats, that a body never sees, unless a body is married, or unless a body happens to see a body's brothers while they are shaving. Talk of women's throats—you ought to see a whiskered throat I saw once—Gracious, how blue I am! Do you suppose it is the weather? I wish the sun would shine out and try me. See the inch-worms on that tree. That's because it is a pet of mine. Everything I like goes just that way. If I have a nice easy dress that I can sneeze in, it is sure to wear out and leave me to the crucifying alternative of squeezing myself into one that is not broke in to my figure. I hate new gowns—I hate new shoes—I hate new bonnets—I hate anything new except new—spapers, and I was born reading them.

There's a lame boy—now why couldn't that boy have been straight? There's a rooster driving round a harem of hens; what do the foolish things run for? If they didn't run, he couldn't chase them—of course not. Now it's beginning to rain; every drop perforates my heart. I could cry tears enough to float a ship. Why *need* it rain?—patter—patter—skies as dull as lead—trees nestling up to each other in shivering sympathy; and that old cow—I hate cows—they always make a dive at me—I suppose it is because they are females; that old cow stands stock still, looking at that pump-handle just where, and as she did, when I went to bed last night. Do you suppose that a cow's tail ever gets tired lashing flies from her side; do you suppose her jaws ever ache with that eternal munching? If there is any place I like, it is a barn; I mean to go a journey this summer, not "to see Niagara"—but to see a barn. Oh, the visions I've had on hay-mows! oh, the tears I've shed there—oh, the golden sunlight that has streamed down on me through the chinks in the raftered roof—oh, the cheerful swallow-twitterings on the old cross-beams—oh, the cunning brown mice scampering over the floor—oh, the noble bay-horse with his flowing mane, and arching neck, and satin sides, and great *human* eyes. Strong as Achilles—gentle as a woman. Pshaw! women were never half so gentle to me. *He* never repulsed me when I laid my head against his neck for sympathy. *Brute* forsooth! I wish there were more such brutes. Poor Hunter—he's dead, of course, because I loved him;—the *trunk-maker* only knows what has become of his hide, and my books. What of that? a hundred years hence and who'll care? I don't think I love anything—or care for anything to-day. I don't think I shall ever have any feeling again for anybody or anything. Why don't somebody turn that old rusty weather-cock, or play me a triumphant march, or bring me a dew-gemmed daisy?

There's funeral—a *child's* funeral! Oh—what a wretch I am! Come here—you whom I love,—you who love me; closer—closer—let me twine my arms about you, and God forgive me for shutting my eyes to his sunshine.

A Hot Day
August 15, 1857

Sissing fry-pans, and collapsed flapjacks, what a hot day! Not a breath of air stirring, and mine almost gone. Fans enough, but no nerve to wield 'em. Food enough, but no strength to chew it. Chairs hot; sofa hotter; beds hottest. Sun on the back stoop; sun on the front stoop; and hot neighbors on both sides. Kittens mewing; red-nosed babies crying; poor little Hotten-tots! dogs dragging about with protruding tongues and inquiring tails; cockerels feebly essaying to crow. Everything sticky, and flabby, and limpsy. Can't read; can't sew; can't write; can't talk; can't walk; can't even sleep; hate everybody who passes through the room to make it hotter.

Now, just see that fly. If I have knocked her off my nose once, I have done it forty times; nothing will serve her but the bridge of my nose. I say *her*, because I am sure it is a female, on account of its extraordinary and spiteful persistence.

"Will I have anything to drink?" No. Wine heats me; lemonade sours me; water perspires me. "Will I have the blinds closed?" No. "Will I have 'em open?" No. "What *will* I have?" Well—if there's an old maid to be had, for heaven's sake, walk her through this room to cool it. "What will I have for dinner?" Now, isn't that the last drop in my brimming cup? Dinner, indeed! Soup hot; fish hot; beef hot; mutton hot; chicken hot;—ugh! Hot potatoes; hot squash; hot peas; hot pudding; hot children;—ugh! Tell that butcher to make his will, or get out of my kitchen. "Lady down stairs wishes to see me?" In the name of Adam and Eve, take all my dresses off the pegs and show her—but never believe I'd be so mad as to get into them for anybody living.

Aunt Peckey
January 15, 1859

"Everybody has something good in them." I beg your pardon. I solemnly affirm that Aunt Peckey hadn't. She was the most malicious, lean, yellow little wisp of a wasp of a woman who ever dried up on strong coffee. She had great, restless, yellow-black eyes, that seemed to swallow up all the rest of her face; they were here, there, and everywhere in a minute, keeping time with a huge pair of ears which actually *flapped for information.* She had a soft, catty way of stealing about and surprising people in the middle of sentences that were never intended to be passed over her wires. Did you open a door? She was sure to be behind it. Did you strike up a light after a confidential twilight-tete-a-tete with a friend? You would certainly see her curled up in some snug corner, where she had sucked the meaning out of every syllable of it. She had a tortuous-*slinky* way of sliding about, which reminded you of her type, the snake. One involuntarily fancied himself bitten, and drew a long sigh of relief when she glided from sight.

She ate—all Pharaoh's lean kine do—like an ostrich; fish, flesh and fowl, hash, soup and stew; it was quite incredible; and she grew so malicious on it; none of the good things of this life seemed to sweeten her blood—I mean her temper—she had no blood. I have seen that vampyre glide out the door, in a storm fierce enough to blow her off her thin, bony legs, with a precious bit of gossip, which she hoped would set some neighborhood by the ears, and return dripping and contented to her hot coffee and dry hose, as if she had been performing a Christian duty.

She had a most obnoxious way of snuffing. (I should be disenchanted with Venus did she snuff.) You never imagined the like; and a horribly suggestive way of applying her handkerchief of a hot day to her forehead and throat, which increased your caloric by fifty degrees.

How she *did* enjoy her tea! She squared up to the table regular boxer fashion, pushed her sleeves back from the wrist, untied her cap-strings, that her bronchial apparatus might be in good swallowing-condition, and twisting either foot round the front legs of her chair, fixed her eager, expectant gaze on the tea-pot. What a sublime moment, when, elevating her saucer, she fixed her great, yellow-black eyes on the ceiling, and took the first swallow! Talk of a "rapt poet!" This done, she would set down the saucer, and resting the tops of the bony fingers of each hand upon the table, elevate her chin in the air, much after the manner of a hen, who has taken an unexpected and satisfactory quaff.

It was fun to commence a story just as she was going through the door, and see her come back to hunt for a handkerchief that never was lost, or a key that unlocked nothing, which search was prolonged indefinitely, according to the length of your narrative, although you out-Cobbed Cobb.[4]

Of course she was oily-voiced; all your catly women are. She had the regular undertaker whine, taking the measure for your coffin with her eyes, while she deplored with her mouth. Aunt Peckey never will die; she grows thinner and skinnier, and bonier and thirstier, and malicious-er and spryer, every year. She flaps in and out, this human raven, at every funeral far and near, for as she pathetically remarks, "she is a lone body, and must have her little enjoyments."

Perhaps you good-naturedly inquire, was there no saving clause? Yes, my dear philanthropist, Aunt Peckey had *two saving claws*, but unfortunately they were always scraping for herself.

Have You Ever Seen Him?
January 29, 1859

Your *blasé* man, who, though yet at life's meridian, has squeezed life as dry as an orange. Who has seen everything, heard everything, eat everything, drank everything, traveled everywhere but into his own heart, to see its utter selfishness. Who is willing, upon the whole, to tolerate his fellow-creatures, provided they don't speak to him when he wants to be silent, or annoy him by peculiarities of dress, manner and conversation. Who remains immove-ably grave when everybody else laughs, and smiles when everybody else looks grave; who lifts his eyebrows and shrugs his shoulders dissentingly, when people who have not like him "been abroad," applaud. Who talks knowingly and mystically of "art," and thinks it fine to shower-bath every-body's enthusiasm with "to-l-e-r-a-b-l-e." Goes to church occasionally, but owing to the prevalence of badly-fitting coats and vests in the assembly, is unable to attend to the service; don't care much what a man's creed is, provided he only takes it mild. Likes to see a woman plump and well-made, but abhors the idea of her eating; likes to see her rosy, but can't abide an india-rubber on her foot, even in the most consumptive-breeding weather; thinks it would be well were she domestic when he considers his tea and coffee, but don't believe in aprons and calico. Thinks she should be religious, because it would be a check-rein upon her tongue when his liver is out of order, and keep her true to him when he leaves her with all her yearning affections, to take care of herself.

And so our *blasé* man yawns away existence, everything outward and inward tending only to the great-central *I*, when life might be *so* glorious, *so* bright, would he only recognize the existence of others. For how much is that education valuable, the result of which is only this? For how much that refinement which lifts a man so high in the clouds, that no cry of humanity, be it ever so sharp and piercing, can reach him? I turn away from his face, on which ennui and selfishness have ploughed such furrows of discontent, to the laborer in his red flannel shirt-sleeves, who, returning at sunset, dinner-pail in hand, has well earned the right to clasp in his arms the little child who runs to meet him. He may be illiterate, he may be uneducated, but he is a *man*; and by that beautiful retributive law of our being, by which the most useful and unselfish shall be the healthiest and happiest, he has his reward.

Going to Move
April 9, 1859

In those three words how many headaches are breeding, carpet-shakers and carmen and upholsterers only know, as they, no doubt, are at this moment contriving ingenious professional ways of bringing the same about. I am to move. I, who can't see a pin or bit of thread on the carpet, without laying down my pen to pick it up. I, who rise and cross the room to wipe a speck of dust off a vase. I, who go mad if anybody so much as whistles at my desk or papers, and consider it an indictable offense to take up my pen or pencil from the exact spot where I laid it down. I, who perspire if anybody leaves my bureau or closet doors open, or miss-mates my gaiter-boots or slippers. I, who hate dust above all earthly annoyances, and abominate turmoil, fuss and confusion. Heaven help me, I am to move. I am to see my bonnet put into the coal-scuttle, and the poker and tongs, wrapped up in my dresses, and great slices taken out of my piano, and arms, legs and noses ruthlessly torn from my statues, and my MSS. used for wrapping paper. I am never to find anything I want for three good months, though I stand in the middle of my household goods, with tears in my eyes and a broomstick in my hands; and everything I *don't* want, and meant to leave behind, is to be continually turning up under my nose, till I wish I hadn't any nose, and twenty people are to be constantly talking into each of my distracted ears, and in the middle of it all I am to sit down and write, yea, *write*, just as calmly as if I were sitting in a meadow, under a broad green tree, beside a little brook, which was telling me all the pretty things which little brooks know how to tell, and birds were singing, and boughs waving, and flowers wooing, till I was as drunk with bliss as a humming-bird in a lily cup. Dear me, I shan't survive it—I know that; so I might as well make my will. Oh, I know the old joke you are about perpetrating, "as if a woman never made her will till she died"; don't insult my misery with your stale jokes; leave that to Jonas Longdrawnout; not that Jonas isn't an acquisition to any circle, still he might have a better memory and not die of it.

Yes—I am to move, I feel it in every nerve. I don't sleep for thinking of it, and diabolical persons are constantly referring to it, as soon as I wake. I can't deny that I've had cowardly ideas of absconding till the whirlwind be overpast; but it is of no use, because if any of my pet things are smashed I shall feel it, let me be where I will. No—there's no escape for me, so I'll meet it—*like a man*—i.e., I'll—say—"my dear, now pray don't have any cooking done on *my* account"; and then I'll run to the best restaurant I can find and order the very best dinner to be had there, and put my feet up and make myself comfortable generally—now and then going home and looking in upon those who are shouldering all the trouble, with—"poor dears, how glad I shall be when 'tis well over!"

A Social Nuisance
May 7, 1859

If there *is* a nuisance it is your boaster; a fellow whose stock in trade is his chance acquaintance with people of note, male or female; who speaks of them in the most familiar manner, as if he were on the most intimate terms of friendship—on all occasions and without occasion;—calling a lady impertinently by her given name, in a saloon or restaurant, that his gaping auditors may infer on what a delightfully free-and-easy footing he stands with her; quoting, more times than there are seconds in a year, the *one* time in which he might by some accident have appeared in public with her; endorsing the same with knowing looks and grimaces, and "you understand, my dear fellow," to the great astonishment of some far-off worshipper of the lady, who, too modest even to seek an introduction to her, innocently exclaims, with uplifted hands, looking at the ill-bred, boasting pigmy before him, "*He* an intimate friend of hers! Lucky escape!"

The harm such creatures may do, where this species of viper are not understood, may be easily guessed. I say "viper," because such a fellow will not hesitate to sting, even while fawning; he will meanly solicit favors which your good nature grants, to repay them with shrugs and innuendos behind your back, where he thinks he can do so with safety to himself.

Every one who has made a success in the world has been bored and imposed upon by this sort of people. Lucky if the impertinence they return for your kindness has not so disgusted the person sought, as to make him or her suspicious of every new introduction. Lucky if it do not compel the naturally trusting, generous heart to miserly pittances of geniality and social feeling. Nevertheless, if you discover that such fellows have passed your threshold, show them the shortest way over it; they were always ready to sting you even while cringing, they can do no worse than that when you rid yourself of their presence.

A Gauntlet for a Vermonter
May 14, 1859

I have a bone to pick with Mr. Saxe.[5] He is six feet in his stockings, but who cares for that? He has a fist like a sledge-hammer, a voice like a wind-harp, and a pen with a nib. He has a wife, and I like him; I trust my pluck is admitted.

In an exchange I find the following from his pen:

"I wrote you, a few weeks ago, about several sorts of travellers, and suggested that the subject was a very large one—large enough, indeed, to form the staple of a good-sized volume. I haven't [time] to write the book at present, but I must give you a sketch, at least, of one whom I often fall in with, and always fall out with—an intolerably selfish person, who, I regret to say, is a woman. I find her in almost every car I enter—on every route—sitting a seat or two in front of mine, *with the window open*—impervious alike to wind or weather, and bearding Boreas in his stormiest habit, as if he were Zephyrus at her Summer gambols.[6] She is not an invalid,—she is not a fat woman, and so disposed, like Falstaff, to 'continual dissolution and thaw,'[7] no, she is simply a devotee to a pet theory on the subject of ventilation. Having learned that our ancestors were sometimes careless, and indeed, rather ignorant, touching the proportions of oxygen and carbon that they were wont to breathe,—whereby, for scientific reasons, they ought to have died (though they didn't) at an early period of their existence,—and being herself thoroughly read-up in this most vital matter, she goes forth in pursuit of fresh air, at all hazards of herself and others. I don't think, however, *she* is in any special danger. The woman is, beyond all her sex, 'fearfully and wonderfully made.'[8] She seems always battling a congenital tendency to asphyxia or spontaneous combustion, I don't know which. Whether anything could cool her into a permanently comfortable frigidity, is a doubt. At any rate, there she sits—or, rather, there she sat last night.

"Methinks I see her now.
With the terrible Northeaster
A-blowing on her brow."

It was the fierce, chill wind of the prairies at midnight. Weary with many miles of travel, and heavy with long watching, I at last fell asleep. I awoke at daybreak from a wretched torpor that was more the work of Boreas than of newspapers, and discovered that I was nearly speechless with an influenza.

The woman was gone; the window was still open, and a damp gale was rushing upon myself and companion at the rate of a thousand yards a minute! I do not approve of profane swearing. I regard the practice as at once ungentlemanly and immoral. I did not swear on this occasion. At least, I gave no voice to my mental maledictions; but I uttered something like an Amen! to the emphatic words of my travelling companion, who, on discovering that the woman's perversity had made him thoroughly sick with a cold in the head, exclaimed, with such obstructed articulation as his distemper permitted—'Codfond eddy bad or wobad (any man or woman) who leabes a widdow (leaves a window) open od such a dight as dis!' "

I also have an enemy. It is a traveller, whom I am constantly falling in with, and always fall out with; an intolerably selfish person, who, I regret to say, is a *man*. I find him in every car and omnibus I enter, by my side, or in front of me—a smoker—*with the window shut*. He is sometimes, my dear Saxe, a nervous, sedentary man, evidently suffering as much as myself, though in a different way, from the vile practice, though, with the pertinacity of the sex regarding anything they *like* to do, he won't believe it. He is not a fool or an ugly man, that we can afford to dispense with him; he is agreeable, sensible and handsome to that degree, that one exclaims, with a sigh—think what he *might* have been—but for tobacco! But having learned that it is the thing to smoke, from his male friends, (who ought to be choked for it, though they are not), and being himself unwilling to be thought behind the age in this clean and gentlemanly accomplishment, and being also thoroughly read-up in cigars, he goes forth in pursuit of *foul air*, at all hazards to himself and others. I *do* think he is in special danger; if not, he is, beyond *our* sex, "fearfully and wonderfully made." He seems always to be battling a tendency to cleanliness, and woman's best efforts to promote it. Whether anything can cure him of this, save a coroner's inquest, I doubt. At any rate, there he sits, or sat, last time I saw him, with my "Scotch cap" on his brow, a man goodly to look at, made to be clean, and yet unapproachable through tobacco. I regard the practice as at once disenchanting, ungentlemanly, and immoral. I don't swear on these occasions; I don't know how. I give no voice in any way to female malediction; I do not say—Sir, I keep *myself* sweet breath-ed, clean, tidy, tastefully apparelled and presentable; but with handkerchief to my "prominent but well-cut nose," I inwardly utter an Amen to the woman who said, If I am never to marry save a smoker or chewer, terrible as is the alternative, may I remain forever unwedded.

Clumsy People
May 28, 1859

I hate clumsy people. Yes—I won't soften it down to please anybody. I *hate* 'em. What right have people to be clumsy? To be all legs and arms? Never to stir without knocking over, or knocking up, or knocking down something? What right have they, whose touch is always certain destruction, and *who know* it, to be forever fingering and pawing delicate ornaments and pretty little fragile parlor fancies? Why must they always select the only table in the room that has flowers upon it, to kick the water over upon your carpet? Why do they invariably sit down on babies, and bonnets, in preference to sofas and chairs destitute of such pleasing incumbrances? Why do they stumble over your toes when they rise, and drop everything in your lap that they attempt to pass you? I can't tell why a body is to endure all this. Why one should polish, and beautify, and adorn that such may recklessly mar. Is this Great Unspanked to be allowed to stumble through creation doing all sorts of disagreeable things under cover of—"*'tis his way?*" Nonsense. Let him learn a better way, or stay away till he has.

Uncourteous Audiences
February 4, 1860

I don't speak in public. If I did I should give those shuffling barbarians a hit, who in their indecent haste to don hats and coats, drown the speaker's voice, and render it impossible for those who are better-mannered to listen to what is often the cream of the whole performance. I never go to a public place that I am not disgusted anew with this ill-bred rudeness. It matters not whether it is church, lecture, opera, or concert, I consider it insulting alike to preachers, poets, and artistes, to whom, if we were not willing respectfully and courteously to listen, we should have staid away. It would be considered quite unpardonable, when taking leave of friends, on an evening visit, to turn one's back upon their parting salutations. We cannot see why it is less so because the circle is wider, and the place more public. That public places are miserably ventilated, and that those who come long distances may gain time by anticipating the press of a crowd, we do not consider sufficient excuse for such discourtesy to those who have done their best to give us a pleasant or profitable hour. We are not to consider that, our fee paid at the door, we are quits with the speaker. In fact we say to everybody, *be civil* or stay away. I deplore this practice, too, for another reason. It is such a bad example to set the young, who have few enough models for imitation left of that delightful old-fashioned courtesy, which now and then strikes us dumb with admiration, in the person of some fine old lady or gentleman "all of the olden time." Wigs and knee-buckles, in this expectorating, "devil take the hindmost" age, have assumed a value in my eyes which it will take "Young America" a long time to depreciate.

While speaking of public places, I wish to ask a question which has often occurred to me while there. Whether it is not possible to make it easy for respectable ladies, who have no one to accompany them evenings, to attend places of public amusement? At present I believe they are not admitted without a gentleman. I am aware of all that can be said on the probable abuse of this privilege. But still it seems to me that the address being given, and seats secured beforehand, all difficulty would be obviated, and a large number of highly deserving, intelligent, and cultivated single women might thus enjoy the relaxation which they often so much need, and from which they are now debarred, for want of that necessary, but often, alas! stupid adjunct—a male attendant. For my own part, I can see no more objection to a modest, well-behaved woman going to opera, or concert alone, or with a lady-friend, than for her to attend devotional evening meeting in this way, as many do. It seems to me the more necessary that this restriction should be removed, as the tobacco-paralyzed male-brain-and-muscle-of-1860 seldom or never thinks of rendering chivalric attentions to women unless it lazily makes up its mind "to marry," or, there are good cigars, wine, or suppers in prospective, as an offset to the exertion.

The Whistling Nuisance
March 3, 1860

Of course you know the whistling nuisance. The fellow in the corner of every car, with his trowsers turned up at the ankles, his legs and hands crossed, and his hat on one side, who, regardless of ingresses and egresses, with his eyes on the ceiling, whistles, shrilly and pertinaciously, through

every known tune from Old Hundred to Casta-Diva. My dear friend—in
mercy tell me, have *you* not wriggled under the infliction? Have you not
dreaded to have the car stop, the scraping and jiggling of which was melody
in your ears, compared with his ceaseless piping? Have not you, too, longed
to tie his neckcloth a *little* tighter? Have not you, too, tried unsuccessfully
to groan—and hem—and look him down? And failing in this, have not
you, too, joyfully consigned yourself, and your habiliments, to the slosh
of the pavements, anything—everything, but that monotonous, harrowing,
ear-splitting "tooting?"

And yet, your whistler is a jolly fellow; but, alas! I am nervous; and
he that putteth his feet on the rounds of my chair, or drummeth with his
fingers on the table, or beateth time, with the orchestra, under my seat
at a concert, may be an angel for aught I know, but he spoils *my* heaven.

"When I Was in Paris"
April 28, 1860

If there is anything that gives me a sensation, like that produced by "the
rolling sea," it is the above phrase, dragged in by the head and shoulders,
on all occasions, and on no occasion, whether the subject of conversation
be books or butter, crinoline or cheese. They who do this oftenest, are they
who have brought away from "Paris," only its lowest vices and affectations.
Self-immortalized by having breathed its air they are henceforth self-consti-
tuted umpires, on all matters of taste to the benighted heathen who have
never crossed the big pond, or having crossed it, take it as too common-place
a matter to be eternally thrusting the fact in everybody's face. One should
see some of these boasting ex-Parisians, male and female, fully to appreciate
the joke of their—"when I was in Paris."

The female specimen wearing on all occasions, and without regard to
wind, or weather, or time of day, a tawdry dress bonnet, in striking con-
junction with very questionable dresses, gloves, shoes and hose. This is the
self-pedestaled she—whose fiat on all matters of taste, is not to be questioned from the *American* side! As for the male specimen,—a total inability
to see the difference between another man's purse and his own,—when
there is anything in the former,—a vaunted knowledge of wines and opera
dancers, and a constant and overpowering sense of "ennui" at everything in
this disgusting country, where oddly enough he and his female fellow-suf-
ferer still continue to martyrize themselves, notwithstanding the frequent

departure and quick transit of our steamers to their beloved "Paris." Here's hoping some favoring breeze may soon waft them over there.

Smoking in the City Cars
July 21, 1860

We notice that smoking on the platform of the city cars is winked at, or overlooked, notwithstanding the rules, by some of the conductors. This is very disagreeable to ladies, who are often on their way out of the city with children, for a mouthful of fresh air, and who *ought not* to be compelled to inhale the fumes of tobacco while in a crowded vehicle. We even saw one of these smokers, the other day, coolly attempt to close the door upon a quantity of already half-suffocated human beings, piled in as only city cars can be piled, *that he might selfishly smoke his pipe in peace!* It is high time the rules on this point were more strictly enforced; as the effect of tobacco, in brutalizing its devotees, leaves no hope for amendment on their part. Will the conductors please protect the ladies from this annoyance?

An Honest Growl
November 17, 1860

I am sick of politics. I am sick of torch-light fizzles. I am sick of "the Prince." I am sick of men who never talk sense to women. I am sick of boys of seven smoking cigars. I am sick of gloomy Pharisees, and wordy, idealess sermons, and narrow creeds. I am sick of lawless Sabbatarians, and female infidels, and free-lovers. I am sick of unhealthy, diseased books, full of mystifications and transcendental bosh. I am sick of "chaste ribbons" and "ravishing lace." I am sick, in an age which produced a Brontë and a Browning, of the prate of men who assert that *every* woman should be a perfect housekeeper, and *fail to add,* that every man should be a perfect carpenter. I am as sick of women self-styled "literary," who think it a proof of genius to despise everyday household duties. I am sick of schools for the manufacture of bent spines. I am sick of parents, the coffins of whose children are already being made, asking teachers to add "another branch" to the already suicidal pile of lessons. I am sick of over-worked, ill-paid female operatives. I am sick of seeing tracts distributed where soup and bread should go. I am sick of seeing noodles in high places, and intelligence and refinement sitting in inglorious ease by their own firesides. I am sick of the encouragement held out to women by the other sex to remain pretty idiots, followed by long moral essays upon the enormity of being such. I am sick of flummery and nonsense and humbug and pretension of every kind. I am sick of this everlasting scrabbling and crowding, and pushing and jostling, on the edge of the five feet of earth which is all any one of us can have at last, after all our pains.

Now, don't lay this growl to indigestion, for I never had it, or biliousness, for I feel as if I were just made, or long arrears of unpaid bills, because I pay as I go. No, sir—as the Episcopals have it, "all this I do steadfastly believe." There—now I feel better.

Compulsory Shopping
February 9, 1861

Raise your eyebrows if you like, but there is such a thing; not for the knowing ones of course, who steer clear of shops where one is not a free agent; who have no time to look at goods they don't want, and select certain stores for their purchases where they are sure of civil treatment, and are free to buy or not to buy. Reader, have you never accidentally stumbled into the description of a store alluded to? Let me describe it to you. Enter the door, and three clerks immediately leap from the scabbard and ask—"what is it?" Of course, you immediately forget any intentions you might have had of buying anything, and before you have time to recall your senses, you find yourself listening to a running inventory of everything in that shop, with the prices, from a cotton handkerchief to a silk velvet cloak or dress. If you are not a lunatic by that time, you make a feeble attempt to get out into the open air; which praiseworthy effort is frustrated by a procession of clerks who accompany you down the store, each with a piece of goods over one arm, which they pat and stroke with caressing fingers, and would be happy to know "if it is eleven or twelve yards you will need for your dress." Speechless with astonishment, and innocent of any "dress" intentions, you hold on to the counter, and stagger along till the door is reached, where the sight of free and happy human beings on the sidewalk gives you courage, and with one bound, you defiantly cross the threshold, and stopping only long enough to note the number and read the sign over this woman-trap, you keep as near a policeman as possible, nor feel safe till you are quite lost in the crowd, and under your own protecting roof, where you register a vow in the family archives, never to go near *that* shop again.

The Reason Why
March 2, 1861
Reprinted in the animal welfare magazine Our Dumb Animals
April 1874

Can anybody enlighten my mind in regard to a point upon which I grope in Egyptian darkness? Can anybody tell me why the *dog* has been selected by the universal voice of mankind to embody everything that is approbrious? Why, if one wishes to convey the extremest idea of forlornness, he should say: "It is a night in which not even a dog would be stirring," or, "one would not even treat a dog as such a person was treated"; or, "a pittance was thrown one as you would throw a bone to a dog"; or, that such a person "leads the life of a dog"; or has "a hang-dog look"; or, that some ne'er-do-well of a family is a "sad dog," or a "sorry dog," or "a snappish cur," or a "good-for-nothing puppy." Then, again, perhaps I may be pardoned for alluding distantly and delicately to the most approved gutter mode of conveying a stinging insult—viz., that such a fellow is the undoubted son and heir of one of the *ladies* of this family of quadrupeds.

Now, I have reflected deeply on this *pug*nacious subject, and without a glimmer of satisfaction to my doubts. I ask, again, of this crowd of persecutors, why—*dog*? Why not cow, or ox, or horse, as well? It is my private opinion the "dog has had his day." Let people now hit somebody of their own size.

Canes
May 11, 1861

Why should a *young* man carry a cane? Does the charm consist in its self-planting property to stick fast in some hole or crevice of the sidewalk, jerking the owner up short at some unexpected moment? Or is it because it is considered good for the head and back to stoop often to pick it up, when jostled from the hand by some hurried pedestrian? Or is it considered a clever trick to stick it under the arm, and then wheel suddenly into a bevy of astonished ladies, who have their hands full to keep their eyes from immediate extinction? Or is it that a vigorous bang on the sidewalk with this utensil gives force to male argument; or that describing a circle in the air with it, is considered to finish a sentence more gracefully than words could do? Or is it because most young men are at a dead loss what to do with their hands? *That's it!*

Noseology
January 18, 1862

In one sense of the word, every human being has a nose; then, again, some people have none. Of the latter class are they who pass certain gutter localities without a perceptible shudder, or breathe a gas-infected atmosphere through an entire evening without a gasp of dissent. Of this class are they who can restrain a cough of disgust when Anna-Maria-Matilda enters with her handkerchief soaked in "musk," or "jockey club," or "patchouli," or some other horrible reminder of a want of personal cleanliness. Of this class are they who pay a sexton a good salary, to keep the church-windows closed from year's end to year's end, lest the fresh air should get in, while the dust gets out. Of this class are they who are impervious to a burnt-bone effluvia from the kitchen range, or an odor of singed woollen of an ironing day, or the very peculiar brand of cigar with which the postman or any other emissary may choose to regale your nostrils and poison your house while waiting. Taking *this* view of noseology, blessed, after all, is he who hath none, especially if Gotham be his residence.

Modern Martyrs
February 1, 1862

Fox's cheerful "Book of Martyrs" strikes us as incomplete.[9] He tells, to be sure, of people who have been roasted alive, cut up, torn limb from limb, disembowelled, and suffered various other trifling annoyances of that kind; but though I have perused it carefully, I see no mention of the unhappy wretch who, coming home at twelve o'clock at night, with frozen fingers, gropes round his room, bumping his nose, and extinguishing his eyes, in the vain search for his match-box, the latitude and longitude of which some dastardly miscreant has changed. Nor do I see any mention of him who, having washed his hands nicely, looketh in vain for a towel, where a towel *should* be, while little rivulets of water run up his shirt-sleeves, or drip from his extended finger-tips. No allusion either is made to her who, sitting down to her time-honored portfolio, misseth one sheet of MS. which somebody has fluttered out, and straightway gone his heedless way. Nor yet of the unhappy owner of a pen, whose pace answers only to one hand, and whose nib has been tampered with by some idle scribbler, in multiplying the name of "Laura," or "Matilda," to an indefinite extent, over a sheet of paper as blank as his mind. I see no mention of her who, sitting down to write, is made frantic by the everlasting grind of a hand-organ beneath the window; that performer's welcome retreat being followed by a shaky old man, with wheezy flute, or the more horrible bagpipe performance, compared with which the shrieks of twenty cur-tailed cats were heaven's own music. I have not noticed any mention of her who, giving her husband a letter to drop into the post, finds the same a month afterward in the pocket of a vest, which he tosses her to mend. I see no mention of the lady-victims of owners of shops, three miles long, who have always *"just the article you want"* at the very farthest extremity of the store; and whom they lure to traverse that distance only to find something in the *shopman's* view "infinitely superior," but about as near the article wanted as is the North to the South pole. No mention either is made of the gentleman with a bran-new-coat, who takes the last seat in the car, next a child fond of wriggling, with a piece of soft gingerbread, or a moist stick of candy in its uncertain gripe. Nor is any allusion made to the friend of the family, who furnishes all the children with holiday toys, every one of which has either a crucifying squeak or a stunning explosive power, which soon fits their amiable mother for a lunatic asylum. Nothing is said, as I can find, of that mistress of a family to whom the morning hours are as precious as gold dust, and who is called down to see a gentleman who, (having read *Jones* on the door-plate,) straightway, with sublime assurance, asks "for *Mrs.* Jones on particular business"; when that lady, descending, finds a well-dressed, well-groomed individual, who, with a smirk and a bow, straightway draws from his pocket "a bottle of furniture polish," which he exhausts all the dictionary and her patience in extolling; or presents to her notice a "cement for broken china," or "samples of needles." Scarcely has she rid herself of this nuisance, when "a boy wishes also to see *Mrs. Jones* on particular business," which turns out to be the hoped-for sale of "six envelopes, two steel-pens, a pencil, a brass breast-pin, a tin trumpet, a corkscrew and four sheets of letter-paper—all for sixpence—and *just sold three next door, mum.*"

Educational Mistakes
April 5, 1862

Now I believe every one is of the opinion that children should be taught civility; but there is one torture through which they are put in the zealous parental endeavor to teach them politeness, which seems to us deserving of the severest reprehension. Some person comes to the house, it may be a valued and worthy friend, who is unfortunately repulsive in appearance and manners. Mamma tells Johnny to "go kiss" the lady, or gentleman, as the case may be. Johnny, like other human beings, has his personal preferences, and in a case like this, especially, prefers spontaneity. He may obey, it is true, but it is a question when a simple recognition would have answered, whether an act involving hypocrisy were not better omitted. I speak from experience, remembering well the horror with which I looked forward, in my childhood, to the periodical visits of a snuffy old person. I think my uncompromising hatred of tobacco in every form dates back to those forced snuffy kisses, followed in many cases by actual nausea, and in all by a vigorous facial ablution on my part, after the repulsive ceremony. To this day, a colored silk handkerchief, of the antique pattern most affected by snuff takers, affects me as does the sight of a red shawl a belligerent rooster or bull.

That horrible colored silk handkerchief! preferred to a white one, for a reason which makes one's flesh creep, and one's blood run cold, fumbled ever and anon from the stifling depths of a huge pocket, and flourished with its resurrectionized effluvia under your disgusted and averted nose. Excuse my speaking with feeling, dear reader, for even in these later days have I sacrificed many a comfortable seat in a public conveyance, that those infatuated lovers of the weed in every shape might have a wide berth for their noisome atmosphere. Now to force a little child, fresh and sweet, with a breath like a bunch of spring violets, to a contact with such impolite persons, for the sake of "*politeness*," seems to me an act of tyranny worthy of a Nero. If people will selfishly render their persons unfit for civilized society, banishment should be the penalty. We are amazed that one who appears to have his *nose*, as well as "his eyes and ears open," should have omitted in his LEDGER list of odor nuisances, the nauseating one of tobacco, from which not even a church is free; for the last act of its self-willed slaves is to indulge up to the last Sabbatical moment, entering the church reeking with their favorite fumes, and not infrequently during the services casting an anxious glance at the clock, as they finger the furtive cigar, which is to compensate them for an hour's self-denial. Indeed, I look forward to the day when each man, lighting his cigar, shall with his feet on the top of the front pew, puff away all pastoral effect of the mention of his many transgressions, of which this vile habit is not the least.

[The "Eyes and Ears" writer, chancing to be in the Editorial Den, is shown this sentence while in the "Proof," and answers it before it is born into publication: We did not profess to exhaust the abominations of the Nose, and aimed chiefly at those sweet affronts which we receive from the perfumery of the fair sex. But, we leave the faults of men to Fanny Fern. And if she will shame men out of tobacco, we will see that a Monument is erected to her honor, a thousand feet high, and every inch marble!][10]

An Unpleasant Truth
May 17, 1862

It is not much to the credit of human nature, that it is generally so anxious to escape the proximity of those who are down in the world. There is a chill atmosphere about them, like a fireless or darkened room, which seems to need much moral sunshine to brighten. The world is apt to require an equivalent in some shape, for its presence and its smiles; and they who have nothing but tears and sighs, and a downcast eye, to offer, may wait a long while for any *earthly* invitation "to come up higher."

Kinks
May 25, 1867

Of all the absurd kinks for a resident in New York is the dislike of living in a house that has been occupied by another person. No wonder you laugh. I laugh at it myself, though "on the wrong side of my mouth," as my irate school-ma'am used to say, when she boxed my ears for talking over the boys' benches. That propensity has never been boxed out of me to this day—but that's a chapter by itself. I tell you I hate to live in a house anybody else has lived in; not on account of the creeping things they may have bequeathed me, but I get nervous going through the different rooms, and imagining the tales they *might* tell, if walls could speak. I want to sleep in a room that nobody has died in, or been born in, which is a great deal worse. I don't want to breakfast in a room where a drunken husband has thrown a china cup at his wife's head, although his inspiration for that chivalrous act, may have been the best champagne. I don't want a dining-room where men have rejoiced over the exclusion of the women of the family, in order that they might bestialize themselves on topics, that women would blush to hear. I don't want scarlet fever to have been rampant in one chamber, and measles, and mumps, and small-pox, and delirium tremens, up stairs and down. I don't want my food cooked in a kitchen, which has furnished silver spoons, and little babies for the ash-barrel. I don't want my refrigerator in a cellar, where Biddy has tapped wine and ale, and administered other delicacies to her "broth of a boy."

I hope you see from this what a blessing it is to have a lively imagination, and how I must enjoy stopping at a hotel. Heavens! how long I have lingered beside a hotel bed before I could jump into it! Think of the men, women and children who have slept there before me! The dusty beards that have been reflected in that looking-glass, and been washed in that bowl! The trousers and dresses that have been hung in that wardrobe! Oh, those Mormon pegs! how can I ever join the community? Perish the thought! my clothes shall be laid over the backs of the chairs; not for their superiority in any respect, or that of their wearer, but, Lord bless you, it is one of my kinks.

Haven't I a right to it? I know a man who believes the road to a poor-house is through a carriage. He will give his wife and daughters money for everything but that. He will let them each get new suits of clothes drenched through, and quite spoiled, rather than spend a quarter of what one of them cost, by hiring a carriage to take them home in a rain shower. That's *his* kink. But that again is a chapter by itself. What I suffer at the promiscuousness of hotel feeding! That napkin! clean, snow-white, grant, but Lord! the mouths it has wiped. Laugh away—a lunatic asylum has no terror for me. They expect people to screech *there* when they can't hold in any longer; and that's a privilege *sane* people don't enjoy. I rather like a lunatic asylum. They never let your "friends" in there. They bury you at night; and put no tombstone over you with Jane, beloved wife of John, and all that, after tucking you up comfortably. I found that out last summer, in my travels, when investigating the subject.

Perhaps you think I'm crazy now. Well, there again I don't care; the craziest people in this world, are they who are never suspected of being so. Now, there's Mr.———, who lives in———st———, and there's Mrs.———, who lives in———Avenue, crazy—crazy as "March hares"—though why "March hares" are crazy, the Lord only knows—and yet they, these people I mean, walk by rule and plummet; bless you, you might time your hours of eating, drinking, and sleeping, by their rigid, punctilious, proper, gettings up, and sittings down. Let me tell you something. It is not the inmates of lunatic asylums who are crazy, it is they who are at large, outside the walls. As you may be looking for a summer retreat, I thought it but kindness to tell you.

My Grievance
From Caper-Sauce, 1872

Some jilted bachelor has remarked that "no woman is happy unless she has a grievance." Taking this view of the case, it seems to me that men generally deserve great praise for their assiduity in furnishing this alleged requisite of feminine felicity. But that is not what I was going to talk about. *I* have "a grievance." My *fly* has come! I say *my* fly, because, as far as I can find out, he never goes to anybody else; he is indifferent to the most attractive visitor; what he wants is *me*—alas! *me*—*only* me! The tortures I have endured from that creature, no pen, tongue, or dictionary can ever express. His sleepless, untiring, relentless persecution of a harmless female is quite fiendish. His deliberate choice, and persistent retention of agonizing titillating perches, shows a depth of "strategy" unequalled in one so young. Raps, slaps, exclamations not in the hymn-book, handkerchief waving, sudden startings to the feet—what do they all avail me? He dogs me like a bailiff, from one corner of the room to another. All the long, hot day he attends my steps; all night he hovers over my couch, ready for me at the first glimmer of daybreak. The marvellous life-preserving way he has of dodging instant and vengeful annihilation, would excite my admiration, were not all my faculties required to soothe my nose after his repeated visits. In vain I pull my hair over my ears to shield them. In vain I try to decoy him into saucers of sweet things while I write. Down goes my pen, while my hands fly like the wings of a windmill in the vain attempt to dislodge him permanently. In vain I open the door, in the hope he may be tempted out. In vain I seat myself by the open window, trusting he will join the festive throng of happy Christian flies, whizzing in the open air in squads, and harming nobody. If he would *only* go, you know, I would clap down my window, and die of stifling, rather than of his harrowing tickling. See there! he goes just near enough to raise my hopes, and then lights on the back of my neck. I slap him—he retires an instant—I throw my slipper after him—it breaks my Cologne bottle, and he comes back and alights on my nostril. Look! here!

I'm getting mad; now I'll just sit calmly down in that arm-chair, and fix my eyes on that Madonna, and *let* him bite. *Some time* he will surely get enough, and now I'll just stand it as long as he can. Heavens! no, I can't; he is *inside* my ear! Now, as I'm a sinner, I'll tell you what I'll do. Good! I'll go a journey, and lose him! I'll go to Lake George. Saints and angels, don't he follow me there too? To Niagara—do the rapids rid me of him? To the White Mountains? Don't he ascend with me? To the sea-shore? Is he afraid of the seventh wave? Look here! a thought strikes me. Do you suppose that fly would cross Jordan with me? for I can't stand this thing much longer.

XI

"... there *are* days when it is simply blessing enough to be alive"

On Life's Simple Pleasures

The key to Fanny Fern's remarkable success as a newspaper columnist was her ability to engage with her readers—to address everyday experiences that were relatable and relevant to her target audience. While mostly known for achieving that connection through her trademark humor and biting satire, she also inspired her readers to appreciate the beautiful moments in their lives. In the selection featured in this chapter, Fern highlights the everyday joys, wonders, and pleasures that her readers may otherwise take for granted, from the deliciousness of a refreshing rain shower to the rollicking fun of an exhilarating sleigh ride or the comforting presence of a compassionate friend.

Breakfast
March 14, 1857

Let the world fly off its axle any hour in the twenty-four, save the breakfast hour. Ruffle me not then, and I promise to out-Socrates Socrates, though it should rain tribulations all the rest of the day. If I am to have but one glimpse of sunshine until nightfall, let it be then. A plague on him or her who sits down to coffee (all hail coffee!) with a doleful phiz.[1] The witches fly away with that female who presents herself in curl-papers, or introduces herself with a yawn. Unassoiled be that grocer, who offends my proboscis with a doubtful egg; garroted be that dairyman who waters my milk; kneaded be that fat podge of a baker who is tardy with his hot rolls.

Tell me no disagreeables—be not argumentative over our Mocha; discourse not of horrid murders, nor yet dabble in the Black Sea of politics. Tell me not the price of any article I am eating, neither inquire of me prematurely what I will have for my dinner. Let thy "Good-morning" have *heart* in it, and touch thy lips to my eyelids as thou passest to thy seat. If thou hast a clover-blossom, or a babe, set it before me; and dream not, because my heart's incense rises silently as its perfumed breath, that I praise not God for the sweet morning.

Fanny Fern on Sleigh-Riding
January 5, 1861

A sleigh-ride! some *he*-then exclaims, with a shrug of the shoulders, as he draws near the little black grating in the wall, which registers the household heat. A sleigh-ride—what pleasure can there be in *that*? Poor thing, he never lived in the part of the country where *you* were raised, and where sleighing was as much an institution as winter itself; your anger changes to pity as you think of his mis-spent life. What pleasure? Good gracious! Six steaming, spanking horses and a driver furry as a polar bear, his nose just visible above the dasher. Two or three dozen merry girls and boys, muffled to their eyes, stowed away with the hot bricks under the buffaloes. The amicable fight of pairs of lovers for the coveted "back-seat," where are no curious eyes to overlook the young man who, tying his lady-love's tippet under her chin, ties his heart in with it; or tucking the buffalo-robe closer about her shoulders, forgets to remove his arm after the operation. What pleasure, with the warm blood tingling in cheeks beneath eyes that flash like diamonds; what pleasure, when snow-powdered trees, fences and houses, fly past like magic to the merry sound of musical bells—spelt with and without an e. What pleasure, when the country inn is reached, where your supper was bespoke the day before, and rolling out of your manifold wrappers, you lift to your lips foaming glasses of hot "mulled wine," of which benighted New York knows not the recipe, and which I too having forgotten, wish somebody would tell me. What pleasure, when we gather round the table, laughing at each other's rosy faces, and discuss oysters and fowl, and more "mulled wine," till bones and empty glasses alone remain; and the waiter having cleared away the table, we have a good old-fashioned "blindman's buff," or an unceremonious dance in our comfortable winter dresses. What pleasure, when after being deliciously warmed and fed, we pile into the sleigh again, nestling close to the one we like best, and telling the driver to go the longest way home, look up at stars that never gleamed so brightly, and defy fate ever to make us shed a tear for anything. What pleasure, indeed? Humph—Ask some steady, well-to-do fathers-of-families I *could* name, but *won't*, and see if their eyes don't twinkle, spite of their "responsibilities" and "the panic."

Spring Time
May 18, 1861

We confess to a delirious pleasure when the season warrants open windows. All the long winter, and it always *is* long to us, albeit we make it a matter of conscience to live out of doors as much as possible, as all scribblers should who value a clear head; still—the winter months even at that—pass at a dead march. We always feel gaspingly like raising the roof off our heads every time we exchange the clear frosty air for a furnace-heated house; where one's head burns and throbs, while one's back shivers. Blessed be the season for open windows we say! To be sure, the sonorous rag and fish men send us flying off our chair in a tangent occasionally, with their prolonged howls; but our breathing, at least, is not suspended, nor do we feel, as in winter, like a caged creature, beating out its life against relentless bars. We forgive every body in spring, and shake hands with universal human nature—the new grass charms the eye as much as if we were looking at the very first blade that ever grew; and the violets and the roses we will match against any in Eden. No sky was ever bluer, say what they will of "foreign lands"; where if a good Providence ever sends us in the capacity of tourist, we trust to preserve our senses during the trip, and our preference for home after our return. But this is a digression; there *are* days when it is simply blessing enough to be alive; when every pulse and sense is brimming with enjoyment; when the gypsy element is uppermost, and gloves, bonnets and roofs are superfluous. When one thinks of the fragrant beds of pine branches, and moss, one has seen in summer tours in the woods, with an old shawl for a curtain, through the rents of which the little birds flew—sang their mating song and away—and the squirrels peeped in for a stray crumb of breakfast, and the kettle hung outside on two cross-sticks, suggesting impromptu breakfasts. Of course this arrangement would not be so pleasant in a driving easterly storm, but who is talking about easterly storms? Can't one enjoy sunshine while it lasts? Of course, a house over one's head is a very good thing in its way; we have seen the time when we thought so; but as we said before, the roof is occasionally superfluous, and insurances, and taxes, and things, are nuisances unknown to gypsies.

Buoyant People
November 23, 1861

There are certain persons whom to meet, is like opening the window of a close apartment on a delicious June day. The first breath is an inspiration. You throw back your locks from your heated forehead, and your weary eyes, and ask nothing but to sit down and let this soother minister to you. All your cares, and frets, one by one creep away, and a new life and vigor seem infused into every nerve and muscle. You are not the same creature that you were ten minutes before. You are ready after all to do valiant battle with life, though you had supposed yourself quite surrendered to its every-day, petty and harassing tyrant necessities. Exuberant animal strength must needs carry with it hopefulness and courage; and they whose nerves have been strained and weakened by past trouble, welcome the breezy, fresh influence of such, like Heaven's own dew and sunshine. It is a tonic, the blessing of which the unconscious giver knows not how to appreciate perhaps, but oh how invaluable to the receiver! A soulful face, an exultant word—a light springing step! We raise our weary eyes first in wonder, then in admiration; and the sympathetic chord thus struck—the brow clears, the eyes brighten, and life seems—not the curse we morbidly thought it—but the blessing God intended it.

Rainy Days
November 30, 1861

It is curious how differently people are affected by a rainy day. There are your cat-sort, who at sight of the first drop, cower in the snuggest, warmest corner, and ask nothing but to be curled in a heap, till the sun shines out, be it two months or two days. The life in them seems quite suspended, or at least they desire but a blinking view of it, till the clouds scatter. I have no sympathy with that class. The fiercer the storm of hail, rain, or snow, the fiercer my desire to start out and brave it. The heavy drops and driving wind stir my pulses like a trumpet-call. I long to go out and wrestle with them; though umbrellas turn inside out, and stockings and bonnet *dye* in the struggle. I would not exchange the delicious glow that comes of it, for all the unwrecked millinery in the possession of the sunshine devotees. But the climax of my felicity is reached of a stormy evening; when dispensing with an umbrella, I let the pelting drops cool my forehead. When I splash through the deep puddles in long, india rubber boots, and am—like a man—independent of the elements; instead of a miserable ribbon-fettered female, shrinking like a canary from spoiling its fine feathers.

Something to Love
January 11, 1862

How strong is the necessity of loving something in every human being. We often see squirrels, birds, dogs, and animal pets of all kinds in the solitary rooms of single people. The sight to us is as affecting as beautiful; as an illustration of the fact that the isolated heart can seldom endure to be *entirely* cut off from sympathy. Soldiers we have seen going off with their regiments, with little kittens perched upon their knapsacks, to alleviate the ennui and loneliness of camp life. Prisoners have been known to pet insects—spiders, and the like—upon which, in more fortunate days, they would not hesitate to place a crushing heel. His heart indeed must be ossified, who is conscious of no such clinging tendencies; who is not pained to stand aloof and alone, with no spoken or dumb welcome for his approaching footstep.

Unsought Happiness
August 24, 1867

Old stagers know that the way to be happy is to give up all attempts to be so. In other words, the cream of enjoyment in this life is always impromptu. The *chance* walk; the unexpected visit; the unpremeditated journey; the unsought conversation, or acquaintance.

Every body feels more or less conscious in their "Sunday clothes." Who does not know the blessing of comfortable every-day apparel, every fold of which has made intimate acquaintance with the motions and postures of the owner; and which can be worn without fear of being spoiled, or rendering the wearer conspicuous. The bonnet which sets lightly on the head and defies rain; the boots which do not constantly remind the foot that a chair would be the greatest of all earthly blessings; in short, that freedom which will let you forget *you* yourself, is like laying down a huge bundle which has fettered you weary miles on a dusty, sunny road, and sitting down unincumbered in a shady spot to dream and rest in delicious care-free coolness. It is just so with the mind. The best things written, or spoken, have *not* been written or spoken "to order." They *"whistled themselves,"* as the terror-stricken urchin remarked to his irate school-ma'am. They came unbidden, in easy, flowing raiment; not starched and stately, rustling prim and conscious. They came without thought of "what people would say." They stepped out because the time had come when they *couldn't stay in.* In a word, they were *natural* as little children are, and consequently delicious and fresh.

The party, the dinner, must be, because so many wires have to be pulled and kept in motion under cover of sociability and hospitality. The politician understands this, and the mammas who have daughters to dispose of. How patiently they go through with the bore of it to attain their several ends! But for comfort or pleasure, heaven knows, nobody would under-take either "party" or "dinner," as custom at the present day requires their elaboration of getting up. Give me the hour just before retiring, when in flowing robe and hair, at an open window, with the moon for a lamp, one can sit and laugh and discuss matters grave and gay, with no inquisitorial tribunal to sit in judgment on language or opinion. Or the breakfast hour, where—the coffee swallowed, with which we can defy fate, Presidents, or politics—the morning paper comes in to set all our tongues wagging on our favorite hobbies, and we rattle on with a devil-may-care looseness, stunning to conservatism, but funny to listen to, and perfectly unattainable in the presence of a "got up" breakfast.

I solemnly aver, that the moment any body *tries* to do or say a good thing, that moment he shall never be delivered of it, but shall only experi-ence throes of mortal pain trying. If you build yourself a beautiful house, and make it a marvel of taste and convenience, in one of its lovely chambers shall your dead be laid; and you shall wander heart-sick away from it, to rid yourself of a phantom that will always follow you, till you turn boldly and face it, and with a strong heart accept its company.

This incessant *striving* to be happy! Never—never shall mortals be so, till they have learned to give it over. Happiness *comes.* It will not be challenged. It glides in only when you have closed the door, and turned your back upon it, and forgot it. It lays a soft hand on your face, when you thought to be alone, and brings a joyful flush of surprise to your cheek, and a soft light to your weary eye, and ineffable peace to your soul.

Notes

Introduction

1. Many scholarly studies have demonstrated the importance of Fern's newspaper writing. Select examples include: Lauren Berlant, "The Female Woman: Fanny Fern and the Form of Sentiment," *American Literary History* 3, no. 3 (1991): 429–54; Robert Gunn, " 'How I Look': Fanny Fern and the Strategy of Pseudonymity," *Legacy* 27, no. 1 (2010): 23–42; Melissa Homestead, " 'Everybody Sees the Theft': Fanny Fern and Literary Proprietorship in Antebellum America," *New England Quarterly* 74, no. 2 (June 2001): 210–37; Laura Laffrado, "I Thought from the Way You Writ, That You Were a Great Six-Footer of a Woman: Gender and Public Voice in Fanny Fern's Newspaper Essays," in *In Her Own Voice: Nineteenth-Century American Women Essayists*, ed. Sherry L. Linkon (UK: Routledge, 1997): 81–96; Sara Lindey, "Overhearing Children's Stories: Children's Rights in Fanny Fern's Newspaper Writing," *Children's Literature Association Quarterly* 34, no. 2 (2009): 138–56; Kevin McMullen, "Turning Over Fresh Leaves: A Reconsideration of Fanny Fern's Periodical Writing," *Legacy: A Journal of American Women Writers* 35 no. 2 (2018): 141–65; Claire C. Pettengill, "Against Novels: Fanny Fern's Newspaper Fictions and the Reform of Print Culture," *American Periodicals* 6 (1996): 61–91; Nicole Tonkovich, *Domesticity with a Difference: The Nonfiction of Catharine Beecher, Sarah J. Hale, Fanny Fern, and Margaret Fuller* (Jackson, MS: University Press of Mississippi, 1997); Joyce W. Warren, "Uncommon Discourse: Fanny Fern and the *New York Ledger*," in *Periodical Literature in Nineteenth-Century America*, ed. Kenneth M. Price and Susan Belasco Smith (Charlottesville, VA: University Press of Virginia, 1995): 51–68; Karen A. Weyler, "Literary Labors and Intellectual Prostitution: Fanny Fern's Defense of Working Women." *South Atlantic Review* 70, no. 2 (2005): 96–131; Elizabethada A. Wright, " 'Joking Isn't Safe': Fanny Fern, Irony, and Signifyin(g)," *Rhetoric Society Quarterly* 31, no. 2 (2001): 91–111.

2. Joyce W. Warren, *Fanny Fern: An Independent Woman* (New Brunswick, NJ: Rutgers University Press, 1992), 7. Warren's book is the main source of the biographical information in this essay.

3. Warren, *Fanny Fern*, 101.

4. Warren, *Fanny Fern*, 108–09.

5. *Godey's Lady's Book and Magazine* 49 (August 1854): 178.

6. While the unauthorized biography, *Life and Beauties of Fanny Fern*, was published anonymously, Fern scholars and biographers point to Moulton as the most likely author. Warren explains Moulton's campaign against Fern in his magazine and in the biography in *Fanny Fern*, 112 and 113.

7. Elizabeth Cady Stanton, *The Una: A Paper Devoted to the Elevation of Women* 3 (February 1855): 29–30.

8. Joyce W. Warren, "Fanny Fern's *Rose Clark*." *Legacy* 8, no. 2 (Fall 1991): 92–93.

9. The absence of discussions of race in Fern's writing reveals the limited scope of her perspective as a white author writing primarily for white, middle-class readers in the US. For an example of the legacy and impact of a prominent African American columnist from the nineteenth century, see Nazera Sadiq Wright's research about Gertrude Bustill Mossell, the editor of an advice column published in the *New York Freeman*. Wright, *Black Girlhood in the Nineteenth Century* (Champaign: University of Illinois Press, 2016).

10. The collections of Fern's columns are digitized and accessible in various online databases and archives. Kevin McMullen points out the limitations of relying strictly on Fern's published collections, given that a large quantity of her articles were not included in her books ("Turning Over Fresh Leaves," 141–65). McMullen also launched *Fanny Fern and the New York Ledger*, a web archive of digitized and transcribed columns covering the first two years of Fern's time with the *Ledger* (fannyfern.org).

I

1. In this open letter to the *New York Tribune*, Fern responds to an article that was published in the *New York Daily Times*, June 5, 1854. Henry Jarvis Raymond, the founder and editor of the *New York Daily Times* (later shortened to the *New York Times*), was a political rival of Horace Greeley, the *New York Tribune* editor to whom Fern addresses her correspondence here. The rivalry between the editors (and their competing newspapers) was common knowledge to readers at the time.

2. Miss Wetherell: Elizabeth Wetherell was the pen name of Susan Warner (1819–1885), US author of the best-selling novel *The Wide, Wide World* (1851), among many other successful works.

3. *The Myrtle Wreath or Stray Leaves Recalled* (1854) was a collection of sketches and poems by Minnie Myrtle, a contributor to the *New York Daily Times*.

4. Mrs. Stowe: Harriet Beecher Stowe (1811–1896), author of the best-selling antislavery novel *Uncle Tom's Cabin* (1852).

5. Fern was one of the first women to publicly praise Walt Whitman's controversial book of verse. See Joyce W. Warren, *Fanny Fern: An Independent Woman* (160–78) for a detailed account of Fern's friendship (and eventual falling out) with Whitman, and her role in supporting his career.

6. Catholic-Hating Know-Nothing: Also known as the "Native American Party," the Know-Nothing party was a nativist movement that took shape in the 1840s and 1850s as a xenophobic reaction against the influx of German and Irish immigrants to the US.

7. an Emerson, and a Howitt: Fern refers to two prominent early responses to the 1855 edition of *Leaves of Grass*: a private letter to Whitman from the famous Transcendentalist author and philosopher Ralph Waldo Emerson (1803–1882), and a review that appeared in the *London Weekly Dispatch* on March 9, 1856, (unsigned, but presumed to have been written by either William Howitt or William J. Fox, according to the *Walt Whitman Archive*, https://whitmanarchive.org). Whitman included both of those responses in his 1856 edition of *Leaves of Grass*, in an appendix titled "Leaves-Droppings."

8. *"prie-dieu"*: kneeling bench designed for use in prayer.

9. Borgia-like: a reference to the Spanish royal family that rose to prominence in the Italian Renaissance.

10. Fern quotes from *The Life of Charlotte Brontë*, by Elizabeth Gaskell (1857).

11. Fern's satirical review of her own book, *Fresh Leaves* (1857), from the fictional standpoint of a stereotypical male reviewer.

12. Likely a reference to Francis Napier, 10th Lord Napier (1818–1898), Scottish diplomat who served as the British minister to the United States from 1857–1859.

13. Although Fern uses masculine pronouns for the author, one possible candidate for the subject of this critique is the popular novel *East Lynne*, written by British author Ellen Wood (publishing under the name Mrs. Henry Wood). Serialized in 1860–1861, *East Lynne* epitomized the Victorian sensation novel, with a plot that included seduction, murder, adultery, fake identities, etc.

14. Yelverton: Likely a reference to the case of Maria Thérèse Longworth Yelverton, a.k.a. Viscountess Avonmore, a British woman who took her husband to court for bigamy. The trial was a sensational news story on both sides of the Atlantic.

II

1. The quotation is from the 1854 book *Mrs. Parrington's Carpet-Bag of Fun*, by Samuel Putnam Avery.

2. In this essay and the one following it, "Tom Pax" is a fictional name Fanny Fern uses for her new husband, James Parton. The couple was married on January 5, 1856.

3. 2:40: slang for high speed; derived from a horse racing record.

4. had to drink Croton: in the second half of the nineteenth century, New York City's main source of water came from the Croton River via an aqueduct.

5. tin: popular nineteenth-century slang term for money.

6. Chesterfield: Fern likely refers to Lord Chesterfield, Philip Dormer Stanhope, 4th Earl of Chesterfield, whose private correspondence with his son was published as *Letters to His Son on the Art of Becoming a Man of the World and a Gentleman* (1774). As Fern's criticism suggests, the letters, which were mostly instructive, reflected the author's misogynistic attitudes about women.

7. Henry Ward Beecher (1813–1887): US clergyman, activist, and author. Beecher was a fellow contributor to the *New York Ledger*, and he and Fern often engaged in good-humored banter through their articles.

8. "Free Love" was a social movement that advocated for individuals' freedom to love, without interference or governing by the state. Many radical feminists of Fern's time, most notably Victoria Hoodhull, championed free love as a liberating alternative to patriarchal marriage laws and customs. Here, and in several other places in her writing, Fern voices her concern that the movement actually posed a threat to women's progress and undermined the cause of women's rights.

9. H. W. B.: Henry Ward Beecher; see note 7.

10. Rosa Bonheur (1822–1899) was a prominent French artist who defied traditional gender norms.

11. crinoline: a stiffened petticoat designed to make a skirt flair out. Fern uses this term in several places to refer to women.

12. Fern refers to John Foxe's *Fox's Book of Martyrs* (1563) and the popular hymn "I Would Not Live Alway; I Ask Not to Stay," by William Augustus Muhlenberg (1824).

13. Lethe: River of forgetfulness in Greek mythology.

14. "vine and oak": a reference to a widely circulated metaphor popularized in Washington Irving's 1820 story "The Wife," depicting the Victorian ideal of a wife's role in the event of her husband's financial crisis. "As the vine, which has long twined its graceful foliage about the oak, and been lifted by it into sunshine, will, when the hardy plant is rifted by the thunderbolt, cling round it with its caressing tendrils, and bind up its shattered boughs, so is it beautifully ordered by Providence, that woman, who is the mere dependent and ornament of man in his happier hours, should be his stay and solace when smitten with sudden calamity; winding herself into the rugged recesses of his nature, tenderly supporting the drooping head, and binding up the broken heart."

III

1. The epigraph quote is from a collection of lectures published by the well-known American minister and author Henry Augustus Boardman, *The Bible*

in the Family: Or, Hints on Domestic Happiness (Lippincott, Grambo & Co., 1851), 55–56.

2. The quote appeared in the domestic advice book *The English Matron*, by the author of "The English Gentlewoman" (London: Henry Colburn, 1846), 28. It was reprinted in the *Freemasons' Quarterly Magazine* (United Kingdom, Bro. G. Routledge & Company, 1848), 68.

3. Fern refers to Harriet Goodhue Hosmer (1830–1908), the most prominent American female sculptor of the nineteenth century, and her sculpture *Beatrice Cenci* (1857).

4. Miss Nancies: nineteenth-century slang, usually a derogatory term for a gay or gender nonconforming man. Fanny Fern often uses the term to refer to finicky men and women.

5. Rosa Bonheur (1822–1899), prominent French artist known for her animal paintings and sculptures. The painting Fern describes here is likely *Portrait of Rosa Bonheur with Bull* (1857), by the French artist Edouard Louis Dubufe. Both of the women artists Fern discusses in this essay were gender nonconforming and had long-term partnerships with other women.

6. Charles Reade (1814–1884), British author.

7. George Sand (nom de plume for Amantine Lucile Aurore Dupin, 1804–1876), French author; "Claudia" is likely a reference to her 1851 play *Claudie*. Madame Emile de Girardin, a.k.a. Delphine de Girardin (1804–1855), French author whose play *La Joie Fait Peur* was published in 1854.

8. Black-leg: term for swindler or cheater.

9. Lucy Stone (1818–1893), American orator, suffragist, and abolitionist. Fern's comment in the following sentence ("I am not sure I should have fought it out with *that* sheriff") is likely a reference to Stone's refusal to pay property taxes without representation, which led to the confiscation and sale of some of her furniture.

10. without a hat at my side: in other words, without a man at my side. Fern often refers to men as "hats" and women as "bonnets."

11. Lantern: a racehorse owned by *Ledger* editor Robert Bonner; Lantern was immortalized in popular Currier & Ives lithographs.

12. John G. Saxe (1816–1887): poet, lecturer, and, as Fern notes, occasional contributor to the *New York Ledger*. Saxe ran unsuccessfully for governor of Vermont in 1859 and 1860.

13. Fern quotes the character Mr. Tulliver in George Eliot's novel *The Mill on the Floss* (1860). The line appears in book I, chapter III.

14. Bismarck . . . Metternich green: types of silk in style at the time.

15. The quoted passage is from *The Ladies' Repository* 35 (1866): 375. George Tyler Bigelow (1810–1878) served as chief justice of the Massachusetts Supreme Court from 1860–1867.

16. Charles Kingsley (1819–1875), British clergyman and author. The quotation that follows mentions the prominent Victorian poets Christina Rossetti (1830–1894), Jean Ingelow (1820–1897), and Adelaide Anne Procter (1825–1864). *John Halifax,*

Gentleman (1856) and *Romola* (1863) were novels written by the famous British female novelists Dinah Craik (1826–1887) and George Eliot (nom de plume of Mary Ann Evans, 1819–1880), respectively.

17. "The Girl of the Period" (1868) was a controversial essay written by Victorian novelist and journalist Eliza Lynn Linton. The essay offers a stereotypical view of modern women as vain and shallow.

18. This is especially true of biographers!: Fern's husband, James Parton, was a prominent biographer.

19. Sary Gamp: Sarah Gamp, or Mrs. Gamp, a character in Charles Dickens's novel *Martin Chuzzlewit* (1843).

20. man-milliner Worth: Charles Frederick Worth (1825–1895): English fashion designer, founder of House of Mirth, a French haute couture brand.

21. "Ginx's last baby": a reference to a famous photograph of a crying infant. Dubbed "Ginx's baby," the photograph was included in Charles Darwin's book *Expression of the Emotions in Man and Animals* (1872).

IV

1. Termagent: a violent, harsh-tempered woman.

2. "tongue is not coated": likely a reference to oral thrush, an irritating infection common in babies and children.

3. *Three Hours School a Day: A Talk with Parents* (1854), by William Lusk Crandal.

4. Greenwood Cemetery in New York.

V

1. This anecdote may be loosely based upon Fern's memories of her father's harsh treatment of her mother. See Joyce Warren, *Fanny Fern: An Independent Woman*, 7.

2. "Hyppolite Hyacinth" is Fern's satirical reference to her brother Nathaniel Parker Willis, founder and editor of the popular magazine the *Home Journal*. (Hyacinth is the name of the character based on Willis in Fern's semi-autobiographical novel *Ruth Hall*.)

3. Suttlers: (sutlers) civilian merchants who sell provisions to an army in the field. "Non est": absent.

4. Libby and Andersonville: notoriously harsh Confederate prisoner-of-war camps located in Richmond, Virginia, and Andersonville, Georgia, respectively.

5. Thirty-two pounder Parrot gun: a type of cannon used in the Civil War.

6. The mercy which lets Jeff. Davis glide safely out of the country . . . : Confederate president Jefferson Davis was indicted for treason but never tried. After being imprisoned for two years, he was released on bail and the federal government

eventually dropped the charges on December 25, 1868. Fern also refers to the federal government's prosecution of women who offered aid to the Confederate army.

7. Forts Pillow and Wagner: Both battles significantly involved African American Union soldiers. At the Fort Pillow Massacre in Tennessee (April 12, 1864) Confederates killed approximately three hundred Union soldiers, most of them African Americans, after they had surrendered, rather than taking them as prisoners of war. The Second Battle of Fort Wagner in South Carolina (July 18, 1863) was famous for the display of valor shown by the 54th Massachusetts, an infantry regiment of African American soldiers.

8. The manuscripts Fern describes in this section are from the Left-Handed Penmanship Contests, organized in 1865–1867 by William Oland Bourne (1819–1901), poet, reformer, and editor of a newspaper for Civil War veterans, *The Soldier's Friend*. The contests showcased the penmanship skills developed by veterans who lost the use of their predominant writing hand, as well as poignant first-hand accounts of their experiences in the war. The submissions were displayed in public exhibits in New York City and Washington DC in 1866.

VI

1. . . . at this time of distress, when so many, by no fault of their own, are without the means of a livelihood . . . : Fern refers to the Panic of 1857, a financial crisis that spread rapidly throughout the US.

2. In a three-part series about her visit to New York's Blackwell's Island, Fern exposed the conditions of the lives of the prisoners, prostitutes, and people suffering from mental illness who were institutionalized there. Her writing in these three pieces (two of which are included here) represents pioneering work in investigative journalism. Fern's writing about Blackwell's Island specifically anticipates a later and more elaborate exposé conducted by the journalist Nellie Bly, who posed undercover as a patient in the Woman's Lunatic Asylum and chronicled her experiences in her book, *Ten Days in a Madhouse* (1887).

3. "The way of transgressors is hard," from Proverbs 13:15. "Neither do I condemn thee; go and sin no more," from John 8:11.

4. . . . if a good and virtuous wife has not a right to expect *healthy* children?: Fern likely refers to cases of congenital syphilis.

5. The epigraph comes from a hymn by the Scottish-born poet and hymn writer James Montgomery (1771–1854).

VII

1. Reflecting a recurring theme in her writing—comparisons between the Boston region and New York—in this essay Fern compares Brooklyn's Greenwood

Cemetery to Mount Auburn Cemetery, located in Cambridge, MA. (Fanny Fern is buried in Mount Auburn Cemetery.)

2. Beecher . . . Storrs . . . Bethune: Fern lists three prominent clergymen based in Brooklyn at the time: her fellow *Ledger* contributor, Henry Ward Beecher (1813–1887); George Storrs (1796–1879); George Washington Bethune (1805–1862).

3. "Morrissey and Heenan": A famous boxing match that took place in October 1858 between John Morrissey (1831–1878) and John C. Heenan (1833?–1873).

4. Five Points: nineteenth-century neighborhood in lower Manhattan, notorious for being the most dangerous and crime-ridden area in the city.

5. Methuselah: Biblical patriarch, grandfather of Noah.

6. The Battery: a public park in New York City. Castle Garden, located inside the park, became New York's first immigrant processing station in 1855.

7. General Butler: Benjamin F. Butler (1818–1893), lawyer and politician, served as major general in the Union army during the Civil War.

8. The Newsboys' Lodging House: Established by the Children's Aid Society, Newsboys' Lodging Houses provided shelter to homeless youth in New York City. The home at 128 Fulton Street was the first of its kind, established in 1854.

9. Mr. C. L. Brace: Charles Loring Brace (1826–1890), philanthropist and social reformer; founded the Children's Aid Society and Newsboys' Lodging Houses.

10. Stewart's: A large department store built in 1862 by entrepreneur Alexander Turney Stewart (1803–1876), Stewart's covered an entire city block in New York.

11. Michelet: Likely a reference to French author Jules Michelet (1798–1874), whose books on love and women, *L'Amour* (1858) and *La Femme* (1859), were widely known.

12. Modiste: fashionable dressmaker.

13. "The Working Women's Protective Union": An organization established in 1863 for the purpose of providing advocacy and resources for working women.

14. "The Mountain House": The Caatskills Mountain House, which opened in 1824, was a famous hotel overlooking the Hudson River Valley. It was visited by prominent and elite guests traveling to admire the beauty of the region.

15. saleratus: a form of sodium bicarbonate used as a leavening agent in baking.

16. Fern is likely referring to an elaborate monument honoring her late father-in-law, Hezekiah Eldredge, who withheld support to Fern and her children when they were destitute.

17. Fern's first husband, Charles Eldredge, and their daughter, Mary, were both laid to rest in Mount Auburn Cemetery. Fern herself was also buried in Mount Auburn.

18. Chief Justice Story: Fern describes a statue of Joseph Story (1779–1845), associate justice of the Supreme Court and first president of Mount Auburn Cemetery; the statue of Story was sculpted by his son, William Wetmore Story.

VIII

1. A certain musical gentleman, whose photograph hangs this minute in Brady's entry: Fern likely refers to the portrait photographer Mathew Brady, who had a daguerreotype studio in New York City at the time. Brady would later become famous for his Civil War photographs. In describing her resemblance to "a certain musical gentleman," Fern may be referring to her brother, Richard Storrs Willis, a musician, composer, music critic and editor.

2. Named after Amelia Bloomer (1818–1894), the famous women's rights activist who popularized the style, "Bloomers" revolutionized women's fashion by providing a liberating alternative to long, heavy skirts. While Fern disliked the look of Bloomers, she recognized the need for women's clothing reform. Here and elsewhere, she championed the idea of some form of pants for women, especially for the sake of women's freedom of movement and overall health.

3. A mother anxiously gazing over a newspaper for the list of killed or wounded: a reference to the American Civil War (1861–1865).

4. Balmoral: a style of petticoat that was popularized by Queen Victoria, who was first known to adopt the style at Balmoral Castle in Scotland. The petticoat was meant to show at the hem of a drawn-up skirt for walking.

IX

1. Sylvanus Cobb Jr. (1823–1887) and Emerson Bennett (1822–1905) were authors of popular adventure fiction and contributors to the *New York Ledger*.

2. With the success of the *New York Ledger*, which reached a circulation number of 400,000 copies, Bonner became a millionaire.

3. Likely a reference to a famous boxing match that took place in October 1858, John Morrissey vs. John Heenan.

X

1. Tom Moore: Thomas Moore (1779–1853), Irish poet and lyricist.

2. "When away from the lips that we love, we'll make love to the lips that are near": Fern refers to Moore's poem " 'Tis Sweet to Think."

3. "Jane Eyre": novel by British author Charlotte Brontë, published in 1847.

4. out-Cobbed Cobb: likely a reference to fellow *Ledger* contributor Sylvanus Cobb Jr. (1823–1887), a fiction writer.

5. Mr. Saxe: John Godfrey Saxe (1816–1887), poet from Vermont and *New York Ledger* contributor.

6. *Boreas, Zephyrus*: Greek gods of the cold north wind and the warm, spring-like west wind, respectively.

7. *Like Falstaff, to 'continual dissolution and thaw'*: Sir John Falstaff is a character who appears in three plays by William Shakespeare. He is described as "a man of continual dissolution and thaw" in *The Merry Wives of Windsor*, Act 3, Scene 5.

8. *"Fearfully and wonderfully made"*: a reference to the Bible (King James Version), Psalm 139:14.

9. *"Book of Martyrs"*: written by John Foxe, the original title is "Actes and Monuments of These Latter and Perillous Days, Touching Matters of the Church" (1563).

10. The response is from *New York Ledger* editor Robert Bonner, who had complained about women's perfume in his weekly column, "Thoughts as They Occur, By One Who Keeps His Eyes and Ears Open," in the March 15, 1862, issue of the *Ledger*.

XI

1. *phiz*: slang term for face or facial expression.

Works Cited and Select Bibliography

Primary Sources

Fern, Fanny. "American Female Literature; Letter from Fanny Fern." *Una: A Paper Devoted to the Elevation of Women* vol. 2, no. 8 (August 1854): 320.

———. *Caper-Sauce: A Volume of Chit-Chat about Men, Women, and Things.* New York: G. W. Carleton, 1872.

———. *Fern Leaves from Fanny's Port-Folio.* Auburn, NY: Derby and Miller, 1853.

———. *Fern Leaves from Fanny's Port-Folio.* Second Series. Auburn and Buffalo, NY: Miller, Orton & Mulligan, 1854.

———. *Folly As It Flies.* New York: G. W. Carleton, 1868.

———. *Fresh Leaves.* New York: Mason Brothers, 1857.

———. *Ginger-Snaps.* New York: Carleton, 1870.

———. *Little Ferns for Fanny's Little Friends.* Auburn, NY: Derby and Miller, 1854.

Works Cited

Berlant, Lauren. "The Female Woman: Fanny Fern and the Form of Sentiment." *American Literary History* 3, no. 3 (1991): 429–54.

Review of *Fern Leaves from Fanny's Port-Folio, Second Series. Godey's Lady's Book and Magazine* 49 (August 1854): 178.

Gunn, Robert. " 'How I Look': Fanny Fern and the Strategy of Pseudonymity." *Legacy* 27, no. 1 (2010): 23–42.

Homestead, Melissa J. *American Women Authors and Literary Property, 1822–1869.* Cambridge, UK: Cambridge University Press, 2005.

———. " 'Every Body Sees the Theft': Fanny Fern and Literary Proprietorship in Antebellum America." *New England Quarterly* 74, no. 2 (June 2001): 210–37.

Howitt, William, or William J. Fox [unsigned in original]. "[Review of Leaves of Grass (1855)]." 9 March 1856. *The Walt Whitman Archive.* Edited by Matt Cohen, Ed Folsom, and Kenneth M. Price.

Laffrado, Laura. "I Thought from the Way You Writ, That You Were a Great Six-Footer of a Woman: Gender and Public Voice in Fanny Fern's Newspaper Essays." In *In Her Own Voice: Nineteenth-Century American Women Essayists*, edited by Sherry L. Linkon, 81–96. UK: Routledge, 1997.

Lindey, Sara. "Overhearing Children's Stories: Children's Rights in Fanny Fern's Newspaper Writing." *Children's Literature Association Quarterly* 34, no. 2 (2009): 138–56.

McMullen, Kevin, ed. *Fanny Fern in the New York Ledger*, fannyfern.org.

———. "Turning Over Fresh Leaves: A Reconsideration of Fanny Fern's Periodical Writing." *Legacy: A Journal of American Women Writers* 35 no. 2 (2018): 141–65.

Pettengill, Claire C. "Against Novels: Fanny Fern's Newspaper Fictions and the Reform of Print Culture." *American Periodicals* 6 (1996): 61–91.

Stanton, Elizabeth Cady, *Una: A Paper Devoted to the Elevation of Women* 3, no. 2 (February 1855): 29–30.

Streitmatter, Rodger. *Raising Her Voice: African American Women Journalists Who Changed History*. Lexington, KY: University Press of Kentucky, 1994.

Tonkovich, Nicole. *Domesticity with a Difference: The Nonfiction of Catharine Beecher, Sarah J. Hale, Fanny Fern, and Margaret Fuller*. Jackson: University Press of Mississippi, 1997.

Warren, Joyce W. *Fanny Fern: An Independent Woman*. New Brunswick, NJ: Rutgers University Press, 1992.

———. "Uncommon Discourse: Fanny Fern and the *New York Ledger*." In *Periodical Literature in Nineteenth-Century America*, edited by Kenneth M. Price and Susan Belasco Smith, 51–68. Charlottesville: University Press of Virginia, 1995.

Weyler, Karen A. "Literary Labors and Intellectual Prostitution: Fanny Fern's Defense of Working Women." *South Atlantic Review* 70, no. 2 (2005): 96–131.

Wright, Elizabethada A. "'Joking Isn't Safe': Fanny Fern, Irony, and Signifyin(g)." *Rhetoric Society Quarterly* 31, no. 2 (2001): 91–111.

Wright, Nazera Sadiq. *Black Girlhood in the Nineteenth Century*. Champaign, IL: University of Illinois Press, 2016.

Index

www.ingramcontent.com/pod-product-compliance
Lightning Source LLC
Chambersburg PA
CBHW031750210525
27016CB00016B/38